WITHOUT BENEFIT OF LAUNDRY

Patricia   with fond love, much admiration
              and good wishes from the author

December 1997

WITHOUT BENEFIT OF LAUNDRY

JOHN PEYTON

John Peyton

BLOOMSBURY

I am conscious of owing much to those friends who have had the kindness
and the patience to read and comment on what I have written. In following
their advice I have gained much. I hope, however, that I may be forgiven if I
mention only a few by name.

Ian Bancroft, who sadly died last year, read an earlier version and gave me
great encouragement which, at the time, I needed. John Bradley, sometime
Professor of English Literature at the Universities of Durham and Maryland,
read more than one version and offered penetrating and constructive comments
on both style and content. Peter Pilkington advised and reassured me on the
last chapter. Simon Hornby, having removed some nagging doubt in my mind
as to whether anyone might read what I had written, played a notable part in
finding a publisher. The Reverend Dr C. E. Stewart has kindly allowed me
to quote extensively from 'Impressions of the Falklands Crisis', a most moving
article which he wrote at that time.

My special thanks are due to Sarah Macnab, my secretary, without whose
patience and skill what I have written might never have got further than the
waste-paper basket. Last, but very far from least in this list of thanks, must
come Mary who, despite initial fears, has read, commented and generously
encouraged throughout.

First published in Great Britain 1997

Bloomsbury Publishing Plc, 38 Soho Square, London W1V 5DF

A CIP catalogue record for this book
is available from the British Library

ISBN 0 7475 3331 8

10 9 8 7 6 5 4 3 2 1

Typeset by Hewer Text Composition Services, Edinburgh
Printed in Great Britain by Clays Ltd, St Ives plc

Contents

FOR TOM AND SARAH,

my son and daughter. They will, I hope, accept it as an expression of love and gratitude and as an attempt to explain the times in which I have lived and also myself. I have come to regret that my father never sought to explain himself to me, and to wonder how carefully I would have listened had he done so. Perhaps they and their children will read what I have written and conclude that, while change builds up barriers between the generations, the search for answers to such questions as who are we, where did we come from and where are we going makes those barriers smaller and less hard to overcome.

Foreword

Why even attempt to put together the pieces of one's life at a time when much has become hard to remember, even harder to explain? Why undertake the labour of scraping away the sediment of the years in order to uncover, not without anguish, things buried and almost forgotten? Why take the risk that no one will be even faintly interested or amused; that there just won't be room on the shelves of publishers and bookshops, already congested with the effusions of others? Such questioning, and my wife's fear that I would be hard to live with in the process, have put me off for years; but I have never quite managed to exorcise this troublesome spirit, which urges me to gather up the fragments – to attempt to explain, as much to myself as to others, to say thank you and to seek forgiveness. An old friend once wrote to me, 'I think we shall each separately, in a dead stillness, look upon ourselves as we are in the mirror of God's perfect justice: it is difficult to suppose that there can be an adequate mercy.' It would be as well to be ready for that moment.

Introduction

In my beginning is my end. Now the light falls
Across the open field, ...
                    T. S. Eliot, from 'East Coker', *Four Quartets*

The Second World War was, for most of those over whom
it cast its shadow, by far the greatest event in their lives. It
reached right down from its cosmic dimensions into their hearts,
minds and bodies, and after its fearful passage left them, as well as
the world, changed; moreover, it widened to an extent previously
unimagined the horizons of further change. These horizons, as we
have come closer to them, have not only made the world a smaller
place, but have diminished our own stature and dwarfed those who
have charge of world affairs to a point at which they seem to be
mere fumblers; such certainties as we once had have been eaten
away. Maybe it is the resultant unease which has brought us to
fall again into that 'fashion of morose disparagement' of which Sir
Arthur Quiller-Couch, sometime Professor of English Literature at
Cambridge, wrote more than half a century ago in the Preface to the
second edition of the *Oxford Book of English Verse*. The passage from
which those words are taken runs: 'Writing in 1939, I am at a loss
what to do with a fashion of morose disparagement, of sneering
at things long by catholic consent accounted beautiful; of scorning
at Man's unconquerable mind and hanging up (without benefit of
laundry) our common humanity as a rag on a clothes line.'

Like streakers at a cricket match, we seem to relish drawing
attention to our own inadequacies and shocking those who
remain shockable. It is possible that, in the crowded and singularly
unbeautiful world which we have been creating, we have left

1

ourselves with little alternative but to sneer 'at things long by catholic consent considered beautiful', to see them as mere baggage from the past which we are too clever now to have need of. 'Hanging up . . . our common humanity as a rag on a clothes line' has become something of a routine: to present it from a more favourable angle, let alone clean it up and give it 'the benefit of laundry', would be to detract from the truth; a more lasting defect would be to make the material ordinary and therefore hard to sell.

My generation grew up dimly aware that history might be about to repeat itself; half knowing that the road we were on was the one our fathers had travelled. In *The World Crisis*, his account of the First World War, Churchill wrote of the 'duality and discordance' which had been the 'keynotes of British politics' in the ten years which preceded its outbreak:

> Those whose duty it was to watch over the safety of the country lived simultaneously in two worlds of thought. There was the actual visible world, and there was a hypothetical world, a world 'beneath the threshold', as it were – at one moment utterly fantastic, at the next seeming about to leap into reality.

What he wrote as history turned out also to be prophecy. Those two worlds with their different levels of perception, each denying the existence of the other, came back to govern our thinking and our policies in the years between Hitler's rise to power and war. At one level there was the familiar, real world, which, for all the problems, the joys and sorrows, the hopes and fears it faced us with, seemed set to go on and on without serious interruption. Then there was that other level, 'beneath the threshold', unexplored and only half real, at which existed pressures and perils, too large and remote for most of us to get hold of, too menacing, perhaps, for us even to want to. We were content instead to hope for the best, even to the point of believing that the sacrifice of Czechoslovakia would buy us peace, with honour thrown in as an extra.

Today those two worlds have converged; instant communication, the speed and ease of movement and, above all, television, have removed the curtain and swallowed the distance which once separated them from each other. Television has brought to us the sights and sounds of a nightmare world from which all traces of human decency, respect for man or reverence for God, things which are the mortar which holds together that ramshackle structure we call civilization, are being systematically swept away. Moreover, it is that nightmare world of civil war, the terrorist, the paedophile and the drug baron which seems the more real as it intrudes upon and overshadows the familiar. Whether this regular parade of horror is intended to spread despair or simply to attract attention to the message doesn't really matter: the result is deeply debilitating.

The weakness and fallibility of human institutions has been sufficiently demonstrated to be no longer a cause for surprise. To dwell upon the fact without either the intention or even the desire significantly to improve them ensures that our problems, and we have enough, not only remain unsolved but grow more severe. One does not have to look far for examples of matters altogether too large for single nations to handle: the huge power of modern technology for good or ill; the population explosion; the warming of the planet on which we all live; the spread of weapons of mass destruction into the hands, maybe, of those mad enough or bad enough to use them, and the chronic turbulence of a world at peace. All these might have brought the nations closer together.

Yet at a time of greatest need, the vision which led to the setting up of the United Nations half a century ago has faded. The determination that civilization should not again be brought to the verge of destruction by sheer brutishness has been eaten away by pettifogging politicians and others, who, like the Bourbons before them, learn nothing and forget nothing. They reject the lessons of history on the perils of national rivalry; they fail to grasp the extent to which modern technology has shrunk our planet to a point at which national frontiers mean not much more than the city boundaries of a century ago; they take no account of the pace of change and ignore the near certainty that that pace will continue to increase, far beyond the capacity of our institutions to handle it.

Our situation reminds me of a tale, which I have been assured is true, of a civil aeroplane flying beneath a blue and cloudless African sky. The captain, becoming bored, switched on the automatic pilot and, leaving the navigator in charge, went back to chat to the passengers. In due course the navigating officer, unwilling to be left out of things, followed him, forgetting for the moment that the anti-hijack door which closed behind him could not be reopened from that side. There are times now when I share the feelings of the passengers as they gradually came to understand that the aeroplane in which they were flying would, unless something drastic were done, continue on course until, when the fuel tanks were empty, it crashed to the ground. In the event, the pilot and his colleague found an axe and were fortunately able to chop open the door and regain control. It seems to me that the world is in need of such a breakthrough in its procedures. But it is a melancholy fact that the most powerful nation in the world, the host country of the United Nations, refuses even to pay its subscription and is the organization's biggest debtor. The possibility of coherent thought and patient discussion between nations is lost in the stage-managed summitry and the need of every leader to get back home and ensure that pressures there do not get out of hand.

Since, however, the purpose of this book is not simply to air ideas about the present or apprehensions about the future, but also to remember, I must now go back. I have learned painfully, in writing it, how hard it is to do so. Memory has no rules or regular habits; it loses much that was important and yet clings on to and preserves quite small things which, like stray, unconnected footprints, have escaped erosion by the winds and tides of time. Recalling people, times, places and events is, to an extent, an affair of chance. Many are lost beyond recovery: of the remainder, some, glimpsed for a moment like a fish in clear, still water, vanish as you move towards them; the outstretched hand comes back empty save for some bits of unmemorable debris from the bed of the stream. Others are easily retrieved, as if from a computer; others again, without aids and regardless of time, are unforgettable, always with you. It is as if memory were a camera, used with varying degrees of skill, sometimes in poor light and at other times, though aimed and focussed, without a film.

I

A Fragile Peace

I believe it is peace for our time.
Neville Chamberlain, 1938

A puncture on the way to the seaside in 1921 at the age of two and a half is my earliest memory: a Wolseley car with lots of brass fittings, a huge horn and the family crest on the door; a chauffeur, Hawkes, who must have departed before I was three; things which I wanted very much to do and objects which I wanted to touch, but which were forbidden; things remembered clearly but unanchored in either time or space; childish headaches and the need to have someone stroke my head – my mother did it best. Shops in Ascot: Marment, the greengrocer; Higgins, where the sweets were sold; Colebrook, the fishmonger, who had a lovely horse-drawn van driven by Mr Buss which brought large lumps of ice. Bowyer, a postman; Dollery, the gardener; Hinkins, the new chauffeur, in a uniform with brass buttons; Mrs Cox and Mrs Biggs, both of them cooks, whom I loved; Cox, a butler, who to my grief departed and became a conductor on buses, which had hard solid wheels and open tops. I always hoped to travel on his bus, but did so only once. Ticehurst, his successor, with flat feet, who seemed never to shave without doing himself almost mortal injury. Mrs King-George, who sent me, when I was only four or five, a chocolate cat addressed to 'the politest boy in Ascot'. I ate its head and, being allergic to chocolate, was quickly sick. Sitting down beside the sea, hating it, protesting, so I was later told, 'Damn the sea.' A dear old man who smelt nice, Dr Paterson, who used to look after us, but who retired and didn't come any more. My father shaving – he made a bit of a ceremony of it –

5

and the pink mouthwash he used. He talked about a place with a funny name, Gallipoli, and people called Turks and shells and flies: I could manage the flies, but not the other two. Later on, when they would have meant more, he never spoke of them. It was only much later, when he was far enough away in time, that I gained sufficient perspective to understand what in his lifetime I could not.

Of my father's childhood and early youth and of his parents and his relations with them I know very little, since he seldom spoke much either of that time or of them. I have only an impression born of fragments that he must have been both lonely and unhappy. His mother had died when he was still very young and his father, large and formidable in appearance, had been entirely engrossed in doing the things which interested him: he lived for much of the time in Ireland, where he enjoyed shooting large numbers of birds; he was keen on racing and had a substantial bet on The Hermit, owned by a friend, when he won the Derby; with his brother, who became a major general, he used to pursue larger game in India; he also commanded a cavalry regiment and, I think, became involved in the Burmese War. Certainly his brother did, for I have a gong with a marvellously resonant tone which he acquired 'after personal encounter' from the Great Dagon Pagoda at Frome in 1852. Such activities cannot have given my grandfather much time to worry about his three children and my father, who was the middle one, spent much of his youth in Italy, living with family friends who brought him up and took care of his education.

None of the three brothers spoke much of their father, and when they did, it was with a blend of admiration and resentment. One remark of the old man which seemed to have stuck in the minds of his sons was to the effect that there was only enough money in the family for one to wear patent leather boots and it was going to be him; they struck me as odd things by which to measure wealth. My grandfather seems to have had little concern for either of his two elder sons; to the youngest one, Bill, he gave the rather lofty advice (circa 1885) that the Army was no longer a career for a gentleman. He was somewhat irritated to find his advice rejected and his son enlisting in the ranks of his own regiment. They made it up later: my uncle, after getting a commission in the 15th Hussars, went on to become a full general.

My father, when still in his teens, set off with his elder brother for Australia where they spent twenty-five to thirty gruelling years sheep-farming; somehow they survived years of drought or low wool prices and in 1910 they were able to sell out and return home, where they hoped to enjoy the security and comfort for which they had struggled. By that time, however, the world was on the brink of change and drifting uneasily towards war.

By 1914, the drift had become an irreversible tide. My father, despite the fact that he was then aged fifty-one, served first in Gallipoli on his brother's staff and then in France. In 1917, he married my mother. I was born in 1919 in a house in Berkeley Street, in a Mayfair very different from that of today. In the following year we moved to Ascot. Looking back now, it seems that while my father had managed somehow to survive and to absorb the shock and horror of that most terrible war, the slump of 1929 brought him to the edge of despair. He was by then older; he had a family for whom he thought he had provided. He saw that the security of an earlier age, to which he had striven to return, had been undermined; he felt that he had achieved nothing. Contentment gave place to worry, principally about his children. Could he continue to pay for our education? Perhaps more important, would we be able to make the most of the start in life with which he was just about able to provide us? He used to scour our school reports for signs of encouragement, saying that to be average was not good enough. His constant urging caused me to look on work as unrewarding drudgery. My brother Tommy, two years younger than myself, handled the pressures better than I did.

My mother had been brought up with a deep Christian faith, which she kept all her life: she did in truth love her neighbour as herself. Twenty-five years younger than my father, she loved, honoured and obeyed him and endeavoured to build something of a bridge between him and us, their children, and to create a degree of mutual understanding. Warmth was more difficult, for my father was, at least on the surface, a stern, strict man and not one to show his feelings. Years later, when they were both dead, I found a letter that he had written to my mother, in which he came

7

near to saying that he would prefer to be proud of his children than to be loved by them. I felt as if I had put my hand in the embers of a fire, supposedly dead and cold, and touched something still hot; I wondered if he had really meant it. He died in 1938, a sadder man than I then understood, hedged in by disappointment, of which he could not bring himself to speak and from which he knew no escape.

My mother was deeply shaken by his death; having loved him, cared for him and depended upon him, she now found herself in charge of her home and family and a year later confronting the changes and sadnesses of war. In the autumn of 1939 she took into her house at Ascot a Waifs and Strays Home, evacuated from London; there were some twenty-five girls of school age, cared for by a matron and sister. My mother did not just make room for them in her house; she welcomed them, immersed herself in their problems and set out to give them some of the things which they had always lacked but which most take for granted. They returned her welcome a hundredfold. One of the girls, Sheila Stewart, later wrote a book about her time at Ascot, *Home from Home*, and another, *Ramblin' Rose*, a remarkable story in the vernacular, about the canal boats and the people who worked them. In 1995 she wrote to me, 'I shall always be deeply grateful to your mother. Thanks to her taking us in as evacuees and canvassing support and funds for the Society among her friends around Ascot, I was enabled to go to Grammar School and College. I only wish she were alive today, I have so much to thank her for.' Another, Dawn Tiffin, wrote at the same time, 'I do hope she knew a little of what she made for us girls, we loved her very much. Because of Englemere Wood, girls were able to travel all over the world, work and make something of their lives and be proud to have been "home girls".'

Matron and Sister, too, were loved and cherished by their former charges, now with husbands and children – even grandchildren – of their own, long after their retirement. I am sure that the love of her new, enlarged family did much to sustain my mother during the long sad years of war, particularly when my brother, whom she adored, was killed in 1942.

In my early years I attended a kindergarten run by a large lady, Mrs Robley-Brown, who insisted on showing us how to march without being very good at it herself; right arm and right leg went forward together and a bit of a wobble resulted. One particularly shocking event is lodged for ever in my memory; a girl called Mary had emptied her fountain pen into the tadpoles' tank in the classroom and they were all found dead in the morning. Mrs Robley-Brown herself, reinforced by a clergyman, arrived in the classroom to denounce such wickedness, made intolerable because it had been revealed on Empire Day: it was, she said, and I remember the outrage which flowed from her, a betrayal of those whom that day we were honouring and who had made our glorious Empire.

The kindergarten was not, I think, a success, for a governess, Miss Saunders, soon followed. A keen Wolf Cub mistress, with a liking for the curate for whom she spent much time writing out texts in diaries, she also used to take a bath after lunch from which she emerged boiled and lobster-red. Well-intentioned and earnest, she was fun to torment and she made me aware that authority had its funny side and could be made to look ridiculous, particularly as she did not have the support of my father. Church on Sunday morning was a ritual, with a parson who put so much of his energy into polishing the woodwork of his pulpit that he had none left with which to enliven the drone of his sermon. Over the altar there was a terrible stained glass window of Christ on the cross; the lead lines, just below the knees, caused me for years to wonder why he should have been wearing socks. There are other fragments, which it is difficult now to fit into the jigsaw: learning from a boy named David Bevan, who used to join us with Miss Saunders, that girls were in some ways different from boys – he had a sister whom he had seen in the bath; holidays at Littlehampton, where I remember a bandstand; at Bexhill, where I had a bit of wood to which I was greatly attached; and at Weymouth, to which we travelled in a special coach hitched on to a variety of trains. I decided to become an engine driver.

Heatherdown School in May 1928: huge boys arriving, some of them in large, smart cars, carrying bats and shining red cricket balls; they didn't notice anything as small as me. A cricket ground called the Polloi for the smaller boys, large conker trees with white plumes, and a rather fierce, no-nonsense matron who came from

Yorkshire and had an accent which I hadn't heard before: my mother took to her at once. An awful piece of verse about 'wee folk, good folk, trooping all together' and a 'white owl's feather'. A master in huge baggy plus-fours swinging golf clubs. It was all strange and very alarming. I found that I couldn't run as fast as most others and, even worse, that I lacked those all-important skills which are involved in making a ball do what you want it to do; I could not therefore hope for any distinction. Mr Day, the headmaster, had captained Kent at cricket and played soccer for the Corinthians: he thought well of boys who might do likewise. I couldn't think of anything to say in twice-weekly letters home; nor, for good measure, could I sing in tune.

Mr P. M. Wilson, or Mr 'Willie', is the one I most remember from that school, and with immense gratitude. He loved what he taught and was determined at least to give those he taught the chance of doing the same. He implanted in me at the age of twelve an awareness of the English language and the sound of it: he opened up Shakespeare and Tennyson; his teaching of the New Testament and the Book of Common Prayer was memorable – I used to know how many times Christ said 'verily, verily' using the word twice; Greek and Latin were made interesting. He gave us all a motto in Latin: mine was *Mihi festinandum est* – I must get a move on. It always took me a long time to organize myself. He painted pictures, each of which illustrated a line from a hymn: those who could identify the line were rewarded by having their initials inscribed on a panel in one corner. One which I remember was of Mr and Mrs Day in their car being towed through the school gates: it illustrated 'Joyless is the Day's Return'. The finest teacher by far of my schooldays, he reappeared in my life some forty years later, living in an old railway cottage at Templecombe in Somerset and in bad health and poor. It was possible then to thank him and help him a little.

Since I could not sing in tune I was not in the school choir, so I used to take my turn at blowing the organ in Chapel. During a lull in the singing one day, I read a letter from my mother in which she suggested that if, in the forthcoming entrance exam for Eton, I came somewhere near the middle, that would be all right. I was greatly and unreasonably incensed

and prayed earnestly that I would take the top level, and which
to everyone's amazement I did.

Eton was better, but lack of skill at games still mattered. Being
free to choose, or so much freer than home or school had previously
allowed, meant that one had to organize oneself, which I found hard.
There were rules to be followed and requirements to be met, and
penalties for failure to do so; but you were on your own. On my
first day I was walking to nowhere in particular, with nothing to
do and wondering how I should do it, when I saw coming towards
me a boy with a friendly face and a huge smile. He said, 'I am Palmer.
You must be Peyton. Come with me and have a biscuit – my family
make them.' Gordon Palmer was one of those people who exuded
welcome, who saw something good in everyone and took pains to
bring it to the surface: he remained the same throughout his life.
Another particularly warm and comforting presence in my house
was the dame (the same as a matron elsewhere), Miss Hichens; she
was described as being two dames round and half a dame high,
had a marvellous tinkling laugh and used to read to you if you
were sick. Fagging was a pest, particularly if one's fagmaster was
large and greedy and stupid, and one of mine was all three. He
ate prodigiously, including sausages for tea, which I had to cook;
he also had a coal fire, which at times withstood all my efforts
to light it.

I learned from my housemaster, Mr Kerry, that life was a mixture
of light and shade; to complain that it was unfair or even to think
so was silly and a waste of time. In those days the standard of
teaching was, at best, mixed. Mr Jaques, my classical tutor, was
kind if somewhat formal. In early days Euclid was a mystery which
the Rev. John Challoner Chute – I remember all his names –
who instructed me in maths did nothing to unravel; he was the
bane of my existence. He used to yell at me in a high-pitched
voice, 'My poor boy, how can anyone be so stupid?' In that
same voice he once admonished a small boy who bumped into
him in the street, 'Why don't you look where you're going, boy?'
To which, since the old horror had a bit of a squint, the reply
came back, 'Why don't you go where you're looking, sir?' The
Rev. Archibald Graham-Campbell taught me classics in my first
term; his particular talent lay in extinguishing any interest which

might, but for his handling of it, have existed in the subject. He could make anything dull, and in his preparation for Confirmation he pretty well did for God. The authorities of the Church eventually despatched him to some overseas diocese as a bishop. There was a terrifying man called H. K. Marsden and known as Bloody Bill; he never taught me, but I used from time to time to find myself doing Trials (a good name for examinations) under his awful gaze. He would prowl round the room, making noises with his finger joints and watching to make sure that no one was cheating: he induced in me something near to paralysis.

The Officers' Training Cops brought rifles and sergeant instructors and field days into my view. Pretence was the order of the day: rattles did duty for machine guns, and a variety of flags for heavier weapons and tanks; a hint of what was to come. King George V's funeral in 1935 was a unique occasion, which marked the passing not just of a monarch but of an age as well. We OTC cadets lined a part of the route in the grounds of Windsor Castle. The command 'Rest on your arms reversed' involved heads being lowered over the butt of your rifle which was pointed downwards. It made it difficult, but not quite impossible, to see from under the peak of a uniform cap that slow-moving procession of kings and princes and statesmen, clad, some of them, in wonderful uniforms, passing only a few feet away like ghosts before their time.

From time to time distinguished people were invited to give lectures to an assembly of senior boys, known for some reason as the First Hundred. Lord Willingdon was one whom I particularly remember; he had recently returned from India, where as Viceroy he had ruled over that huge, teeming sub-continent in real majesty. In appearance he was magnificent, immaculate in a grey frock coat, a true patrician and the archetype of an imperial statesman. He quickly let the air out of that with his opening words: 'The proudest day of my life was not when I became Viceroy of India, but when I put on a light blue cap and played for Eton at Lords.' It cut no ice and diminished almost to nothing his account of life in one of the most enthralling positions a man could hold. Visiting politicians used to make the same sort of error, feigning nervousness and trepidation where they felt none.

Twice I went in for the Loder Declamation Prize; the judge

on the first occasion was Winston Churchill. I remember three things about that rather awe-inspiring occasion: first, his neat, well-polished boots; second, my own chagrin when he awarded the prize not to me but to the headmaster's son, Patrick Alington; and lastly, some of the words which we were required to declaim from John Donne's tremendous sermon on death: 'It comes equally to us all and makes us all equal when it comes.' The passage goes on to speak of the dusts of the churchyard, a mixture of patrician bran and plebeian chaff, and to pose the question, '. . . who then will undertake to sift those dusts again?'. They were words magnificent in sound and meaning, but 'sift those dusts' were not easy ones to articulate.

Much of what is taught and learned doesn't stay for long: it is like roughage in the diet which passes through, leaving something from which bone and blood and muscle and fat are made. Out of the mass which is put in by way of instruction, something is retained for the building of memory and intellect. Greek is at the root of so much human activity: it is the language of the poets of tragedy and comedy, the gateway to philosophy. Without Latin, it would be hard to do more than glimpse the scope of Rome's power and its law or gain an impression of the 'great majesty of the Roman peace'. The thought somewhere expressed by Tacitus that the only thing to which the Germans responded was a 'repeated dose of blood and iron' was one which stuck. I dabbled – I was neither clever enough nor energetic enough to do more – in the classics, although I was fortunate to be taught them for one year by John Wilkes, known as Jeeves. Despite myself, I absorbed and remembered a surprising amount. *The Frogs* of Aristophanes particularly has stayed with me; it is the tale of the visit to Hades of Dionysus, God of the Theatre, to bring back the recently dead Euripides. In the event, he is called upon to act as the judge in a contest between Aeschylus and Euripides to decide which is the greater poet and which should return to reverse the decline of the Greek theatre. The two of them speak lines which are weighed in cheese-scales; those of Aeschylus are pronounced the weightier of the two and he is therefore proclaimed the winner; the frivolous criteria and processes of judgement that are mocked in the play have many modern echoes.

Maths and science, poorly taught, became, at least for me, commonplace and dull; giants such as Copernicus, Galileo and Newton were quickly flattened out by such treatment. No one spoke of the resentment and anger which consumed the authorities of the Church on being told that the world was not as they said it was. No one told of Newton, who overturned the world of physics and saw himself as 'a boy playing on the sea-shore, whilst the great ocean of truth lay all undiscovered before me'. Archimedes was interesting only because a bath seemed an odd place in which to make his important discovery.

We were required, one week in March 1936, to read the Sunday papers and be ready the following Tuesday to make a speech about their content. They reported the German re-entry into the Rhineland, ordered by Hitler in defiance of the Versailles Treaty. The French were ready to move against them, but not alone. Britain counselled patience; after all, as some worthy said at the time, 'the Germans have only gone into their own back garden'; we were, as ever, slow to recognize evil, and the chance of stopping Germany was lost. As Churchill wrote ten years later in Volume I of *The Second World War*, 'Virtuous motives trammelled by inertia and timidity are no match for armed and resolute wickedness.' Wishing to make an impression, I said that the events of the weekend would lead to war. Why ever should Hitler turn back from success which had been so easily won? Why forfeit acclamation and risk rejection? Why grovel and confess that he had got things wrong when he had read the stars so well? Why, seeing our meek acceptance of his first challenge, should he hesitate in the future? I half expected a rebuke for being melodramatic. But instead Mr Wilkes, for whom I had great respect, commented favourably and seemed even to agree. I was pleased, but I began to feel afraid and to wonder what was going to happen to the world in which I was growing up and which was beginning to seem good.

Eton was, I think, my first conscious encounter with history. Old and beautiful buildings in brick and stone – School Yard, College Chapel, the Cloisters and Upper School – spoke of those whose vision they had been. They also told of the unending procession of boys who had passed through them, taking away with them an imprint of the place and leaving their own upon it. The long list in the cloister beneath Upper School of those who had given their lives in the First World War was a reminder that civilized life was not just a part of the natural order of things and that some had paid a steep price to preserve it. Before long, that sad list was to be reopened to include the names of many of my contemporaries, my brother's amongst them.

I went up to Oxford to read law in October 1937. Trinity was a small, beautiful and friendly college, and my rooms were those once occupied by the elder Pitt as an undergraduate. The door into my staircase was watched over by a bust of John Henry Newman, who had written in 1867 of his wish 'to oppose the coward despairing spirit of the day'. Adjoining the quad was a garden, lovely and timeless. The College was Head of the River in 1938 and again in 1939: no fewer than seven of the crew of that last year were killed serving with the RAF in the years that followed. Dick Hillary, a particular friend of mine during our first year, later achieved fame as a fighter pilot in the RAF. Shot down and badly burnt, he wrote a wonderful book called *The Last Enemy*. Having done so he went back to flying, unable to stop himself, until the almost inevitable end.

The College was presided over at that time by the Rev. Dr Blakiston, known to all as Blinks but never so addressed. Once some undergraduates had whitewashed the word 'Blinks' on a wall by the Lodgings. Confident that they had not been seen, they were surprised and dismayed to be summoned before him. He had told the College 'Boots' (there is no such position today) that he wanted the names of all those whose shoes bore traces of whitewash. Dr Blakiston was a bachelor who determinedly avoided contact with the female sex. Writing to a colleague to congratulate him on the birth of a daughter, he rather spoiled things by adding at the end, 'Better luck next time.' To a lady who wrote asking for a night's lodging, he replied tersely, 'Bring your own sheets'; she went elsewhere. He was not at all sympathetic to the idea of women at Oxford, detested the New Bodleian and loved mosaics. On these subjects he could talk with eloquence; for all others he needed time to prepare. Once during a sermon he found that a page of his notes was missing; he stopped in mid-stream and waited while someone went back to the Lodgings to fetch it. Ordinarily

Dr Blakiston wore a square bowler hat, but when out for a drive, on reaching the city limits he would exchange this for a catfish skin cap, trimmed with fur, which he had acquired on holiday in Norway. Legend has it that, driving an Austin Seven which he had recently acquired but not quite learned to master, he said to his companion as they approached the Martyrs' Memorial in the middle of Oxford, 'You look that way and I'll look this way.' Both looked their respective ways; the car, lacking instructions to the contrary, continued on its course straight into the Martyrs' Memorial. When the visiting head of an American university came to call, dressed in full academic robes, Dr Blakiston caught sight of him standing at the front door and demanded: 'Who are you out there all dressed up like that?' Having then, with some reluctance, allowed the visitor to come in, he faced him with the somewhat terse instruction, 'All right, be brief, be brief.' On another occasion when he was escorting Lady Astor, then a new MP, to an encaenia, he dealt summarily with her comment on the age of those receiving honorary degrees and her fear that she would have to wait a long time for hers. 'Madam, that is a contingency so remote that I don't think we need spend time in contemplating it.'

During the First World War a bath-house had been erected in the College by the Government for its own purpose. With the peace came the suggestion that the College should pay for it. 'We don't want it, you must take it away and make good the site,' insisted Dr Blakiston. The bath-house remained, and the idea that it should be paid for was dropped. There would be no place for him today, which seems a pity; he stood for something not easily defined, and for that reason will be long and fondly remembered.

The man who most influenced the College was the bursar, Philip Landon, who taught law. He thought it important that the College should excel, and rejoiced in the success of those who shone on the river and the cricket field, in rugger and athletics. He was a bachelor who had fought in the First World War, and his life and love were Trinity and the law. He was said to be a snob; he was certainly a fervent believer in the aristocratic principle, which to him meant the rule, not of the richest or of those with titles, but of the best. The plea of the younger Pitt after Trafalgar, 'May the liberties of the people never be trampled in pieces by democracy', was one which he echoed. He tried very hard to get me to work; but I couldn't. The restraints of school and of home were things of the past: my father had died in 1938, six months after I had gone up to Oxford.

For the first time in my life I found myself out of range of good advice, and I enjoyed it. War appeared certain; though some of those whose duty it was to prepare for it persuaded themselves and others that it was not. Study, examinations and thoughts of a career seemed unreal, irrelevant, and although I made some kind of acquaintance with the law, I did not let it trouble me too much. Eating my quota of dinners at the Inner Temple provided a good excuse to go to London. I became over-fond of racing and bet more than I could afford. I dabbled in politics – not much, but enough to become addicted later. I spoke from time to time in the Union, once 'on the paper', as it was called, in support of the Prime Minister, Neville Chamberlain; I could think of nothing very convincing to say and made a dreadful hash of it. Oxford is a beautiful historic place, very much alive with a huge variety of people and things to do. I was, I knew, lucky to be there. I knew also that it would not last. We were coming to the end of a chapter; the next one would tell a different story.

Some five years later, when Germany was in ruins and Hitler lay dead in his bunker, and so many of those whom I had known at Oxford had been trampled down in the ghastly process which he had launched, I went back to Trinity and spent an afternoon in the garden. I wondered which was real; how could that unchanged, quiet and lovely place have co-existed with the horror which had destroyed so much and brought such grief and anguish in its train?

I looked back then to that brief period in which the last embers of hope were dying. The Anschluss, Hitler's annexation of Austria, had put paid to that country in 1938. Sudetenland – the last item, so Hitler said, on his menu in Europe – was eaten up later in the year. Munich had brought the short-lived relief of a couple of aspirin. Neville Chamberlain's claim to have brought back 'peace with honour' sounded almost improper and certainly ridiculous; it was as if he thought that, by putting on the clothes of the past, he could gain present respectability. His purloining of Hotspur's words, 'Out of this nettle danger we have plucked this flower safety', only made it worse. I can see the news film now of him descending from an aeroplane, waving a piece of paper which Hitler had signed without hesitation and whose message he meant not at all. It was terrible how flimsy and futile the man of peace had been made to look when pitted against the ruthless and the vile. The seizure of Prague less than six months later had only confirmed what had already been clear, that bargains struck with wicked men – the word 'wicked' seems inadequate, but I know no other – are perishable. When in August 1939 Hitler struck at Poland, the Allies whispered weakly 'No' and delivered an ultimatum which the aggressor predictably ignored. He had already challenged the world; he had grabbed what he wanted and no one had moved; he was armed and prepared for war; he knew that those against him were not. He had been convinced by events that those who pleaded for peace would never go to war. In that, he judged wrong; but the price of his error was one which millions paid.

The seizure of Prague had removed any doubts that remained and, with conscription in the offing, I preferred, unwisely as things turned out, to make my own arrangements rather than wait and have them made for me. I applied for and received a commission in the Supplementary Reserve of the 15th/19th Hussars. In the summer of 1939, I served what was originally intended to be a two months' attachment with the regiment in York. Horses had been replaced in the previous year by a mixture of light tanks and carriers. The Light Tank Mark VIB, to give it its full name, deserves ignominious mention. Though light, it was not fast nor was it easy to control: downhill, because its steering depended upon the clutch, it had a way of going in the opposite direction to that intended. Its armour was flimsy. Inside it was a mass of sharp edges, protrusions capable of doing far more serious injury to those within than its guns could inflict upon an enemy.

A stout and pompous little full colonel in the RAOC visited us in camp at Ganton a bare two weeks before the outbreak of war and warned us of the sanctity which attached to grass verges: allowing any track vehicle to mount one was an offence which could lead to a court martial. I have often wondered what happened to him, and how he coped with the storm when it came. Was he with his futile little rule book swept away by it? Or did he perhaps find some niche in which he remained high and dry, out of reach of the tides of war, putting his head out every now and then to nip the unwary? He remains in my memory, not because he made any impact upon my life, but as a reminder of how ready we are to find a role for the officious and room for the self-important.

II

The Devil's Turn: 1939

It was as if a paralysing pestilence had visited the place; it was simply the stupefying numbness of war.

Laurie Lee, *A Moment of War*

On 3 September 1939 I heard William Temple, then Archbishop of York, preach in York Minster. He knew – as we all did – that by the time the service had finished we would be formally at war. We were, he said, to love our enemies. I was not at that time able to understand, nor can I now, how anyone can be expected to set out to kill who is not moved by hate or fear or greed. How was it possible, in any ordinary sense of the word, to love the Germans, who were at that moment poised to release such massive evil upon the world? At the end of the service, the Archbishop confirmed that the ultimatum to Hitler had indeed expired; we were at war; the destruction of Poland would go on. There were two realities present on that lovely morning. The fabric of the Minster was real enough: it was something you could touch and see and feel, shining with light and grace. Yet there was something other, just as real, though you couldn't see it: it was haunting and full of menace. A single man had conjured up forces, which it seemed could put out the light and which had nothing to do with grace – forces which could destroy the fabric of that beautiful place and much else. God, it seemed, had had his moment; it was now the Devil's turn.

There ensued a gap in time – almost a vacuum – during which the stage was being cleared for the first act of a play, of which only the prologue had at the time been written. The Army started at once to grow – in numbers at least: it began by retrieving those who were in its cold store, the reservists. One morning I had to march to the station some two or three hundred of them who, having been recalled to the colours and dressed up in uniform, were to be assimilated and digested into the system, reconditioned as soldiers. They were a wonderful, cheerful and irreverent lot, who could have easily found their way to the station without my guidance. In so far as my commands were audible, they fell in with them: some even managed an eyes right to the Commander in Chief, Northern Command, whom we passed unexpectedly. If they were concerned about what lay ahead for them, they kept their concern at bay with a mixture of beer and that strange instinct which, when things become serious, leads the British people to find something good in each other and something to laugh at as well. The highlight of my life in York had, however, nothing to do with the Army. On my first evening there I sat next to a girl named Mary Wyndham at dinner, danced with her afterwards, met her again the next day at an agricultural show, fell in love with her and never completely got over it.

I was in due course despatched with John Brooke-Hunt, who became a lifelong friend, to join the 54th Armoured Training Regiment at Perham Down, near Tidworth in Hampshire. It was not armoured, it didn't train anyone for anything, nor was it recognizable as a regiment. Rather it was a cold store, in which a motley collection of dug-outs from the previous war who had long forgotten anything they had ever learned about soldiering, and young men who knew even less, were collected and kept until someone thought of something to do with them and found some place to which to send them. Those in charge were uninspiring. The commanding officer was a regular soldier for whom his own regiment had no present requirement. My squadron leader, hauled back to the Army out of London Transport, was a dull man who saw it as his duty to keep a jaundiced eye on all that went on around him; he regularly filled me with sympathy for drivers and conductors of buses who had endured his rule. For good measure there was an adjutant who had, until a few months before, been playing the organ in Lower Chapel at Eton. He was a considerable musician and, I am sure, a kindly man, but the move from organ console to orderly room desk had changed him into a martinet and caused him to bestow upon King's Regulations the enthusiasm and devotion which he had once applied to the Te Deum.

There were neither duties to be performed nor pleasures to be enjoyed; the atmosphere – too lively a term, perhaps – was the essence of anti-climax. No one knew what was coming and most thought it better not to guess. It took time to realize that our superiors knew as little as we did about what was going on; the war became the 'phoney war', and we seemed to be quietly slipping back into peace. But that was too much to hope for and there were signs that things were not quite as they had been: ration books; gas masks; large numbers of elderly people in uniform, often with armbands proclaiming their importance; and trains which took twice as long as before to reach their destinations. A song declaring that we were going to hang out our washing on the Siegfried Line seemed a bit wide of the mark; the fact was that we had got into something for which we weren't ready and which would not easily be ended.

The stultifying dullness of life at Perham Down was considerably brightened by the arrival of Toby Milbanke, who was a source of much-needed light and laughter. He had been a regular soldier in the 10th Hussars. Discouraged by the thought of remaining for long years a subaltern on a rate of pay that was derisory, he had sought and found more acceptable employment. He dealt in Perrier Jouet champagne, Benson and Hedges cigars and rum from the West Indies, spending such time as he could spare in the pursuit of foxes. Having become accustomed to an agreeable way of life he didn't find the restrictions involved in a return to Army life at all congenial; even less the people who imposed them. Told by his commanding officer that he did not like his subalterns sitting in the Mess after lunch drinking Kümmel and smoking cigars, he responded, 'Well, you can fucking well make me a captain.' Usually he was content, without the need for words, to convey an impression of profound disrespect for those who had charge both of us and, at that time, of our country.

Toby had once won a bet that he could hit a golf ball from the steps of White's Club to those of St Paul's Cathedral in under three hundred shots. He did it, helped by a friendly policeman, early one Sunday morning. His father had won a VC, at Gallipoli, and he dreamed of doing the same; he had a host of amusing friends and

22

was full of laughter and fun. His dachshund, called Goering after the Reichsmarschall, being both small and unwarlike hardly lived up to his name. I met up with Toby again after the war; he had been badly beaten up in Yugoslavia by some Russians to whom he had declined to give up his jeep. Not long afterwards he shot himself, a delayed casualty of war and a terrible reminder of the length of its shadow.

It was something of a relief to find that those on high were not only aware of our existence, but felt it appropriate to give us an inkling about what was going on and how they saw the future. All junior officers in the Tidworth District were assembled one fine September afternoon in the Bulford gymnasium to be enlightened. The presence of the Chief of the Imperial General Staff, Field Marshal Ironside, and a senior official from the Home Office gave the occasion an air of seriousness. The principal item on the afternoon's agenda was a film of the Maginot Line with a commentary to match. It was, we were told, impenetrable; it had a depth of three or four miles; it stretched from the Franco–Swiss frontier to a point just south of the Ardennes. The considerable gap between its ending and the North Sea was a matter of regret, but it was unlikely, so the argument went, that the Germans would wish either to incur the odium of attacking the neutral Low Countries or to fight their way through the difficult terrain of the Ardennes. The civil servant, however, saw things in a less hopeful light. Nothing has ever erased his closing words from my memory: 'We must face it; we are going to have a tooth out and by God it's going to hurt.' I had a nasty feeling, which I shared with my neighbour, that it was one of our teeth that he had in mind. That afternoon's glimpse of authority's thinking was not particularly informative; even less was it reassuring.

In due course the process of what was at the time considered to be training got under way. Courses of a month each on driving and maintenance at Bovington and gunnery at Lulworth; a little later intelligence for a week or so at Aldershot. The threat of signalling for a month at Catterick disappeared, to my great relief, for I could never manage the Morse code. It was at Bovington, the headquarters of the Royal Armoured Corps, that it began to be clear how little thought we had given to the likelihood of war and how unready we were. We made the acquaintance of a range of track vehicles, few in number and wretched in performance. The Light Tank Mark VIB, to which I have already referred, grew worse on further acquaintance. Off the tarmac road, it bucked and reared over even minor bumps and; due to its interior arrangements, was a source of discomfort, even of danger, to its occupants; while, to an enemy, it could never have been more than a minor irritation. A larger one known as the Mark IX Cruiser carried eccentricity too far, in that if it survived contact with the enemy for more than twenty minutes it was inclined to set fire to itself. Better things on the way, was the hope of our skilled and competent sergeant instructor; he presented to us one morning, with something of a flourish, the Infantry Tank Mark 3 – Matilda to its friends – which moved at a maximum speed of four or five miles per hour and had a two-pounder gun and a respectable covering of armour. One rather inconvenient characteristic was that if it stalled in third gear the crew had to get out, open up the armour-plated backside and lever it into neutral with a nine-foot crowbar. It was, we were told, in mass production – three per month; a single old tank on a pedestal in the road, a survivor from the previous war preserved as a monument, at least looked more impressive.

At Lulworth we learned how to strip, clean, reassemble and fire those weapons which concerned us; a .5 Vickers machine gun which was said to be armour-piercing, a smaller .303 which was not, a Bren gun and a .5 Boyes anti-tank rifle. The course culminated in a battle practice – with Mickey Mouse and others popping up momentarily out of the gorse to be shot at. At Aldershot we studied aerial photographs and learned in some detail about poison gas: phosgene, chlorine, mustard and some sort of new nerve gas, which didn't sound at all nice, by name Arthur. Then back to Perham Down, where we hung about with, as before, nothing to do, forgetting much of what we had been taught and wondering uneasily when this eerie interval would end and what horrors would follow when the curtain rose at last on the next act. It was a relief to learn in March that a number of us, considered fit and ready for war, were to join our various regiments in France. The prospect of movement in any direction would ordinarily have been welcome. On the other hand, having become more or less engaged to Mary, there was the anguish of parting after two weeks of embarkation leave had vanished almost before they began; they were the last moments of happiness for a long time to come. A slow journey by train from Ludgershall to Southampton, a night sailing by troop ship to Le Havre, leaving behind us a country which, endeavouring to get on with its business, gave an impression of total unconcern with the non-event on the other side of the Channel, but tolerant of those sufficiently eccentric to wish to take part in it.

We spent a week or so in tents at Pacy, far from an ideal site: it took only a shower of rain to turn it into a quagmire. But apart from the distasteful chore of censoring letters life was a pleasant and leisurely affair, with plenty to eat and drink; there was no sign of the austerity which we had been quick to impose on ourselves at home. Lunch with John Brooke-Hunt on a lovely Sunday in late April at Bonnières was rounded off with a bottle of Château Yquem 1918; I had never drunk such nectar before. Returning drowsily to camp, we found orders for John and myself to join our regiment near Lille. A journey with many stops, and at a pace which an inquisitive tortoise could have managed, got us, rather surprisingly, to our destination. In the two weeks or so which followed, the curtain of hope which we had erected between ourselves and reality began to look more and more threadbare. We all knew that the Germans were about to move, and waited in the most gentlemanly way for them to do so at whatever time they chose.

In the unfounded hope that the Germans would respect their neutrality, the Governments of Belgium and Holland laid it down that the Allied Forces which had come to defend them should not enter until and unless the Germans attacked. It was, of course, an absurd arrangement and one which we must have been daft to accept. On 10 May the Germans did exactly as they had always planned to do and attacked both Holland and Belgium, at which point we were allowed in, having thus made sure that the Germans were not in any way disadvantaged. As the first Allied troops to enter Belgium, we were greeted along the route by cheering crowds as deliverers from the invading horde which now threatened their small country once more. Our vehicles were strewn with lilac;

we were inundated with gifts of food and wine. We provided those cheering crowds with a flicker of hope, which lasted only days before being extinguished by the onrush of German might.

The operation – it was really not much more than a gesture – might possibly have made sense to Don Quixote; to those taking part it made none. There had been no chance to prepare, nor did anyone have any clear idea what was expected of us, still less how we might achieve it. I recall a feeling of almost total bewilderment. It was a confused dream, with unrelated incidents intruding into memory like mountain tops emerging through the clouds beneath them. I don't remember being consumed by a great desire to do anything particularly heroic. I didn't at all want to be killed, wounded or captured; nor, much as I detested Hitler, had I any great wish, since he was not available, to kill anyone else. What I do remember is the misery of that helpless stream of humanity which flowed along the roads. It had been their misfortune to find themselves in the invader's path and now they were crawling miserably away, severed from their roots, carrying with them all they could manage; their misery was topped up from time to time as the Germans bombed or machine-gunned them from the air. We saw nothing of the RAF until one day, suddenly, three fighters appeared in pursuit of two German planes, one of which we saw shot down. The effect on morale was instantaneous; men revived and washed and shaved and bade each other 'Good morning'. The announcement in a BBC news bulletin that the greatest tank battle in history was raging in the Louvain area came as a surprise, for the only tanks around at that time were our own, which were not up to much. It was then that I first became aware of the eyes of the Empire, which, the bulletin went on to say, were fixed on the town. Subsequently, those same eyes fixed themselves in turn with similarly disastrous consequences on Crete, on Singapore and finally on Tobruk, after which they mercifully remained closed.

Meanwhile, on the ground there was nothing we could do but sit and wait for the Germans to come, knowing only that they were on the move and that there was no one and nothing in front of us to stop them. As regimental intelligence officer it fell to me to make one or two sorties on a motorcycle, either alone or in a sidecar with a despatch rider, eastward towards Maastricht, Liège and the

Albert Canal some fifty miles away. Although I covered a good deal of ground, what I best remember now is the total emptiness and silence; no one moved on the roads or in the village streets; shops were closed; in the fields there were only unmilked cattle whose mournful complaint was, beyond the clatter of my own motorcycle and an occasional German aircraft overhead, the only sound I heard. Here and there sad bits of debris at the roadside told of German air attacks: a wrecked gun carriage with underneath it the charred and barely recognizable remains of what had been a man, and from time to time a pram or a home-made cart left loaded with belongings which someone seeking safety had hoped to take with them but had been forced to leave behind. Once I chanced upon the headquarters of a Belgian division; I met and talked to a general and his staff, but any hope that they might be able to tell me either what was going on or their own plans soon vanished. A bullet hole suddenly appearing just in front of me in my sidecar during one of those journeys served as a reminder of my personal involvement. Apart from that, I was just a looker on at a scene in which there was no movement and from which no sound emerged: its message of despair was one you couldn't miss. In words written by Laurie Lee about the Spanish Civil War, 'It was as if a paralysing pestilence had visited the place; it was simply the stupefying numbness of war.'

I had an accident on my motorcycle one morning, damaging my knee. Slightly hurt, I went in to report to the colonel and was alarmed to find him closeted with General Montgomery: even in those early days Monty created the impression of understanding the situation and being the only one who did, and above all having a clear idea about what might happen next. He was kind and sympathetic about my injured knee, and even interested in what I had to report. I narrowly escaped what I saw at the time as the ignominy of being despatched in an ambulance as a casualty: later I saw things differently. After a few days, but still without having had contact with the enemy, we moved back across the River Dyle. Somewhere along the way we came across a chateau from which it was clear the owners had moved out in haste. It seemed almost like a stage set from a film studio, with a well-kept garden and beautiful lawns – an island on which the sun still shone, untouched and totally remote from war. There was also a well-filled cellar, from which we borrowed a bottle of wine with which to wash down a quick lunch; then we moved on out of a short and pleasant dream.

A man who was said to have been signalling with a torch from a window was brought to me in the night: someone had had the idea that I was the one to deal with him. Clutching a New Testament, he shook and shivered and foamed at the mouth. Aware that, with nerves very much on edge, those who had found him were expecting drastic action from me, I wondered what on earth to do with him. There was nowhere to lock him up and nowhere to send him; I couldn't – and didn't at all want to – persuade myself that he was dangerous; I judged him mad and let him go. We were moving back; by that time there was no thought in anyone's mind that we could do otherwise. Unhappily and for no reason that I ever understood, we were transferred to the Fourth Division, none of whom I ever saw, but whose retreat we were to cover.

Waiting in the night by a crossroads, cold and silent, looking along a road expecting Germans to emerge at any moment from the darkness; a few shells burst at first light, but no one came; then we were moving back again. We were said to be cut off, at least to the extent that the bridge immediately behind us over the River Dendre was in German hands. The commanding officer, Donald Frazer, sent me off to tell 'C' Squadron of this and suggest that they should try to cross the river at Liederkirk. On my way to see which, if any, of the bridges were not in enemy hands I met up with John Livingstone-Learmonth, a troop leader in my regiment, and took a ride on the back of his carrier. As we entered a small town, I shouted to him to tell his driver to keep into the side under the shelter of the houses. I remember very clearly how, a moment later, a ball of light appeared, coming, it seemed, quite slowly towards us. It hit John full in the chest, killing him instantly. I got back to 'C' Squadron and reported what had happened.

After that, my memories become confused and fragmentary. Separated somehow from my motorcycle and sidecar, I joined others running in what we hoped was the right direction. I remember taking shelter in a field of standing corn which, I began to understand with some relief, lifted the bullets as they zipped through it; then moving for better protection to a pig-sty where I met up with Co Peterkin, a cheerful Scottish lawyer who had joined my regiment in France not long before I did. We decided to wait until dark before moving out; we hoped that if, meanwhile, the Germans should arrive, they would not be interested in the pigs and would not notice us. It was not long before they did arrive in swarms, out of nowhere; they had the air of men who understood what they were doing, knew that they were winning and were enjoying themselves. Any relief that I may have felt at finding myself still alive was soon overtaken by confusion and the first twinges of an enduring anguish.

III

Prisoner of War: 1940–1945

By the waters of Babylon we sat down and wept.
Psalm 137

Six of us locked in a small room together in the Grenadier barracks in Brussels, unable to go out save for visits to the lavatory. No room for anything save the beds – not very comfortable ones, but the last we were to see for years. A long, slow, sad and hungry march eastwards from Brussels through Tirlemont to Maastricht. I have dim memories of the days, none at all of the nights. One more move, this time by train, and we were in Germany. Some days in a school at Bocholt which served as a prison: days in which there was little to eat and nothing to do, except begin to take in bit by bit and painfully – you couldn't manage it all at once – the size and horror of what had happened: that the Germans were winning, that they were not going to be stopped and that we were to our shame their captives. Endless games of piquet played with a pack of cards which, having gone through many dirty and greasy hands, had achieved two or three times its original thickness. On the back of each card was an advertisement for a liqueur: a bottle or so would have been welcome. A Belgian banker with a beautiful tenor voice sang songs. Our plight was the same as that of the Israelites, who, captive and having lost Jerusalem, sat down beside the waters of Babylon and wept. 'Gott mit Uns' was the claim on the German soldiers' belt buckles; certainly at that time he didn't seem to be with anyone else.

A long train journey south, with glimpses of the Rhine and of a seeming fairyland which both entranced and sickened. Arrival at Laufen in Bavaria, not far from the Austrian border and Salzburg,

30

and almost within spitting distance of Berchtesgaden, meant a world of barbed wire, overcrowding, hunger and dirt. No news save from contaminated German sources; worst of all, separation, to which there seemed no end, from just about everything that made life worth living. By way of welcome the Germans gave us numbers, took our photographs and shaved our heads. This made us all look different, prematurely old; it was, so the Germans said, to get rid of the lice, though at that time we were free of them. They came later, the result of primitive living conditions. In my room 117 people lived, ate and slept; half that number would have been a crowd. We slept on straw paillasses on top of wooden slats in three-layered bunks, as many as the room could hold. Books were scarce and those which came my way seemed tantalizingly to be all about food, of which we had very little.

In those first months there was little to do except continue the process of absorbing what had happened. The dinginess, the squalor and the overcrowding, the meagre rations, the shaven heads and twice-daily parades to be counted were the principal ingredients of our existence: there didn't seem to be a future. As a special concession we were allowed into a cellar full of rotting potatoes to search for any that might be edible; the stench was unforgettable. There was an odious and greasy interpreter, Couffietta or some such name, who on roll-call parades used to declaim to us the various camp orders which the Germans thoughtfully issued for our guidance. One, which never failed to raise a laugh and which was repeated at intervals, warned that British officers prisoners of war were strictly forbidden to have connection with German women; a breach of the order would be punishable with imprisonment for life or, in severe cases, even with death. Occasionally, and from only a few places in the camp, it was possible to catch sight of a woman – usually looking like a pantomime dame, in no way tempting and anyhow impossible to reach. On one of our twice-daily parades all Jews were bidden to step forward: Clifford Cohen, later a County Court judge, bravely did so, having no idea what to expect. It proved to be nothing more serious than an exercise in humiliation, but he didn't know that at the time.

After some months a few food parcels from those parts of Europe as yet unconquered began to filter through. A friend of mine, Tim

Bailey, received one or two from the wife of our Ambassador to Hungary, still free from Nazi molestation, and generously shared out their delicious contents. A quantity of tinned hams, also from Hungary, would have been particularly welcome but was received with caution by the British authorities, who decreed that they should be put by for a rainy day; one wondered what more would have to happen before our circumstances could be so described. When, many months later and prior to a move to another camp, the tins were opened on German orders, they exploded, the contents having by then acquired the characteristics of dynamite.

Isolated incidents from those early days keep emerging from the mists. Without warning, a moronic sentry shot and killed a young officer simply because he was looking out of a high window, nowhere near the wire. In the absence of news from any untainted non-German source, rumours known as 'Latrinograms' were rife. A monk who regularly visited the camp for no obvious purpose was said to have sidled up to one prisoner, nudged him, turned over the cross he wore and pointed to the WD (War Department) sign; another version was that he had whispered, 'MI5! Not to worry – we've got them fucked.' From some source or other the content of one of Churchill's most famous speeches reached us, and with it a faint gleam of hope that all was not lost. I had never got on terms with music before, but found there was comfort to be had in listening to Henry Coombe-Tennant, who had been captured in Boulogne with the Welsh Guards, playing the piano by the hour, from memory and without repeating himself. Music took you into a world beyond the reach of words: Bach's 'Jesu, Joy of Man's Desiring' and 'Sheep May Safely Graze' came as the faintest of echoes from a world which had no resemblance to the one in which we found ourselves.

Strangely, the wine for the German officers' mess was stored in a cellar which, though protected by a number of locked doors, was actually inside one of the prison blocks. It was only a matter of time, once the wine was known to be there, before Michael Edwards of the Royal Welch Fusiliers, who had a way with locks, was able to get at it. Once we had got access to the wine, it seemed only sensible to remove as large a quantity as possible while the opportunity remained. There was, however, a problem of concealing it in a building which had been stripped of anything that was not absolutely necessary and afforded little cover. We had little choice but to drink it in huge quantities, with the result that stomachs, somewhat empty and unaccustomed to such a deluge, rebelled. On balance, it was an enjoyable occasion; not only did we have a liberal supply of drink to cheer us up, but one of the more unpleasant German NCOs was seized by such an explosion of rage that, had he not been held together by his belt, he would have been disintegrated by the force.

Victor Fortune, as the commander of the 51st Division which had been cut off, surrounded and captured at St Valéry, had been as much stricken as any of us. Yet from the moment of his arrival he showed a greatness of heart and a dignity which were a marvellous example and encouragement to those who, far younger than himself, were not all that far from despair. He had had assigned to him a special guard whose orders were to follow him whenever he left his room – to protect him, so the Germans absurdly and characteristically said, from us. His response was to walk the little so-and-so off his feet. Looking back now, I remember General Fortune, his courage and his dignity, and am grateful for the example he set. The knighthood he received after the war was well earned.

We also had with us another 'General'; his real name was Captain Foa, and he was accorded this honorary rank to mark the fact that, smartly dressed in the uniform of the 3rd Hussars, even to wearing breeches and gaiters, he looked sufficiently distinguished, compared with the rest of us, to deserve it. He was an unusual character who, so he told us, had been given an allowance by his father of £400 a year on the somewhat novel condition that he stayed south of the Equator. Employed on a sheep farm in South Africa, and required one day to take a flock of sheep to market, he lost the majority en route and finally arrived with only four of them tucked up in the back of the South African equivalent of a Daimler Hire. There were other characters who for one reason or another took root in one's memory: a second lieutenant in the Tank Regiment called O'Hara, whose name and complexion ensured his being called Scarlet; he talked in a rather well-watered voice of the places in which he had, as he put it, dipped his wick. By way of contrast there were two who, in course of time, became dukes: John Brackley (Sutherland) and Ian Campbell (Argyll). There were two who worked in the kitchen, supervising the daily production of a substance which was given the name of soup; they seemed to maintain their body weight better than most. Bryan McIrvine, a young actor who, with make-up on and dim lighting, sang a song of those times called 'The Deepest Shelter in Town' and convinced his audience that Florence Desmond, who was then singing it in London, could not have done it better. There was a substantial quota of majors who were known as 'Corunnas', I suppose to mark the fact that they had been involved in some previous war; it didn't much matter which. There were as many as sixty or so of my Eton contemporaries: Phil Pardoe, captured in Calais with the 60th Rifles and Roddy Macleod, taken with the rest of the 51st Division at St Valéry, had both been in my house.

The Germans had no reason to be concerned with formalities such as the Geneva Convention governing prisoners of war: they had swept all before them; they had occupied or enslaved much of Europe; and the Third Reich, so Hitler told them, would last for a thousand years. Prisoners of war were a low priority – to be kept in and, so far as possible, alive. Germans, we learned, have little difficulty in going along with 'my country right or wrong', nor for that matter in accepting that whatever it does is right. They spend time and intelligence in putting together their plan; they march towards its fulfilment, impatient and contemptuous of those who have doubts. Chancellor Kohl's angry comment in 1996 that failure now to accept his guidance and German supremacy in Europe would mean war later suggests that not much has changed.

It was surprising how, even in 1940, the Germans showed on occasion concern that we should have right thoughts about themselves. Having concluded that we needed guidance on the Polish question, they provided each of us with a detailed narrative in English, with supporting documents, of the events which led up to the invasion of Poland. Supreme examples of Goebbels' art, they showed how in incident after incident decent peace-loving Germans living on either side of the frontier had been oppressed, ill-treated, robbed and insulted by their Polish neighbours. They had so persisted in their criminal misconduct towards the German minority within their borders that the patience of the German people and of Adolf Hitler had been exhausted: there had been no alternative but to resort to force. It was a tale in which facts were reshaped and truth stood on its head, but told with such skill that one needed to remind oneself of its tainted source.

After some months, letters, clothes, food, cigarettes and books began to arrive from home via the Red Cross, which became our lifeline. I don't think we ever realized what a strain it must have been on resources, nor until later were we sufficiently grateful. It would be difficult to exaggerate the effect of things like a change of clothes and pyjamas to sleep in; to explain what they did for body, mind and spirit. Letters, particularly from Mary and my mother, were a joy; for a few moments things that were so far away became close. Those letters brought with them the message that at home morale was high; that our country had been spared the fate of France; that there had been a struggle in the air over Britain which the Germans had not won; and that there was someone leading the Government who understood and detested Nazism, who meant it when he said that we would never surrender, that eventually we would win. The rather faint hope which we had cherished, that somehow in the end things would come right, acquired a vestige of reality. It began to be possible to dream of a world other than one ruled by Hitler in which every human virtue was either trodden in the mire or misused.

In the early months of 1941 I slipped on some ice and became lame with housemaid's knee. I consulted George Hadley, a doctor who had been a registrar at the Middlesex Hospital in London before the war. Could I make something of my knee, something altogether more severe, which might induce the Germans to send me to hospital from which I might escape? He came up with the idea of disseminated sclerosis. I acquired a limp and a medical history, and achieved some skill in controlling my reflexes. In due course I was put in front of the German doctor, who required that I should have a lumbar puncture in order to eliminate the possibility of VD. George Hadley warned me that, with the equipment available, this could be painful – and it was. Moreover, the package containing my precious spinal fluid was lost in the post, which meant that I had to go through it again; but on this occasion our doctors were able to steal some morphine. A day of total bliss ensued, the only one in five years; I drifted happily above it all, no fears, no worries, just a contented, somewhat detached, spectator to whom life was quite comfortable and even amusing.

The second lumbar puncture having excluded the VD possibility, I was sent, rather surprisingly, to see a specialist in Munich and spent a fascinating day travelling there and back by train with a guard of my own and an interpreter; good-looking and courteous, he was known as Childe Harold. On reaching Munich, I was told that I would now have to walk some miles to the hospital. Fearing a trap, I said I had a bad leg and was so lame that I couldn't. My escorts couldn't provide a car and were not allowed to take me on a tram. I said I couldn't believe that we had come all that way for nothing. They decided to ask the railway transport officer if he could give me permission to use public transport. He was a surprise: as I entered his office he rose to his feet and asked me if I would mind shaking hands. Where did I come from?

'Laufen,' I said, 'with the prospect of going back there all too soon.'

'I am so sorry. I meant, where is your home?

'Ascot,' I said.

'Oh,' he said, 'I have often been to the race meetings there and to Cowes.'

Then he gave my escort, whom he had told to wait outside, a permit for me to travel by tram to the hospital. He was so charming and friendly that I almost asked him if he would be so kind as to help me leave the country.

The German neurologist was thorough in his examination, but made no attempt to hide his feeling that he had better ways of spending his time. On the way back to the train, I paid a brief visit to my guard's home, where I met his wife and child. They were simple, kindly people who, gathered up and swept along by the storm, were afraid; it was hard to think of them as enemies. That evening, back inside the wire, it was barely possible to believe that I hadn't dreamed it all. In due course, however, a medical report arrived via the International Red Cross, diagnosing disseminated sclerosis but saying that it was not severe enough to warrant repatriation at that time. That had never been my aim, for even if it had been offered it would have meant taking the place of someone whose wound or sickness was real. It was a disappointing end.

One most important development was the acquisition of a wireless in the camp, I know not how and don't remember when. The BBC news was taken down daily and read out in every room each evening; it came to us like an injection of oxygen into bad air. Carefully hidden and operated only with the utmost caution, the set was never discovered by the Germans, who must have known of its existence and who regularly turned things upside down in searches. The routine of guards in a prison camp, unexciting and safe, should have allayed their vigilance, but it never did. They had read and studied carefully all the books about escaping which prisoners in the last war had written. There was in every camp an officer responsible for security – usually bright, more often than not nasty, always observant.

In the summer of 1941 Hitler invaded Russia, and in October the German press reported: 'Red Army destroyed before Moscow.' At about that time we moved camp to Warburg in Westphalia, a desolate spot with a sprawl of temporary huts built on clay, which any rainfall soon turned into a sea of heavy mud. It was home, I think, to around three thousand prisoners including some hundred or so RAF and a few Indians. At one end there was the Brick Block, so named to distinguish it from the other buildings, cheap wooden structures which kept out the rain but certainly not the cold. I lived in one of these not far from the canteen, a place which, so far as I remember, the Germans closed following the discovery of a tunnel. It was also near the latrines, a crude construction the emptying of which tended to ignore the requirements of hygiene. There was also a shower block where a reasonably hot shower was to be had once a week. Russian prisoners of war working in the area used to come in occasionally for the same purpose. With no food other than what the Germans gave them, they had been reduced by a process of hard labour and hunger to a low state. It was said that one of them one day had fallen into a concrete mixer: one of the German guards had then been sick; the remaining Russians all laughed, which caused the other German guard to be sick.

The wooden hut in which I lived was about thirty yards from the wire. There were a dozen rooms, six on either side of a corridor; each housed twelve people, who slept on two-layered bunks with straw paillasses laid on slats. At either end of the hut there were two small rooms allocated to men of the rank of major or above. Douglas Bader, who had no legs and even less fear, occupied one. His courage and total conviction that nothing was impossible had carried him to glory. He was one of those larger-than-life characters who tend to arouse the hostility of those whose importance they fail to recognize.

My hut was a bit far from the perimeter for tunnelling, but my companions and I, all subalterns, were of a mind to try. I had the task of securing the permission of the British authorities. There was already a team at work in the next-door hut, which was nearer the wire; the colonel who ran it did all he could to persuade the escape committee to refuse us permission, because, he said, we were bound to make a mess of things and so attract the attention of the Germans to the area. The committee, however, felt it would be invidious to tell a lot of subalterns that they weren't fit to do what was said to be their duty. So we were given permission, but were told we would be on our own when it came to supplies of timber, tools and so on. Our neighbouring colonel, when he learned that we had started, contented himself with the comment, 'Oh well, it won't last. It will fall in on them before long.' A few weeks later his own tunnel – in soft clay and too near the surface to survive heavy rainfall – fell in when he was himself underground: ours, much deeper and in harder material, was proof against such misfortune.

Much skill and ingenuity were devoted to the construction of our tunnel. At the end it was some eighty-five yards long; its diameter of about two feet was just large enough to crawl through. It was necessary to keep the size down in order to limit the amount of spoil to be dug, hauled from the face and then disposed of throughout the camp. Every twenty yards or so there was a chamber six feet long by three feet high and two and a half feet wide, with a man whose task it was to haul bags of earth piled on small home-made sledges. Five lights, one in each chamber and a movable one at the face, took current from a home-made cable of copper-coated wire wound round with paper (both from Red

Cross parcels) and then covered with pitch. Air was pumped to the face through a pipe made of tins which had originally contained Canadian milk powder; the inlet was concealed underneath one of the brick piers on which the hut rested. The atmosphere in the tunnel was made bearable by means of this rather Heath Robinson affair, but despite it there were times when the air became foul. A supply of electricity was obtained from the circuit in our room, the 'switch' consisting of a razor blade inserted between two nails which looked as though they belonged in the tongue-and-groove partition wall. It worked: it didn't give anyone a shock, nor did it fuse the lights or cause a fire.

Access to the shaft was through a hatch in the corner of our room. Opening it required great care since the floor was regularly examined for tell-tale marks by the Germans, who on one occasion went so far as to remove all the beds and cupboards and sweep it with snow to make sure; they even stuck bayonets between the floorboards. However they found nothing since, by a stroke of luck, it had been someone's birthday. As a result we had decided to take a few days off and had not only replaced the hatch with more than usual care but; quite exceptionally, screwed it down.

A crawl of a few yards on soft earth under the hut brought you to another hatch which covered a twelve- to fifteen-foot shaft; this in turn took you down to the point where the tunnel itself started. That hatch too had to be meticulously cared for; it consisted of a tray some six inches below the surface on which were placed bags of earth that could be easily and quickly removed. Human ferrets used to make regular visits under the hut, prodding the soil with bayonets in a search for soft patches of recently disturbed soil, which would have alerted them to what was going on. It was essential that there should be no sign that anyone other than themselves had been under the hut. The air outlet or inlet – we tried it both ways – was, as I have said, concealed well enough to survive frequent inspections: it remained, however, the Achilles heel.

A storage place for tunnelling tools and equipment and escaping gear, similar to one which had been made in our roof, was discovered one morning in a hut at the other end of the camp. We had the German lunch interval from noon till two o'clock to move all the stuff out of our roof in a hurry and store it temporarily in the tunnel itself, which we were forced to close down for the time being. Soon after we had finished, the Germans were in our roof, looking in vain for signs of activity there. One moment of delight relieved our anxiety when a stout, unpleasant German officer fell through the trap door in the roof, missing only by inches castration on the fixed bayonet of the sentry, who was walking up and down in the passage below. We then faced the problem of what to do with all the equipment, now safely stored underground but completely blocking the entrance to the tunnel. I was able to persuade two friendly majors in one of the small rooms at the end of our hut to allow us to carry out some alterations. The tongue-and-groove inner wall was brought out into the room so as to increase the gap between itself and the outer wall to some nine inches. In this shelves were placed, giving us sufficient space to store all our stuff. The inner wall was divided into two sections which could be removed simply by unscrewing a clothes hook. Although the idea was mine, the difficult part was done by George Robinson of the Durham Light Infantry, who had before the war worked for Rolls Royce. He did a splendid job, and the Germans never found our hiding-place.

It was more than three months later, when the tunnel was around eighty-five yards long and had broken surface in a cornfield about fifty yards from the wire, that one of the ferrets by a million-to-one chance struck the outlet of the air pipe with his bayonet. The Germans still couldn't find the entrance to the tunnel, however, and threatened dire consequences for all who lived in the hut if we didn't tell them where it was: the fact that we had people working underground at the time and had no other way of getting them out settled the matter. Desmond Llewelyn, who subsequently acquired fame as 'Q' in the Bond films, and a couple of others were then hauled off to the cells for several days' solitary confinement. Since it was a Saturday and the Germans wished to avoid trouble for themselves over the weekend, they dug a trench intersecting the tunnel and poured in a substantial quantity of raw sewage from the nearby latrines which as usual were full to overflowing. They became, however, quite incensed and upset when someone chalked the word '*Kultur*' on the side of one of the shit-carts; they tended to be sensitive to such gibes.

That tunnel had been the centrepiece of our lives for some six or seven months. Suddenly it had gone, leaving a void: there was nothing to do, nothing to absorb our energies, nothing to focus on; what was worse, there was no prospect of escape from the gloom and squalor. The hope, no matter how slender, of getting away had taken our minds off a war which showed no sign of ending and in which we had no part. It was only later that it began to dawn on me what a blessing it had been, filling our waking moments for months and giving us something to dream of as well. It had also been something of an experience. A small group of people not in any way hand-picked, finding themselves by chance in the same room, had between them contrived to dig through some eighty-five yards of earth, in some places hard gypsum. They had done this with tools which could hardly have been more primitive; they had solved the problems of lighting and ventilation and had disposed throughout the camp a huge quantity of spoil. Even more remarkable, perhaps, they had got on with each other. Tom Preston and Jack Mercer, both sappers, had planned the line of the tunnel, controlled the actual digging and decided how much timber was needed for revetting and support. Tony Lister, brought in later to provide the light, was known as 'the genius'; he had been closely involved in radar in its earliest days and had rather carelessly been left behind in the retreat to Dunkirk. Douglas Moir from the Royal Tank Regiment was tough, with heroic potential. The others were James Calderwood, Alan McCall, Andrew Craig-Harvey, Jimmy Mellor, Peter Parker, Jocelyn Abel-Smith, Duncan Nash, Dan Cunningham, Desmond Llewelyn and myself. Some of them are, I know, dead; I wish I knew where the others were: I would so much like to thank them for what they did for me.

In late April or early May, a few days after the tunnel had blown, I had a letter from my mother: my brother Tommy, twenty years old, had been killed in a commando raid on St Nazaire. I could only guess at the pain and the heartbreak, and wonder at her endurance. I remember walking alone around the barbed wire perimeter of that unholy, muddy wilderness with its sprawl of huts, almost drowning in the misery of it all, though tears were not possible in such a place. I tried to make sense of my thoughts: my brother had been killed; a tunnel, which had been my life for months, had been discovered; a thousand RAF bombers had been over Cologne, and the Germans had had a dose of what they had been handing out to others. There are those who now from safe perches condemn such things, but they have never felt 'the stupefying numbness of war' or known its bottomless misery; the same people spread paint on statues of brave men and hold themselves to be superior and enlightened. On that day, I think, I did manage to wonder what it was like for ordinary Germans, who maybe were enjoying the war no more than I was, to find themselves hammered by so fearful a storm. But such feelings would almost certainly have given way to a grim satisfaction that those who had launched all this evil and madness upon the world had now received a foretaste and a warning. Those whom they had considered beaten, whose neck Hitler had promised to wring like a chicken's, were striking back.

A month or so later, in June, there was a major break-out of around forty people. They went over the wire in four teams by means of home-made ladders, the entire lighting system of the camp having first been put out of action. By an extraordinary oversight the Germans, normally so thorough, failed to realize that in one hut there was a point in the system from which it was possible to extinguish all the lights, including those around the perimeter without which the sentries could see nothing. Three of those who got out, Henry Coombe-Tennant, Albert Arkwright and Rupert Fuller, actually went the whole way. They had a long journey on foot to the Dutch frontier, after which they moved with greater comfort and speed to the Pyrenees, into Spain and finally home.

At that time hope did begin to stir, even in that dismal place; the skies did slowly and imperceptibly become lighter. One clear memory I have of prison life was how in moments of misery one was somehow propped up by friends and others who generated an atmosphere of tolerance and understanding. They all had their own problems, worries and fears; but somehow they found from within themselves a bit extra with which to help others, almost without knowing it. There was, I think, a general will to help those to whom life had begun to seem insupportable to see that it was not so; that there was such a thing as the future; and that, since the means of preparing for it were at hand, it would be foolish not to use them. Gradually, and thanks to the efforts and imagination of the Red Cross, books became available and arrangements were made for examination papers to be sent out. I decided to embark upon a study of the law, this time with the definite intention to work and to take my Bar exams.

In the late summer of 1942 we moved camp again, to Eichstätt in Bavaria. This, by the standards to which we had become accustomed, was an improvement. The accommodation, still basic, was less squalid: washing facilities, though crude, were more easily accessible, the latrines less foul. Not only was the area within the wire an improvement, but the surrounding countryside afforded the welcome reassurance that there was still colour in the world. Although the sun must have shone at Warburg, it never made much impression on that grey-brown wilderness.

There were some whom prison life never seemed to change and who marvellously remained calm, kind and generous. Bruce Todd was a Roman Catholic and a wine merchant. His manners remained at all times exquisite, and he found it in his heart to be concerned for those less equable than himself. One cold night in September 1942 I turned my face to the wall, muttered some imprecation and said good-night. 'Never mind, John, the war will be over by Christmas,' he responded. I cursed him for his foolishness and bet him five pounds that it would not. A few months later he enquired how I would like to be paid, in cash or in kind. 'From you, in kind,' I said. Some time later I received a note from his company saying that they had reserved three bottles of Scotch for me and hoping that I would be back before long to enjoy them. Bruce had one great worry: arranging his rug by the side of his bunk so that there was no chance of the moon lighting upon his face in the night. That, he feared, would make him mad.

The Australians, when they first joined us in Eichstätt in the summer of 1942 after being captured in Greece and Crete, were a problem to us, as we were to them; they thought us stuffy, we thought them barbaric. Six of them lived in the same half of the same room as I did; only a blanket hung on a piece of string separated us. For a couple of months I never even spoke to them, for no better reason than that they were strange and didn't seem to like us and I was locked into my own misery. Such idiocy, however, couldn't and didn't last. One night, when we were expecting the Germans to blow their trumpet in the small hours and get us all out for a count, one of our Australian neighbours showed his irritation by walking round the room endlessly in clogs. I suggested, in language which I thought he might understand, that he should stop making such a din and go to sleep; after which, rather surprisingly, all was quiet.

Flushed with triumph in the morning and feeling I might have been a bit too rude, I armed myself with an olive branch and paid them a visit. I had been lucky, they told me, not to have my head knocked off; the others had had to sit on the noisy one and hold him down and so save me from a violent counter-attack. Once we had got over that first 'coolness', things became very different. I remember thinking that if ever I was on a desert island and the other fellow with me had lots of food and drink and I had none, I would hope he would be an Australian, for then I would be sure of being given more than a fair share and a laugh as well. Harry Halliday, Don Quartermaine, Murray Daly and others became friends. Harry came briefly to stay at Ascot after the war, but after that, sadly, we lost touch.

The Australians, cricket-mad to a man, thought there should be a Test match on the rather rudimentary pitch in the camp and challenged England. The English declined, saying it would not be worthwhile, since they had a number of established players while the Australians had no one of note. It was quite a time before the English yielded and a match, which the Australians won quite easily, actually took place. The English, rather stuffily at first, refused a return match, but gave way and were again beaten. The Australians had a good laugh at the Poms' discomfiture.

It had begun to be clear, even before our move to Eichstätt, that the tide of the war, if it hadn't turned, was no longer flowing irresistibly in Germany's favour. Following Pearl Harbor in 1941, America had joined in. In the autumn of the following year Alamein marked the turning point of the war in North Africa, and not many months later the German defeat at Stalingrad delivered the emphatic message that the tide had turned also in eastern Europe. In a prison camp, people had a way of preserving seemingly worthless things and then digging them out later. Someone had kept a *Völkischer*

Beobachter news-sheet of 1941 with the headline: 'Red Army destroyed before Moscow'. In the changed times it was pinned up in a place where the Germans would see it, alongside one dated January 1943 proclaiming: 'One million heroic dead at Stalingrad'. It was their first experience of a reverse so massive that there could be no hiding it. The noise of bombers overhead by day and by night, and the air raid alarms in the camp, confirmed for us the message that the tide was indeed turning. What had at one time seemed a distant dream, and had only recently become a hope, quite suddenly became an established prospect which even stranded spectators such as ourselves could share and enjoy.

Early on in Eichstätt days there was a British commando raid on Alderney or Sark, during which some German soldiers were captured and temporarily handcuffed. The Führer, having heard of it, decreed that a number of British POWs should receive the same treatment. A parade was called and the last hundred or so, of whom I was one, were separated and marched off into one block which, having been emptied of its previous occupants, was cordoned-off from the rest of the camp. We were then put in handcuffs, which were taken off at lights out and put on again in the morning. For a time it was exceedingly tiresome. Apart from the obvious inconvenience, it interrupted the study of law on which I had just embarked. Gradually, however, as the stupidity of the whole thing became clear, German vigilance diminished and our skills at removing the handcuffs improved. Moreover, the constant contact between guards and prisoners had consequences which Hitler had not intended: cigarettes, of which we, thanks to the Red Cross, had plenty and which the German soldiers lacked, became currency, and what had started as a reprisal became a trading opportunity. Sacks of flour labelled 'For our brave comrades on the Ostfront' and other items, useful to us, found their way into the camp under cover of the laundry or by other means.

After a couple of months or so, someone else took my place in handcuffs and I was able to get back to my study of the law. My fellow students and I were fortunate to have a number of highly qualified people available to help us. Foremost amongst them was Jack Hamson, an academic lawyer of distinction, from Trinity College, Cambridge; he had been caught in Crete. The

45

arrangements for the examination papers for the Bar and other professions to be sent out via the Red Cross had been firmed up: the opportunity was real and it was a huge blessing. Not only did it help time on its way, but it provided an aim and a challenge more immediate than just getting ready for life in a world with which we had lost touch. The Germans' behaviour had noticeably improved once the lesson of Stalingrad had sunk in, though they still managed from time to time to do something crass and stupid. When, during an air raid alert, one prisoner took a few steps outside the hut which served as the camp hospital, he was shot and killed; another attempting to bring him to safety met the same fate. The obvious regret of the German authorities and the way in which they handled the funeral arrangements served to take the edge off, but not to remove the hate and contempt which such wanton and deliberate acts generated.

On another occasion, when the Germans had an unpleasant announcement to make, they expected trouble and let down the flaps which ordinarily covered the machine-guns on the watch towers which surrounded the camp. As squads of SS and plain-clothes men marched in along the road above the parade ground, we all began to sing, 'Heigh ho, heigh ho, it's off to work we go'; that and the laughter which went with it puzzled and annoyed the Germans, and tension mounted. While I cannot any longer remember what it was all about, what I do clearly recall is Jack Higgon, the senior British officer at the time, telling us what the Germans had in mind and going on to say that, though he had protested, he had no alternative but to accept. He reminded us of the story of two men walking towards each other along a narrow pavement on a rainy day. As they met, one said, 'I never get out of the way of a cad'; the other replied, 'I always do', and stepped into the gutter. 'That,' said Jack, 'is what we have to do.' There was a roar of laughter which went on and on.

The need for laughter to pierce the dullness and light up the gloom was constant; it was the one need which the Germans, earnest and pompous, could be relied upon to meet. When someone said in a letter home that he couldn't take much more of the Huns, there was an immediate and angry reaction. The writer was summoned before the more than usually nasty commandant – an Austrian, who sentenced him to several days of solitary confinement and shouted that the Germans were not Huns; he even threatened us with a course of instruction to prove that they were not the linear descendants of Attila. Alas, it never happened: it would have provided considerable amusement. From time to time we had a visit from a Swiss official, representing the Protecting Power, to take a look at our conditions. Normally these visitors took care not to offend the Germans, but one less supine and more spirited than most asked the commandant to explain how the paillasses on which we slept were dripping with water. 'It is well known that all British officers are bed wetters,' was the characteristic reply. The Swiss turned on him and, to our immense satisfaction, tore into him with vigorous disapproval.

A private soldier who worked at a camp not far away – we officers were not permitted by the Geneva Convention to do so – arrived one day in our rather rudimentary camp hospital for treatment. He was a cockney, adaptable and quick to recognize opportunity, particularly when it involved sex, of which he had had more recent experience than any of us. Women were also employed at his work-place. With the arrival of Red Cross parcels, the British soldiers had soap; the women, Czechs, Hungarians, Poles and others, had none and were keen to acquire it. As he put it, 'They had their soap.' German girls, feeling left out, protested: why couldn't they have some soap? 'So they had their soap too.' Asked, when he was about to leave, if he needed anything, he replied on the instant, 'I could do with a bit of soap, sir.' He was given a box full of the stuff with a load of good wishes only slightly contaminated with envy.

Escaping was difficult: few got out. One particularly good effort was made by Colonel Tubby Broomhall, dressed as a German general with accompanying staff. Reaching the gate and finding it shut, one of his escort who spoke German yelled at the guards: '*Machen Sie auf!*' It was opened immediately by a trembling NCO, who then spoiled everything by ringing through to the Kommandantur to say that the general was on his way, he was sorry to have held him up, but he had not been told of his presence in the camp; the party was then quickly rounded up.

A growing awareness on the part of the Germans that they were not going to win brought a few concessions which would have been unthinkable in earlier times. Once or twice we were taken to film shows in the town, and parties were allowed out on parole to gather fuel in the woods. It was a very strange experience to find myself in a wood and with no wire. I wrote in a letter home:

> I went out of the camp to collect wood; it was the first time that I had had some measure of liberty. It was an exciting experience to find oneself alone for even a short time, to be in a wood again, to see the miracle of colour that exists in a single leaf. After even a short period of two hours, the restraint and leaden inertia of the prison camp began to fall away. I found myself face to face with life and beauty; those things which for a long time have been matters of hope and belief were proved as facts before my eyes . . . [CENSORED] . . . I was happy to see that things of nature were still as I dimly remembered them.

A strange and unusual figure dressed in a belted camel-hair coat and a black trilby hat was at that time to be seen about the camp. Herr von Fetter was from the German Foreign Office, and his mission seemed to be to seek out and befriend those who had titles or who were thought to have good connections at home; I was not one of them. The idea was, I imagined, either to show that Germans had another face to the one with which we were familiar or, more likely, to identify those who might one day be useful as hostages. Most of those with whom he made friendly contact were sent along with persistent escapers to Colditz, a castle from which escape was thought to be impossible – though not, as it turned out, for Airey Neave and one or two others.

Searches and parades did sometimes have a lighter side, particularly at night when the Germans found that the darkness presented them with problems. On one occasion a night parade had been called: we all had to get out of our bunks, dress and go outside to be counted. A little sentry came into our hut, yelling his head off about getting up. Told to piss off and not quite clear in his mind as to what this involved, he hovered for a moment between thrusting his bayonet into the offender and fetching the officer. Happily, he opted for the latter, who enquired what was the matter.

'I am sick. I am not getting up.'

'Ferry well, if you are sick you shall stay in bett, the Chermans also are chentlemen.'

In the course of a major search of the whole camp, some of our SS visitors took post in the latrines where they did a lively business trading schnapps for cigarettes. It may have been the same day that one of the plain-clothes men – we called them Gestapo, and they looked the part – rather carelessly put his briefcase on one side; it disappeared on the instant. Great rage, in which there was an ingredient of panic, ensued, for the briefcase contained a pistol. The matter was reported to the commandant, who threatened terrible things; there was some kind of ultimatum. The senior British officer was sorry, but he knew nothing about the briefcase – whose it was, what had been in it or how it had come to disappear. Nor had he any means of finding out: he just couldn't help. Deadlock and more threats followed. Then the thought came to someone that perhaps, if the search were to be called off, the briefcase might just turn up; and indeed it did.

Early in the spring of 1945 the order came that all POWs were to be moved – on foot – to somewhere south of the Danube. We could take with us only what we could carry, and the remainder of our belongings were left in store. Incredibly, mine caught up with me at home not all that long after the war ended. There was a tragic start to the march: we had just got clear of the camp when a number of our own fighters, flying very low, appeared overhead and, thinking we were a German formation, made several runs over us with machine guns. There were casualties; some friends who had been prisoners ever since 1940 were killed. Shocked and horrified, and ignoring German shouts that the march would go on, we all turned round and went back to the camp. The following morning we set out again on our journey; it took a week or so, moving mostly by night and sleeping anywhere by day – sometimes in haylofts, which were dry and far more comfortable than what we had become accustomed to, and meeting up with chickens and eggs and other things which we had not seen in ages.

Eventually we reached Moosburg, a huge camp with a vast

population of prisoners of war from many nations. By that time the Germans had about as much idea about what was happening as we had; they vanished completely when General Patton arrived, bringing his army with him. I remember seeing him larger than life, swaggering through the camp, two mother of pearl-handled pistols at his belt, looking for all the world as though he had won the war single-handed; he was a very welcome sight. Notices began to appear indicating that War Crimes Investigation Team number so-and-so had arrived and was ready for business. We were free in theory. War Office instructions, however – they may have been sensible, though they didn't seem so at the time – decreed otherwise. We were to remain inside the wire and even take turns at keeping each other in. After nearly five years in German custody I did more or less stay put, but I couldn't manage to turn myself into a camp guard. Many years later I heard from a friend who, quite unknown to me, had also been present, of how an American GI standing next to him had reacted as he saw the Stars and Stripes go up over the church tower: 'Gee my fucking balls, the Flag' – an unusual form of greeting to 'Old Glory'.

We spent some days at Landshut in Bavaria, at first crowded together in an attic. Then some American soldiers, meeting us in the street and hearing that we were old lags, knocked up a terrified German family. They told them that they were American SS troops and that they had better look after us, otherwise they would be turned out of house and home and shot, perhaps after torture. The Germans, believing that we might afford them some protection, complied and made us most comfortable. During the days that followed the GIs paid us regular visits to check that we were being looked after, and kept us well supplied with PK rations. Beyond that most important fact, I remember only the fear of that German family in whose house we spent just a few nights. I felt sorry for them as I realized how little they had had to do with it all; now it was their turn for misery.

IV

Three Special Prisoners

Still are thy pleasant voices, thy nightingales awake.
W. J. Cory

Living in any closed community brings with it a special awareness
of those around you, a belief that you understand them and
they you. I have spent much of my life in three such communities
– school, prison camp and Parliament – all of which entailed a
measure of separation from the outside, or real world as it is fancifully
described. In a prison camp there was always that cordon of barbed
wire, watched over by guards, to remind you of the separation.
Even the letters and news and supplies which filtered through
from outside seemed somehow to intensify the separateness; the
letter you were reading was an echo from someone whom you
hadn't seen face to face or heard speak for years. Whether you
would ever do so again depended upon events in which you had
no part. Within the cordon there were, by contrast, no barriers;
you were always within sight and sound of others, eating, reading,
walking, sleeping, even in the latrines. There was only the barest
minimum of duties or obligations; for the time being at least, there
were in material terms neither rewards nor penalties.

At the beginning most of us sought to explain, more to ourselves
than to each other, how it had come about that we had been taken
alive and unscathed and that here we were comparatively safe, taking
no part in an all-devouring war. Such explanations as emerged were
hackneyed and unhelpful, too much of the genus 'There was I,
when round the corner came two German tanks.' Although the
pointless search was fairly soon abandoned, the haunting question
of how it came about remained, and with it a sense of shame at

51

having failed. It was something which I found hard to handle and of which writing this book has powerfully reminded me. It would have been easier had I then realized the extent to which others felt the same; but it isn't easy to talk of shame until it has lost its sharpness or unless you know for certain that the sense of it is shared.

Time moves the scenery around and moves people into what seem like other lives; age blurs the imprint of people and things that once seemed unforgettable: some have vanished, others are seen only as scarcely defined shadows just out of reach. Yet there are some with whom I was in prison more than fifty years ago whom I shall never forget, partly because we were able to move our friendship into the post-war years and sustain it and partly because I am conscious of having received from them more than I could ever repay. There were three in particular. Jack Hamson, a law don from Cambridge who later became Professor of Comparative Law, taught me law in prison and helped me out of the pit into which I had dug myself in 1942. He also gave me, if not his total and deep-rooted faith, at least a few cuttings from it which, transplanted into my more meagre soil, have survived. Dick Troughton, who was called to the Bar with me in 1945 and became chairman of W. H. Smith and later of the British Council, had a way of mixing laughter and concern which made him something of a salvage expert. Henry Coombe-Tennant was a regular soldier in the Welsh Guards, who in prison provided music and with it a gleam of hope and comfort at a time when there seemed to be none; later, as a monk, he taught silently and by example what faith and discipline are about.

Jack Hamson had found the combination of his own capture in Crete and the British failure to hold the island a shattering experience. In a book written in prison camp, *Liber in Vinculis*, he described that failure as a profoundly disgraceful performance: 'It is a mighty spur to a man to know for certain, with conviction to be persuaded, that there is for him no issue out of the coils of his predicament except only by and through his actual success; and such a spur might perhaps have stung into a semblance of activity the dull and sluggish inertness of our leaders.' The Prof, as he was called, was a marvellous teacher; his enthusiasm kept pace with his learning and his words show it: '. . . to understand the Common Law of England – a rich and enthralling prospect . . . My love of it has not decreased . . . it is a grand and magnificent system of law, of living law.' That deep and very real regard for the Common Law did not necessarily extend to the judges who administered it; he was accustomed to comment freely and trenchantly upon their errors. He particularly enjoyed teaching law in those early days in camp before the books arrived; he then felt free to say what the law was without fear of contradiction, a degree of security which not even he had enjoyed at Cambridge.

In a prison camp he cut a strange and most unmilitary figure. His boots, light brown to orange in colour, were unusual; they had, in response to his mother's urgings, been specially procured for him in Italy by a future Pope and delivered to him by some quite unusual agency. A regulation khaki side hat, perched on the middle of his head and on top of a balaclava, looked more like the headgear which Mahatma Gandhi made famous than an item of uniform. Corduroy trousers and an odd assortment of woollen garments rounded it off and completed the impression that here was someone rather different. A total belief in the goodness and the power of God, profound respect for the Common Law, and devotion to Cambridge and to Trinity were the sources of energy which lay beneath an unusual surface.

In those dark days before Alamein and Stalingrad I had contrived almost to lock myself into despair; hope was at best seminal and faith little more than the remains of an old habit. The discovery that, unlike the one hemmed in by barbed wire and watched over by guards, this prison was one of my own making, for which the key was still in the door, was quite a shock, and it was due in no small measure to Jack. It had not previously occurred to me that a man as wise as he could possibly be as lost and prostrate as I felt at that time. Yet, as he talked and wrote, I realized that his case was not all that different from mine. He spoke of his wife Isabella and of his daughter Janet, whom he felt he had somehow deserted when he left to take part in the defence of Crete. He spoke too of its failure, which he saw as a defeat which could and should have been avoided; and of the shame which that defeat and his own capture had caused him. His gradual emergence from the shock and misery, and the conscious effort which he applied to getting his feet back on to the firm ground on which he had built his life, were more than an example to me: they were a lifebelt which I had neither looked for nor expected. Of the faith which guided him he said one day, and I can recall the moment, the place and his voice, 'I know that I am in the powerful hand of God.' He developed a hope, almost a belief, that somewhere hidden but not too far away there might be an idea which could guide us all when peace returned. Although he never found it, he showed how important was the frame of mind which caused him to search.

The thoughts of that time echoed again and again in things he said and wrote throughout the rest of his life. Not long after our return he gave me a book called *Gothic England*, full of pictures of buildings of extraordinary grace. He wrote on the flyleaf, 'To remind you of the temptation we once in Germany jointly suffered – namely to believe that the remote country herein depicted might, and even did, exist.' He summed it all up in 'Prelude to Prayer', a homily, which, at the age of eighty-two, he delivered in Trinity College Chapel in 1987. It was right that he should have delivered it at Trinity, which he loved and which for many years was his home. It was not only his last word, for he died some six months later; it was also his total witness, with many echoes of all those things which had engaged his mind in Germany more than forty years before. 'Captivity had fallen upon us brutally' and he had with others begun to see things anew; much 'as the poppy of the First World War had been seen and had acquired incomparable dignity and importance in its own right'. He had become aware of previous blindness and of having been 'driven out of the carapace of your established self', and of 'a vulnerability, increased by an overpowering sense of shame at your present condition'. His words come nearer to encapsulating for me the impact of captivity than any others I have heard.

He spoke often of the Virgin Mary, and in that farewell at Trinity he returned to his theme. While he declared the Magnificat to be wholly outside the range of his discourse, he seemed immediately to prove that it was not only within range, but almost the core of what he had to say; he described it as:

a torrent of praise and thanksgiving, an outburst of joy and confidence in God and His sure providence, the more remarkable if you consider her human condition when she uttered it – a teenage girl who on her marriage found herself with child by a person other than her husband, and that not in our permissive and licentious cosmopolitan society, but in a Jewish village community two thousand years ago.

He was, he said, suggesting that 'it may be possible for us to catch a glimpse of the existence of God as the sustainer of the marvels of the creation about us'. By the urgency and eloquence with which he was accustomed to declare his belief, he could rekindle flames which others have almost extinguished by their droned litanies on social injustice.

'To understand the Common Law of England, that was a rich and enthralling prospect; and it has the power almost to enthrall me still.' Jack's words remind me now of how lucky we were at that time to have the chance to sit at the feet of such a man, to learn and to be in our turn enthralled. He saw the Common Law of England as an edifice of civilization, a structure built over centuries to enable men and women to live in peace with one another, to offer at least a measure of protection to the weak against the strong, be the latter king, feudal lord or employer; to provide a means of settling disputes and define, in changing times and as nearly as words allowed, the duties which they owed to each other. He gave life and meaning to the old writs of Quo Warranto and Habeas Corpus, by which the subject might obtain redress against abuse of power by the state. His respect for the institution did nothing to dim his awareness that those who dispensed justice and applied the law were inclined from time to time to fall into grievous error, and he did not hesitate to tell them so. His opinions about the quality of modern Statute Law were unflattering.

He was much attached to Gray's Inn and was proud to be its Treasurer in 1975. He saw the Hall as 'the memorial of the will and determination of a great variety of men acting together to make and maintain that which seemed to them good and right.' The memory of it had been for him, 'in days of grievous trouble when the world was collapsed and in pieces, a potent source of comfort and profound encouragement.' During his year as Treasurer, Jack asked me to dine with him at Gray's Inn. Sitting next to Elwyn Jones, then Lord Chancellor, I enquired how it was that the

Treasurer of so distinguished a Society was not a QC. Elwyn replied that he hadn't thought of it and wondered if Jack would like it. His name was included in the next list of Silks.

When I wrote to tell him of my decision to enter politics, Jack gave me some sharp advice:

> You know that in general I disapprove of a young man going into politics. I think politics to be profoundly corrupting of a person's integrity. He becomes infected with a perfectly unreasonable idea of the 'possible', I mean as judged by the cautious calculation of the politician who reckons himself to be 'sound' and prudent. And this in my view is deadly, particularly to a young man who may be apt to accept the judgment of his apparently established seniors.

He warned:

> the pursuit of politics today [1948] excessively removes the individual from the actual event; and if it does not stultify him, gives him a ridiculous and destructive sense of omnipotence; so that, losing himself in the exciting and infantile intricacies of his game, he brings to bear upon the actual event a merely empty and inane caricature of a mind.

'Profoundly corrupting of a person's integrity'; 'losing himself in the exciting and infantile intricacies of his game'; those two phrases, which I suppose I barely noticed at the time, now make the nerve ends twitch, for they seem to explain that instinctive mistrust which the looker-on and the voter feel for those who, aiming always to please, are obliged as often as not to tailor facts and varnish truths.

In writing of this extraordinary man I have called in aid many of his own words, for they carry with them his flavour and vigour; his love of language, his respect for institutions and for custom; his awareness of human fallibility, including his own; his faith in God's goodness, his acceptance of judgement and his hope of mercy. If, in letting him speak for himself, I have not made clear the extent of what I owe him, it is because the debt is too great.

Dick Troughton was one of those who studied law with me in Eichstätt, where he was known as Trapper; I have a hazy idea that it was because of the headgear he wore. Soon after the war, at a time when we both still intended to practise at the Bar, he gave me a book entitled *First Steps in Advocacy*. He had written on the flyleaf these words of Thomas Traherne: 'You will never enjoy the world aright, till the sea itself floweth in your veins, till you are clothed with the Heavens and crowned with the stars.' We had talked of them together in prison. He succeeded beyond anything I could manage in absorbing them, in making them a part of himself. He gave me other books from time to time, including Churchill's *World Crisis*, which he inscribed generously, 'With thanks for a great deal', and *Collins' Book of Epigrams*, inscribed even more generously, 'Coals to Newcastle'. I would very much like to have deserved either tribute.

Dick possessed a high degree of awareness of the wonders by which he was surrounded. He used to breathe it all in in great gulps – people and things; he enjoyed them all so much that when with him you couldn't help but do so too. Love and laughter belonged in him. Simon Hornby, a later Chairman of W. H. Smith, got it about right when he wrote of Dick that it was impossible not to feel better after being with him. Dick's father, whom I met on only a few occasions, had that same way of almost gasping with delight at something seen or heard. We were talking after dinner at his home, when I first stayed there, of words, of things said or written, which contained in them the ingredients of hope and help. For me, he said, Job's words spoken from the depth of misery surpass anything else: 'I know that my Redeemer liveth.' In saying that he explained himself and perhaps Dick as well.

We were both members of Boodle's and used, particularly in the early days after our return, to meet there from time to time. He found great joy in studying the Club's suggestion book, particularly the entries made during the months after the Fall of France when there was first the prospect of invasion and later the actuality of bombs. These suggestions had nothing to do with the war or its prospects: one which Dick claimed to have found, dated September 1940, was simple and short: 'Why the devil can't we have strawberries?' One evening, when we were having a drink together, we saw one of the older members sitting alone and looking sad; we asked him if he would like to join us. He did so and quickly became more cheerful; at one point and without any particular relevance he broke off what he was saying, looked long and hard at us, and came out in stentorian tones with 'I am so sorry for you young men, you never knew the Empire.' Neither of us knew quite how to respond to this unexpected expression of sympathy, and if we had tried to do so we would have got it wrong; for after a long pause, he went on to make it clear that it was not the Raj and all that, but the Empire, Leicester Square (a music hall in his youth) and the girls whom he had enjoyed and we had missed.

Dick had a wonderfully successful career. John Burgh, in a moving obituary, told of a time when the British Council was facing swingeing cuts and Dick, emerging from a forty-minute meeting with Mrs Thatcher, had given this account of it: 'After the meeting, I said to her private secretary, wiping the sweat from the back of my neck, that I would not wish to repeat this experience. He retorted that he had never before seen her listen for so long and behave so gently.' It was not, however, the important positions which he occupied which set him apart and made him so rare; it was the way in which he gave himself, heart and mind, to whatever task he took up and to those who worked with him and for him. There was no trace of greed or self-seeking in him. Generous and thoughtful in his praise, he was not one of those who smiled with easy tolerance upon all that went on around him.

Dick was fierce in his disapproval of powerful people who were either less concerned than he thought they ought to be – or not at all – about the feelings and the rights of others. The takeover of Collins the publishers, of which he was a director, disturbed him greatly. In a letter to me in January 1989 he wrote:

The bitterness is that Lord Young and his gang [the Department of Trade and Industry] will not, or it appears so, consider anything other than competition as worthy of consideration. National interest means nothing. So we will have 2,000 decent Scotsmen working so that the product of their work goes to paying the interest on the 3 billion that 'News' [international] borrowed to buy in the USA. Will the money be ploughed back in the business in the UK? After all when Rupert Murdoch tried to buy a 'media' business in the USA, he had to give up Australian citizenship and become an American. No requirements here. However, I shall get over it by next week. But the people who have spent their lives in it will not.

Nor, in the event, did he.

In another letter, which he wrote to me at the end of 1989, he spoke of a united Germany: 'I wish I could enjoy the freedom of East Germany, but all I can think of, and with dread, is a United Germany dominating, as it will, Europe economically, or militarily, or both.' I share that dread to the full and with increasing sharpness as those who would distance our country from Europe are able to build up support for the notion that we can safely stand aside.

Dick and Gosh, the wife whom he adored, had left London behind them twelve months before and gone to live near her old home on the shores of Loch Broom. 'Here one is, or I am, on a vertical learning curve in learning about Rhododendrons and Azaleas. The Arboretum is a perpetual source of happiness and exercise.' He appreciated the care of their many visitors, who over a period had left between them as litter just two cigarette ends and one piece of paper. In 1991 Gosh developed a cancer from which there could be no recovery. As it happened, and perhaps mercifully, Dick, struck down by a heart attack, died before she did; life without her would for him have lost much of its joy. He had once written me a letter which I cannot now find, in which he reflected about Moses seeing from Mount Pisgah the Promised Land, towards which he had guided the Israelites but which he himself was not to enter. Dick, I think, had a clearer sight than most of us of the Promised Land, and a better understanding of the things which stand in our way.

Henry Coombe-Tennant, born in 1913, philosopher, musician, soldier, intelligence agent and monk in turn, was, in words taken from his obituary written by a fellow monk at Downside Abbey, 'something special, met with perhaps only once in a lifetime'.

Aloof and self-contained, he gave the impression, only half true, of not needing other people. A note about him dated 1934, in a Trinity College, Cambridge magazine, contained this discerning comment: 'Sure to be interested in you, if he notices you.'

I first met him, or rather I first heard him, in that dirty, over-populated German prison camp at Laufen in the summer of 1940. In that time of darkness and defeat, I listened to him playing the piano hour after hour. Music had never meant much to me before, but at that time and in that place I listened and found relief. Many of the things he played came from another age and another world, far removed from ours; but they brought with them the faint suggestion that somewhere in the darkness there might still be light.

With Albert Arkwright and Rupert Fuller he escaped in 1942 from the next barbed wire settlement in which we found ourselves; one even more depressing than the previous one. It was a bold project, prepared over many months with great thoroughness. After the camp lighting system had been put out of action forty or more people crossed the fifteen-foot-high barbed wire defences by means of somewhat crude half-ladder, half-bridge contraptions. Henry and his two companions were the only ones to make it all the way.

They made it a rule only to move at night. They kept to it until, after three weeks in the open, they reached the Dutch frontier: they were by then so low and exhausted that they simply carried on and crossed it in daylight. Seen by a boy, they hid in a ditch and waited and hoped. Men came after dark, took them to a farm, fed them and locked them up in a barn with a loft and dry straw. They slept. Taken later to Brussels and put on a train for France with a guide each and papers, they were told if questioned to say nothing except '*J'ai des affaires à Lille*' and to show their papers.

The train stopped at the French frontier: Henry and Albert got by with only a cursory examination, but Rupert couldn't get the words out and was taken off the train for questioning. Somehow he got his wits back and to every question responded with something out of his papers. Then, in an inspired moment, he walked to the other side of the table where his inquisitors were seated, tapped on the important-looking badge of the principal one as if it was a door knocker, threw his head back and dissolved into helpless maniacal laughter. The Germans, outraged, picked him up, threw him on to the platform and chucked his papers after him. The other two, sitting anxiously on the train, saw with relief Rupert pick himself up, collect his papers, wave goodbye to the Germans and climb back on to the train.

Henry, not one to boast, told me that bit of the story. Years later Albert, soon after Henry's death and not long before his own, spoke to me of Henry's skill at map-reading and his knowledge of the stars. He was, in Albert's words, 'a skilful and reliable pathfinder'. He had never, he wrote to me, got to know Henry in camp prior to their escape. He had struck him then as being 'always diffident and very reserved, almost to the point of being shy and unsociable, not like his real self'.

In 1944, just before D-Day, Henry parachuted into the Ardennes where he fought with the Resistance. After the war he worked for the Foreign Service and MI6, mostly in the Middle East. It was then that he began to take note of the force that Islam is in the lives of Muslims, and, having looked again at his own beliefs, to emerge from the agnosticism into which the residue of public school Christianity tends to evaporate. In 1958 in Baghdad he became a Roman Catholic and seven years later, to use his own words, decided that he 'might as well go the whole hog and become a monk'. He spent nearly thirty years at Downside Abbey, where he died in 1989. I saw him fairly often during those years, for Downside is in easy reach of my home in the West Country. To be with him was to be aware that he was indeed 'someone special'. He was a quiet man; he didn't say much, but what he said you remembered. He spoke of Wittgenstein as 'the only genius that the twentieth century has produced' and quoted words which had become almost a part of him, 'the things whereof one cannot speak, thereof one should be silent'. Of life in the monastery he used frequently to say, 'If you can't face up to the problems outside, you'll never be able to do so inside.' In so saying he revealed for me something of the purpose and value of monastic life. Before he came to stay with us – and he was a frequent and most welcome visitor – he wanted to be assured that there was in the house a room which could be set aside for him to say Mass.

Whatever problems he may have faced, he appeared serene; he was serious without ever being solemn. When Jack Higgon, who had been with us in prison camp, died in 1984, Henry gave the address at the Memorial Service in the Guards Chapel. Tall and wonderfully good-looking in the habit of a Benedictine monk, he looked and was magnificent. After the service he came back with a few other ex-prisoners to lunch in the House of Lords. Out of the blue he suddenly remarked, 'You know, I should have told them of what Jack had said in prison to some Australians with whom he had been discussing what was the best material from which to make riding breeches. The Australians had favoured moleskin. Jack, after a moment's thought, replied, "I see what you mean, but there would be this drawback: moleskin is airtight and if you chanced to be wearing a broad-brimmed hat and then farted, you would blow your hat off."' A Benedictine monk telling that tale from the pulpit of the Guards Chapel would have been something out of the ordinary.

Henry died in 1989. His last years were sad; two hip replacements and a bad fall left him with a burden of pain. He may have felt disappointed by what he saw as his failure to master the pain, which closed in on him; but he still retained that grace and serenity which were a part of him and in our world so rare. His role as a pathfinder was not confined to the three weeks of his escape from a prison camp in Germany; it was his role in life. With all his great gifts and talents, his path cannot have been an easy one either to find or to travel. His success in doing so took others along with him, at least for some of the way; his example was one which you could neither ignore at the time, nor ever forget.

The three men, all of them from Trinity, of whom I have written in this chapter lit the world around them with their intelligence, their perception and their kindliness: for that they will be long remembered by those who had the good fortune to come within their orbit. They had, in addition, that indefinable quality of grace, which, because it saves its possessors from the quicksands of conceit, enabled them to come as near as anyone I have ever known to loving their neighbours as themselves. For that, not surprisingly, they were in their turn greatly loved.

V

Freedom for Me,
Independence for India

Wandering between two worlds,
One dead the other powerless to be born.
                    Matthew Arnold, *The Grande Chartreuse*

On leaving Germany at last in 1945 we flew first to Reims in
American Dakotas; then it was home in Lancaster bombers,
landing at an RAF station somewhere near Aylesbury in the dark,
just as the bonfires of the first VE day were being lit. We had tea and
cakes and some kind words from the station commander's wife. It
was the first woman's voice I had heard in five years; the sound
was so strange that, when she started speaking, the words were
almost drained of meaning. We were taken by bus not to some
military establishment, but to a small private house, in which the
only question I was asked was what would I like to drink; I had half
expected to be sat down and asked who I was, where I had come
from and what I had been doing. The reception arrangements could
not have been more relaxed; someone had thought them out with
kindness and imagination. It seemed a long way from that Belgian
pig-sty in which I had been caught five years before.

As soon as I could, I telephoned to my mother: I felt more
numb than elated and the words which should have flowed easily
did not. She, I think, felt the same, for we both spoke in rather
flat, everyday tones, as if the past five years had not intervened;
but they had and, to me at any rate, they were more real by far
than this new world which I had once known, but of which I
was no longer a part. The ordinary simple things of life: being

63

free, unconstrained by barbed wire, to come and go; eating and drinking at a table with china and glass; sleeping in a bed between sheets; having a hot bath; pulling a plug in a lavatory; travelling in trains or cars; perhaps above all the possibility of being alone – such familiar ordinary things had for so long been only memories that they seemed remote and unreal. It was strange too to be with people who had not spent years together and in the same or very similar places, whose experiences of war had been altogether more eventful, full of change; people who had known danger and pain and had fought in battles which had been won.

I travelled to London next day and rang up Lionel Massey. We had lived for a time in the same corner of the same room at Eichstätt; he had slept in the bottom layer of the same bunk as I did. He had been severely wounded in the leg in Greece and, since no treatment was available, had suffered considerable pain. After long and patient negotiation by the International Red Cross, the Germans agreed to an exchange of badly wounded prisoners and he was repatriated. I had, I think, been of some help to him, or so he had told his parents, Vincent Massey, at that time the Canadian High Commissioner in London, and his wife, Alice, for they smothered me with kindness and insisted I should dine with them that evening. I was relieved to have an opportunity to get my breath back and to find some relationship between my feet and the new ground upon which I was walking before going home. I needed to put off questions to which I could not find an answer, and found it easier to be with people who wouldn't probe too deep. At dinner that evening in the Dorchester Hotel – another strange experience – Vincent Massey took me by surprise by asking suddenly what I thought of the Germans. They made me, I told him, think of the man in the parable who, having turned out one devil, kept his house swept and garnished, thus making room for seven devils worse than the first. They had made room for Adolf Hitler, they had drunk his awful brew and had brought terrible anguish to us all and finally to themselves. I didn't expect them to feel much in the way of shame or guilt, only that they had been unlucky or hadn't known what was going on. That answer still seems uncomfortably near to the truth.

I had never liked the house at Ascot, which had been my home and in which I had grown up, and I found to my horror that I had no desire at all to go back there. I dreaded the process of untangling the years, of attempting to explain to my mother, who I knew would want to hear. It would involve, too, being for the first time in a place where my brother Tommy belonged; now he would not be there. Questions, forever unanswerable, which I couldn't even utter – why him? why not me? – just wouldn't go away. Mary, whom I loved and hoped to marry, was about to marry someone else; the war had gone on too long. Coming home should have been wonderful. I was shocked to find it hard. I was free, but still locked into something from which it was harder to escape than barbed wire.

I went before some sort of resettlement board and was told I was to be retrained. Was I required to go to the Far East to take on Japan? No, I was not eligible to go. Wouldn't it be a waste of time and effort to retrain me? Wasn't there something else I could do, other than be prepared for a life which I wasn't going to lead? By the rules, they said, they could not give me a staff job; but if I could find one for myself, I could have it. I managed to find myself a not uncomfortable, but far from exciting, niche as staff captain in the HQ of Western Command in Chester. My boss, who had had a not unpleasant war in Cairo, used to go on long tours of the Command, judging their success by the number of eggs which he was able to acquire on the way; there were few to be had in the shops. Apart from the twice-yearly Honours List, which was to him a matter of consuming interest, he was content to leave the day-to-day work, which was unexciting, to his two staff captains. Army Council Instructions (ACIs, they were called) poured out from the War Office. Although the war was by now over, the machine which had run it was still there, seeking things to keep itself and others busy and somehow finding enough paper to keep in-trays well filled.

I persuaded the authorities at Western Command that, having lived for years jammed together with others like sardines in a tin, I should not be made to go and live in the Command Officers' Mess, and that it would be better for all concerned if I were to live instead in the Grosvenor Hotel. To my joy I found myself in the next room to John Brocklebank, whom I had known dimly at Eton and rather better in a prison camp. He contrived to laugh about most things; he had, he said, been caught in Cos 'cowering in a nullah'. He had been something of a cricketer, was a keen follower of Everton Football Club and endeavoured unsuccessfully to make one of me. He later became Chairman of Cunard, by which time we had begun to forget that we were an island and shipping and shipbuilding had been allowed to go into irreversible decline.

My military career fizzled out in a suitably undistinguished manner. I contracted what was called dry pleurisy, which a clever osteopath quickly put right. I applied for and was given sick leave, but only on condition that I was first medically examined. An X-ray revealed, so they told me, a shadow on a lung, which might be TB. After a fortnight's leave and further investigation, the shadow was said to be still present and the diagnosis was confirmed. Alarmed, I sought the advice of a Harley Street lung expert who dismissed the idea with one impolite monosyllable. He advised me to seek an early opportunity to pass on his opinion to the military authorities: there were, he said, too many people on the loose who took pictures which they didn't know how to read. My days in Chester were over, but I was still in the Army and officially sick.

Concerned about my future, I had soon after my return made contact with Walter Monckton, in the hope that he might find a place for me in his Chambers. Anxious now to start work, I sought his advice; the timing could not have been more fortunate. He had for some years been the Constitutional Adviser to His Exalted Highness the Nizam of Hyderabad and Berar. The Labour Government declared early in 1946 their intention to terminate British rule in India; three Cabinet Ministers, headed by Sir Stafford Cripps, were about to depart for India to prepare the way for this momentous change. Walter had to leave almost at once for Hyderabad; he required a personal assistant; would I go? I was thrilled by the prospect, but had first to extricate myself from the Army a month or so before my due date, something which the regulations did not permit. In the view of the Army I had tuberculosis, and would continue to have it until their medicals said I hadn't; moreover, I was entitled to a pension. My plea that I hadn't got the one and didn't want the other got me nowhere.

I did the rounds high and low in the multitude of buildings which the War Office then occupied, in the hope of finding someone with both sense and clout. At last I ran to earth in Eaton Square a general who, having listened to my tale, said how ridiculous; of course I must go to India; I would go before another medical board; the TB would be removed from my records – it had never existed in my lungs; my demob formalities could wait until I got back. It was a huge relief to find someone who understood the silliness of the rule book and favoured common sense.

We flew to Delhi in March 1946 from Hurn in a York aircraft, via Rome, Benghazi, Cairo, Basra and Karachi: thirty hours of flying with night stops in Cairo and Karachi. It was the first time that such places had ever come within my horizon. The aircraft had room for only twelve passengers, who included four or five of the Governors of the provinces of British India. Two I remember particularly: Sir Francis Mudie, a Scot, Governor of Sind, who was our host in Karachi, and Sir Evan Jenkins, a Welshman, Governor of the Punjab, who had until recently been private secretary to the Viceroy. He seemed to know everything that there was to be known about India – its history, its customs, its leaders and its peoples. He spoke, so it was said, the two main Punjabi dialects perfectly; during the long hours of flying he read Homer in the Greek. He seemed to be everything that a Proconsul ought to be. What a gain, I thought, it would be for our country that such men would now be available at home where there was a need for them. In the event, no one seemed inclined to make room for men of his size.

Now, half a century later, we do not produce them or, if we do, do not know how to use them. We prefer our rulers to come in smaller sizes, nearer our own level; safer, less visionary, more amenable and with fewer imperatives of their own. Leaders are all very well, but there is no knowing where they might take us. Better have men whom we can keep an eye on, who know the things we want and are ready with assurances that we can have them – men who will sit in the driver's seat moving the controls, waving cheerfully to us all, but with the engine switched off, going nowhere. Lord Lloyd had them in mind when in 1937, as Rector of St Andrew's University, he observed that it was 'a monstrous misunderstanding of the tasks of leadership to congratulate yourself upon catching the bus which you yourself are supposed to be driving'. That rather greasy process of self-congratulation has now become the regular stock in trade of the political parties.

I had been out of the Army for a few days only, out of a German prison camp for less than a year, when I arrived in India for the first time, still having something of the prisoner's hangover. At home, where so much had changed in the huge upheaval of war, even those once familiar, everyday things which had stayed the same had been new and strange to me. India, always a shock to the unprepared newcomer, presented me with something almost beyond the reach of words. It is a land of vivid contrasts and endless variety, one in which the opposites meet, mingle and almost embrace.

It was not until much later that I came fully to understand how extraordinarily lucky I had been, to find myself so placed as to have a close-up view of that great flood of events which brought the curtain down on British rule and swept India to independence. What amazing good fortune it had been to be able to meet so many of those who played leading roles in the drama; to gain at least an impression of how it seemed to the British who had brought and held together that huge and diverse sub-continent with its teeming masses; to glimpse the aspirations and the rivalries of those to whom government would soon pass. As the ending of British rule came nearer, and with it the withdrawal of a system which favoured neither Hindu nor Muslim nor Sikh, a vacuum of power began to appear – in the jargon of the weather men, 'an area of low pressure'. Into that vacuum were drawn the winds, all the conflicting interests, the hopes and the fears of some hundreds of millions of people.

The British presence in India had evolved in a characteristically pragmatic and rather untidy way. Originating in trade, continuing in international rivalry, it had ended in sovereign rule. There had developed over time an intent to hand over power as soon as there emerged some Indian organization capable of exercising it over the whole of the sub-continent. While the Government of India Act of 1935 had moved things on to a modest extent, the war had brought us other things to think about. By the time it was over, the Congress Party had achieved a position in the sub-continent from which it felt entitled to demand British withdrawal and the reins of power for itself. In 1946 the British Government indicated its willingness to depart and began to get ready to do so.

It was one of those decisions to which hindsight and history give the appearance of inevitability, but it did not seem so at the time. Once made, however, it set in motion a train of events, the course of which few could foresee and none could control. There was at first no thought in the mind of the British Government that partitioning of the sub-continent would follow; certainly they did not envisage the tearing apart of whole communities which had grown together like some living mosaic, sharing the air they breathed, the streets they lived in, the services they used, but worshipping different gods. Indeed, those Ministers who came to India on a Cabinet Mission declared themselves, soon after their arrival, as 'unable to advise the British Government that the power, which at present resides in British hands, should be handed over to two entirely separate sovereign states'. Nor, I am sure, did the British Government contemplate the unilateral setting aside of the solemn treaties which governed the relationship of the Indian States, so-called Princely India, with the Crown, on the ground that continuing to honour them had become inconvenient. Yet before long Partition was seen to be inevitable and the treaties were left in the pending tray to be unceremoniously discarded as refuse by the new Government of India.

Previously each State had its own ruler who, in accordance with treaties, agreements and understandings reached separately and at different times, acknowledged the sovereignty of the British Crown and enjoyed its protection. There were six or seven hundred of them, ranging in size and importance from those like Hyderabad and Kashmir to smaller ones which were not much more than large country estates. Foreign affairs and defence were the responsibility of the British Crown, the Paramount Power. At first there seemed to be some prospect of something on these lines continuing. In a statement dated 16 May 1946, the Cabinet Mission and the Viceroy set out the 'basic form' which the constitution should take: 'There should be a Union of India, embracing both British India and the States, which should deal with the following subjects: Foreign Affairs, Defence, and Communications.' This last bold and unqualified statement by British Ministers did for a time reassure the States. It was not long, however, before it began to be eaten away by events and expediency; it was finally jettisoned by the British Government without anything much in the way of an explanation or apology. Not surprisingly, the States felt that they had been betrayed.

It was Walter Monckton's duty, as Constitutional Adviser to HEH the Nizam of Hyderabad and Berar, to advise him how best to secure the future of his state and to ensure that the British Government neither overlooked the interests of Hyderabad nor conveniently forgot the formal obligations which they had undertaken towards Hyderabad under a succession of treaties. It was Walter Monckton's near-impossible task to remind all concerned of things which they wished very much to put aside; the British Government and the leaders of India of the rights of the states, confirmed in innumerable treaties; and the states themselves of the need to accept the inevitability of change. The British Government's aim was to depart free of all governmental commitments, leaving India in total charge of its own affairs. The leaders of the new India were of the same mind, insisting that the transfer of power should be complete and final; moreover, once Partition had been accepted in principle, they became even more determined to be masters in their own house. Hindus for the most part, they had little regard for the aspirations and concerns of a despotic Muslim ruler, the large majority of whose subjects were Hindu and who had made no move in the direction of democracy. Hyderabad in 1946, despite some signs of unease, gave the impression of having been set apart, undisturbed by the storms of war, a tranquil oasis which had somehow contrived to get left behind in time and not be the worse for it. It was both fascinating and sad to see, in part through Walter Monckton's perceptive eyes, the way in which events swept on to a conclusion which only seemed inevitable after it was reached.

I had never had such a role before, nor have I again been in such close day-to-day contact with a man in whose make-up there existed so large a measure of kindness, intelligence and eagerness to understand. There were some who, lacking it themselves, suggested that his undoubted charm did duty for other abilities. While he possessed it in abundance, it was a part of him; it welled up from within him, reflecting his love of life – it was never put on like a suit of clothes out of deference to important people or respect for a special occasion. He listened to people, giving them his whole attention, holding nothing back; in doing so he found a way to their hearts and minds which was barred to others. He was at the time a leader at the Bar; his voice was so easy to listen to that it compelled attention; he could put complex things simply; he had, when he wished to use it, a seemingly inexhaustible patience. He possessed a degree of energy which led Colin Pearson, one of his Juniors and later a Lord of Appeal, to describe him as 'the most over-engined man' he had ever met. His ability to apply himself and get to the heart of a problem was well concealed behind the relaxed and seemingly effortless manner with which he subsequently deployed his arguments.

I have heard him addressing audiences as different as the Court of Appeal, the Hyderabad Cabinet, the House of Commons and his constituents. With all of them he showed the same courtesy and genuine concern, not to instruct, but to help them with any difficulties. If someone had something to say, a question to ask, he didn't simply wait for them to finish, he listened, digested what they had said and responded, giving them the feeling that to him they and their opinions mattered. Such qualities came to the fore in the Abdication crisis, when, as Attorney-General to the Duchy of Cornwall, he advised first Edward VIII and then George VI. He continued, after it was over, to enjoy the friendship and confidence of both. He was fond of telling how, at the King's request, he had at the height of the crisis consulted Churchill, who responded with this message: 'Life is a tease; you must tell him, and tell him from me, that joy is the shadow of sorrow and sorrow the shadow of joy.' Asked by King George VI whether there was anything he could do for him, he replied, 'Yes, sir, walk with me to the door'; he hated walking backwards.

Walter drafted also the abdication statement of King Farouk of Egypt, who, he said, had complained about the pen and the quality of the paper provided for the occasion. As Minister of Labour at a time when the trade unions possessed great power, he had to satisfy those who said, 'Don't give in – but mind you, we don't want a strike.' It was not an easy task, nor was it obvious how

71

his critics would have done better. In later more forgiving times, when being divorced was no longer such a barrier, he would almost certainly have become Lord Chief Justice. Be that as it may, it was perhaps in India that Walter's impact was greatest, his character and his talents most appreciated. The Nizam himself and his Ministers, Ali and Zehra Yava Jung and the Nawab of Chhatari, trusted him, admired and loved him as much as and more than they did any other European. The Nawab of Chhatari once said to me, 'We love Walter. He takes such trouble to understand us. He is always so very polite and has such good manners, and that is so important to us.' There are many, and I am one of them, who have cause to remember him with affection and gratitude.

HEH the Nizam of Hyderabad and Berar was a prince, a descendant of Moghul emperors, one who saw himself as entitled to rule, who saw no need for change and feared it. His position had been reinforced by treaties with the Crown; he had had conferred upon him the title of 'Faithful Ally of the British Government'. He now looked for a treaty which would establish a similar relationship with the new India when it came into being. The Nizam was said at the time to be the richest man in the world, so rich that when the Government of India withdrew the one thousand rupee note issue he needed extra time for his to be counted. He was, despite his wealth, something of a hermit who was disinclined to entertain or to spend money. The Nizam was not a man whose nature was to look for a middle way, and was easily swayed by extremists within his own state who counselled him against doing so. He trusted and listened to Walter, but could never quite bring himself to accept his advice to accede to the new India on the best terms available. The great majority of his Ministers listened likewise with respect to Walter, but clung to the belief that the changes of which he spoke would not happen, at least not just yet: moreover they had no wish to incur the displeasure of His Exalted Highness, to whom alone they owed their positions.

Ali Yava Jung was the Hyderabad Minister most closely concerned with the discussions and negotiations about the future of the state. He worked closely with Walter. When in Delhi he and his enchanting and beautiful wife, Zehra, and their children lived in the Hyderabad Guest House; we saw a great deal of them and became friends. They had two children, Minoo, who promised to grow up like her mother and did so, which was as much as anyone could ask, and Azzad. Aged four, he appeared one day, immaculate in a white suit, vanished for a while and then reappeared looking as though he had been in a slaughterhouse, having covered himself and his clothes with his mother's nail varnish and lipstick. For that I dubbed him 'The Brute', and the name stuck. Ali was, for the most part, an easy, delightful person to work with; during the fast of Ramadan, however, no matter what the pressures of the moment, he withdrew to pray and was hard to reach. Following the transfer of power, although as a Muslim he might have been expected to throw in his lot with Pakistan, he opted for India and became in turn Ambassador in Cairo and in Paris; Chancellor of Aligar University, where he was nearly killed by rioting students; and finally Governor of the province of Maharashtra. He died sadly and suddenly at a time when there was much left for him to do. At the time of which I am writing, he was alone amongst the Nizam's Ministers in understanding how the cards were stacked against Hyderabad.

Others who had the ear of the Nizam simply could not see that the war had changed the world and that that small and charming enclave in the middle of southern India, of which they were a part, had no chance of remaining unaffected by its convulsions. They failed to a man to grasp that King George VI, as a constitutional monarch, could not instruct the Ministers who ruled in his name; nor could they understand that the British could do little to preserve Princely India, even if a Labour Government had been so minded; that in the hard new world treaties were more likely to end in the rubbish bins than live in history. Neither the ties of friendship, nor the flow of memoranda, representations and petitions, could prevail against the irreversible tide of change which was flowing. Ali saw it all and understood as clearly as any Indian the positions of the British, of the leaders of the new India and of the princes, but was able to make little headway against counsels which the Nizam found more to his taste. He and Zehra helped me to understand at least something of the whole extraordinary and complex scene. I remember Zehra explaining sadly at lunch on my first day in Delhi the huge differences of culture and language which separated rich and poor, and which made it almost impossible for them to talk with and understand each other.

Many of those who came to India for the first time saw and heard only what they expected to see and hear and were quick to assert that they had understood. One British MP, with a police inspector as guide and interpreter, paid a visit to one of the more deprived areas of Bombay and, having talked briefly with one or two out of the teeming masses who lived there, emerged with the claim that he had understood the soul of the people of India. If an Indian speaking no English, with police inspector as interpreter, had made a like discovery in this country, it is at least possible that someone might have laughed.

The Nawab of Chhatari was President of the Council and Prime Minister. A kindly man, gentle, and with marvellous manners, he found it hard to come to terms with the times and to make the decisions which they required. He, like Ali, listened to Walter's warnings, but could not bring himself to urge upon the Nizam those things which he knew would be unwelcome. An aristocrat and a landowner, he belonged halfway between the old world in which the Nizam and his other Ministers dwelt and that new one towards which they were all being swept. For most of the time he was aware of the tide running against the princes, but on occasion he managed to persuade himself that a friendly greeting from a member of the Cabinet Mission reflected something more positive than a wish to avoid awkwardness. Time has a way of leaving such people stranded, looking unreal and faintly ridiculous, easy targets for those to whom any sign of dignity is an invitation to sneer.

New Delhi, the base from which the Cabinet Mission was to operate, looked from the air like a planners' paradise. Compared with Old Delhi, it stuck out like a well-manicured thumb which somehow had got stuck on to a wrinkled and rather grubby hand. Central and dominating were the Viceroy's House and Government Buildings. Lord Wavell, the tenant for the time being, was a man of few words but knew and loved those of others, as he showed in his anthology, *Other Men's Flowers*, in which he gave more than a glimpse of himself. Early in the war, with scant resources at his disposal, he had soon put paid to the Italian forces which faced him in North Africa. It can fairly be said of him that his exceptional qualities far surpassed the rewards which he received.

His temporary guests in April 1946, the members of the Cabinet Mission, were a strange mixture. Sir Stafford Cripps, its leader, was a serious man, a socialist, a lawyer and a vegetarian, clever, not unkind, but austere, with a rather jaundiced view of people who didn't share his opinions and scant regard for many of those who did. When he came to us for a meal, he was given such food as almost made a vegetarian of me. During the war he had been Ambassador in Moscow. At the beginning of my prison life, before the German invasion of Russia and when German–Russian communications were still open, I had written a postcard to him, even though I hardly knew the man, pointing out that I was hungry. Now at last I was able to thank him for two splendid parcels which he had sent me.

A. V. Alexander, First Lord of the Admiralty, was a man of a very different kidney. Outgoing and jolly, he would tell you all about himself and his habits: four cigarettes while getting up in the morning – paying, so he said, little attention to Mrs Alexander's objections. Given an audience, a piano and some beer, he enjoyed sitting down in the evening and singing sea shanties. He rather surprised the Nawab of Chhatari on one occasion with the warmth of his greeting, clapping him hard on the back: 'Hello, Chattiari old man. How are you?' He never could get the name right.

A. V. asked me if I knew any girls; I said I didn't, that I thought they were all in the hills and I didn't know where the hills were. He told me that a most glorious girl, a Wren officer, had just come up to join him from the naval base at Trincomalee. He would, he said, give a dinner party to which he would bring this gorgeous creature so that I could meet her. He was as good as his word, but she, statuesque and chilly even in the heat of Delhi, didn't quite match up to the hopes which he had raised.

I liked A. V.: he told me to be sure to come and see him when we were all back in London, and was very surprised when I did. Lord Pethick-Lawrence, Secretary of State for India, I only remember dressed in an old-fashioned bathing suit, floating gently in the pool at Viceroy's House, waiting to be discovered like an elderly Moses, but without the bulrushes.

In Hyderabad, we lived in great comfort in a large house with many servants, a lovely view, but hideous furniture; Walter suggested it must have come from a Second Empire brothel. We were guarded by soldiers of the Nizam's army, whose orders, I discovered, were, first, 'Sentry must not sit down'; second, 'Sentry must not pick flowers.' The food was cooked by a chef whose courtesy matched his cooking; it was superb. He collected testimonials, which, set out on a large piece of paper, he was accustomed to present to prospective employers. 'Most respected Madam', the document started, 'may I present the following for your kind visualization.' The opulence which surrounded us would have seemed something out of the ordinary at any time. Coming so soon after my prison camp years it was a prodigious shock, yet one which I managed to survive. Not surprisingly, there was a constant flow of guests. I once got into a bit of trouble by saying, when a famous German expert on ethnic matters arrived two hours late for lunch, that I was sorry there was no food left: I didn't like him and had told the cook to say that the food had all been eaten. John Graham, the Chief of Staff of the Nizam's Army, feeling that he could put things right, went out and discovered, of course, that there was food – plenty, and the man was fed. Walter, when I confessed, was for a short time furious; he forgave me later, when a beautiful lady who had been at lunch interceded on my behalf.

On the point of leaving for Delhi one day, we were suddenly told that the Deccan Airways Dakota which we were to use had developed trouble with its undercarriage and was declared not to be airworthy. The Air Vice Marshal commanding the RAF in the area kindly agreed to lend us an Anson. We met this ancient vehicle and its two-man crew at Begum Pet airfield. The pilot, who came from Glasgow, was far from reassuring: 'This is no plane for a VIP. In fact I hate flying the brute myself.' I passed this on, but Walter, who was in a less than sunny mood, brushed it aside. 'We have to get to Delhi today – how else can we do so?'

We took off, myself in a state of considerable apprehension. The navigating officer embarked upon the lengthy process (fifty-two turns of the handle, I seem to remember) of winding up the undercarriage. Ali, sitting behind, kept nudging me and pointing, as I thought, to the beauties of Hyderabad City. I said yes, I had seen them, and confined my attention to the newspaper, full of advertisements for remedies, not at that moment appropriate, for constipation. He continued to nudge and to point until at last I understood what was on his mind: a quite impressive column of smoke was coming from the crude and uncovered electrical circuit just above the window. I said to the navigating officer that I didn't much like the look of it. 'No, my God, nor do I,' he replied, and, pointing out the trouble to the pilot, started immediately to wind down the undercarriage. We landed safely and returned to our house, where we drank a quantity of gimlets; all pre-lunch drinks were so named regardless of both colour and content. Since I could not lay hands on another aircraft, we had to resort to rail: special carriages of the Nizam's were to be attached to the Delhi train, which departed soon after sunset on the following evening.

It was my first journey by train in India, and the comfort of our carriages made the intense heat easier to bear. Outside on the station platforms and in the rest of the train things were different; swarms of people covered every inch of space, seeking to go somewhere, struggling to get into or on to trains already crammed and literally covered with people. Somehow they fitted in packed together, without even the oil which sardines are given for their comfort. The most lively were those who sought to sell food, drink and a huge variety of trinkets, and the children, even those without an arm or a leg, who moved with amazing agility. The babel of sound was unceasing; the crowd like a tide which never ceased to rise, but was withal endlessly resigned, marvellously patient.

In Delhi we called on the venerable Sir Sultan Ahmed, Constitutional Adviser to the Chamber of Princes, and one of a growing number who saw Britain as getting ready to let down her friends. We visited the Naidus, mother and daughter, who were comfortably ensconced in a palatial house belonging to a well-heeled supporter of the Congress Party. They had staying with them a strange English lady whose favoured attire was four small Persian tablecloths, with, across her bosom, the legend: 'To this wide spread are welcome friend and foe – I'm neutral.' Mrs Naidu, who later became the first Indian Governor of the United Provinces, was an impressive figure. Clad, as I remember her, in a purple sari, she looked rather like an ageing Roman emperor. Her daughter Bibi, concerned as ever that her relationship with Nehru should not be overlooked, once offered me a three-foot-high vase to be used as an ashtray; 'I have taken the only one in this room up to my bedroom for Jawaharlal.' On another occasion, having invited Walter to pay a personal call on Nehru, she welcomed him with warmth: 'Oh, Sir Walter, so good of you to come. Jawaharlal has been much looking forward to seeing you. Do you mind coming up to my bedroom to talk with him?'

'Of course I don't, though, now I come to think of it, I have never before been invited to a lady's bedroom to meet another man.'

There had been talk, towards the end of April, of a conference in the cool air of Simla, at which all concerned would have the opportunity to present their views to the Cabinet Mission and for the Ministers then to pronounce their conclusions. For some days the conference was off and on, but it finally got under way around the end of the first week in May. As with many of those exercises in summitry, to which we have since become accustomed, expectation dwarfed achievement. Gandhi, Nehru and Congress held all the cards and were not disposed to allow others to take many tricks. The hard line taken by another of the Congress leaders, Vallabhai Patel, who was jealous of Nehru's popularity, further reduced any prospect of accommodation being reached between Hindu and Muslim or of promises made to the Princes being kept.

The Nawab of Bhopal, representing the latter, was quick to point out that the attitude of the British Government had left him with no option but to curry such favour as he could with the Congress leaders. Chhatari commented gloomily to me, 'Now, John, you will be able to go home and tell your friends how the princes of India have been deserted. Only a year ago, there were dangers of German bombs and Japanese invasion; we were then side by side. Now we are alone and have nobody we can rely on.'

Quite suddenly, in the evening of the second or third day, and out of the blue, everything changed; it was as if the gloom had been washed away by the torrential rain. Nehru had become President of Congress; he and the Muslim leader, Jinnah, had met alone together and were to do so again. Gandhi's pronouncement, 'The clouds have rolled away', confirmed the good news.

A. V. Alexander, who came round for dinner, was beside himself with joy; within minutes of arriving he had seized upon the piano and embarked on a number entitled 'Doodle-de-do'. Within three days of this rejoicing, the froth had subsided and it became clear that the conference had achieved nothing.

On the Sunday morning of the conference we had drinks before lunch with the Congress leaders. Pandit Nehru, elegant and charming, a natural leader, was the host; he did the rounds, talking to everyone in turn.

'Do you realize,' he asked me, 'that you and Sir Walter Monckton and the Nawab of Chhatari are the only ones in this room, and I include the women, who have not been in prison for at least two years?'

'But no,' I protested. 'I have done almost five years in a German prison camp. Surely that counts.'

'Yes, of course. Please tell me which you prefer, solitary confinement or to be with others?'

What he himself had found most trying was being with seventy-five other people in what he described as very crowded conditions. While he may have had something of a recluse in him, I felt certain that he had never endured what must be the worst part of solitary confinement – not knowing for how long, what will come next, or what your gaolers have in mind for you, or the effects of exceedingly low-grade accommodation and living on meagre punishment rations.

Rajagopolachari was urbane, civilized, good-humoured and slightly cynical. 'Of course,' he remarked, 'you will say that we are not able to govern ourselves. Quite right – but then nor can you.' Mrs Naidu and her daughter were also there. The latter had been a reluctant starter for Simla and had only agreed to come on the promise of some azaleas. Since the only ones in flower at the time were in Jinnah's garden, Nehru was deputed to ask for some. Jinnah said, 'Of course', but, uncertain as to which flower was meant, and not liking to ask, sent none. Much was made of this by the Congress leaders, who had already cast him in the role of scapegoat, the one who, by his intransigence, had caused the conference to fail. From all that we heard, however, it seemed that the blame lay elsewhere, particularly with Patel.

Mohammed Ali Jinnah, Founder and President of the Muslim League, was, like Nehru, good-looking, courteous and immaculate in both Eastern and Western dress, though more withdrawn. But whereas Nehru had with him a collection of Congress members of personality and ability, Jinnah was on his own on the Muslim side and at least the equal of the leaders on either side. Like the rest, he was swept along by events; he had no alternative and knew it. He said very clearly to Walter, 'I would not now be joining in the cry "Quit India" if I could trust the British Government.' He was, however, looking for something which by that time they had not the power to give; for, as they saw it, their purpose of an orderly withdrawal depended for its fulfilment upon their being able to satisfy whatever demands the Congress leaders made upon them.

Following the demise of Simla we flew to Bhopal with the ruler, who could not resist the opportunity of getting some free legal advice. As Chancellor of the Chamber of Princes he had a position of some prominence; with a somewhat diverse flock and neither troops nor money, however, although he was listened to with courtesy he had little influence on events. As a fifth or sixth son he would never have inherited the Gadi – the throne – had it not been for his mother's determination; she had fought for him at every level up to the Privy Council, who found in her favour. Her son honoured her memory at a special shrine in the Palace, with readings round the clock from the Koran. Colin Garbett, the Resident, had a tale about a young British official serving in India, who had sent a cable to his bride-to-be saying how much he was looking forward to her arrival and that he was having his tum-tum painted green against the happy day. She replied that Mother thought his message disgusting; she agreed and would not think of marrying him. He had not thought to explain that a tum-tum was a variety of buggy.

While in Bhopal we had the opportunity to see Sanchi, surely the most splendid of India's Buddhist shrines. More than two thousand years old, built in red sandstone and situated in the very middle of the sub-continent, it is unforgettable. The principal features are the four gateways which lead to the main stupa or dome, and the exquisite carvings which cover the whole of the monuments. I particularly recall our very learned guide – a Muslim – pointing out to us how in the earlier parts of the shrine the Buddha is represented only in symbols, the most usual being a tree. Only in the later and outer ring is he shown in human form, a development coming after his absorption by the Hindus, who, conscious of the advances of Buddhism, accepted him as one of the latest incarnations of Vishnu, I believe the ninth; the tenth and last is still to come.

India is a land of many layers; it is at once open and unfathomable. In a sense all is on display: you cannot miss the poverty, the slums, the dirt, the primitive ways, the animals wandering aimlessly about amongst the huts which do duty for human habitation and the dogs belonging to no one and somehow managing, like the people in the layer just above them, to get by. Beggars young and old, some horribly disabled, press their claims upon the passer-by with attitudes which vary from saintly resignation to something more threatening. One small incident has stayed in my memory of a dog which had got locked into a bitch and was being dragged behind her, screaming with pain, as she ran through an empty village street in the midday heat; no one noticed, it wasn't important, only the heat was real, absorbing what there was of life. Driving in the countryside, you became accustomed to seeing groups of women walking. From a distance, you thought from their bearing that they were Queens; closer to, you saw them to be old, with lined faces, owing their seeming majesty to the fact that they had carried vessels of water on their heads daily all their lives. You saw people by the roadside squeezing sugar cane, threshing crops, carrying stone in the only way they could, having no wheelbarrow – on their shoulders. Yet the poverty, the starkness and the cruelty which shock so many are only half of the account; by the side of them there exists a gentleness and mercy and kindliness which we in the West, who think ourselves superior, cannot match.

Departing by air from Delhi I had mixed feelings: relief at getting away from the heat and the dust and even the drama; delight at having been there and seen things I had never dreamed of. I wondered if I would ever go back. A lift was offered by the Maharajah of Bundi from Hurn Airport to London in a majestic Daimler Hire which would have given Queen Mary, sitting erect in the back and waving graciously, plenty of room. After three punctures, the last at Bagshot – such a thing had never occurred in India – I bailed out and rang my mother at nearby Ascot, who came and collected me.

Invited by Walter to return to India early in 1947, I at first refused, foolishly thinking that I should continue to sit in chambers, hoping for legal work. I had joined the chambers of Patrick Devlin as a pupil of Colin Pearson, who had left the Monckton chambers. The work of the chambers was heavy, solid stuff from which few crumbs were left for beginners. One of my first briefs was in the House of Lords; it sounded rather grand, but the role was a very minor one. Our instructions came from a substantial firm of solicitors so well known and respected that they took time before they got round to settling small accounts such as mine. Devlin, cold, reserved, led our side; D. N. Pritt, who, for all his rather strange enthusiasm for Russia, seemed warmer and more human, led the other. Out of court and over lunch he talked constantly in Communist jargon, measuring his fee, which was huge, against the number of months which it would have taken a heavy labourer in the Soviet Union to earn the same amount. My task was simply to take a note, which, so far as I knew, no one subsequently read. On another occasion I had to attend court to receive a deferred judgement. My function, simple as could be, was to listen to the judgement and, when it was over, the decision having gone in our favour, to ask for costs. I was exceedingly nervous, so much so that I saw two judges sitting side by side on the bench, where I knew there was only one; I was so alarmed that I quite forgot to do what I was there to do. Mr Justice Lynskey kindly rescued me, saying, 'And of course the Plaintiff shall have their costs, if they ask for them.' 'Indeed I do, my Lord,' were the first words I ever uttered in a court of law. A few poor persons' divorce petitions to draft at, I think, one guinea or at the most two a time were the usual diet. Sitting around rather miserably in chambers hoping that something would turn up seemed a poor way of spending the time to which in prison days I had so looked forward. Urged by Ralph Snagge, who at the time was in the Lord Chancellor's Department, to apply for the vacant post of assistant private secretary to the Lord Chancellor, I did so and duly attended for interview.

Lord Jowett was a handsome man and knew it: he would have adorned any stage.

'When did you pass your Bar exams?'

'In 1943 in a prison camp.'

Lord Jowett was not impressed. 'What kind of degree did you get?'

'I was awarded a war degree, because after two years at Oxford I left for the war and did not therefore sit my Finals.'

That moved him even less. 'How do we judge these young men, George?' This to Sir George Coldstream, the Permanent Secretary. 'We have no yardstick. . . . Whose chambers are you in?'

'Yours, sir.' He was still the titular head.

'We will have to give the matter some thought, and of course there are the Civil Service Commissioners to be considered. You will hear from us.' With a skill which could only have been acquired through long practice, in a single sweep of his arm he placed his full-bottomed wig in exactly the right position on his head and went on his way to the Woolsack.

A few days later Hawkins, the clerk of the chambers, was summoned to see the Lord Chancellor, who enquired about me. Hawkins told him that he thought it was most unlikely that I would accept: I had better things to do with my life than spend it in his office. That was sufficient for Lord Jowett and I was at once offered the job. Urged by Hawkins to do so, I turned it down and felt for a moment rather smart – until, of course, the fact caught up with me that I had little or nothing to do. Colin Pearson, my master, was a very able lawyer: he became in due course a Lord of Appeal, but in those days he hadn't enough work for himself and certainly no crumbs to offer me. He was even thinking, so he told me over lunch one day, of applying for a County Court judgeship.

Turning down the offer of a safe job in the Lord Chancellor's Department may have afforded me a temporary puff of self-satisfaction, but it still left me earning nothing in chambers at No. 1 Brick Court. Out of the blue at lunch one day, Percy Wright, who after the war had set up as a Lloyd's insurance broker and made a considerable success of it, suggested I should join his firm. He was persuasive and I was bored and poor, and there seemed to be prospects. Moreover, it did seem to offer some kind of financial base from which in the future I might launch myself into politics, which had by that time become my foremost aim. I accepted, but since, in the meantime, I had been again asked by Walter Monckton to go back to India, I put off the move until my return.

I had to leave at once, but, having Walter's power of attorney, I needed to pass it on to someone else before doing so. A Commissioner for Oaths who would be in his office on a Saturday morning was something of a rarity; one was, however, located in a small firm in Suffolk Street. Eighty years old, he looked as if he had led a full life and enjoyed it. As I left him, he shouted, 'Young man, I've been sixty years in the law. What do you think I've learned?' He answered his own question in stentorian tones, 'If you want a bloody good row, keep it in the family.'

I had just closed my last suitcase before leaving for India, when Mrs Hardwick, the cook-housekeeper who looked after three of us who shared a flat, enquired if I was ready. She added in a doom-laden voice, 'I wish you weren't going in one of them aeroplanes. They don't just kill you, they maim you'; on which happy note I departed.

Power was due to be transferred to the new Indian and Pakistani Governments around the middle of August. There was to be a dinner about that time given by the Hyderabad Government, presided over by the Nizam himself; white ties to be worn. Walter would need his medals and stars and I had them with me. The journey was uneventful until we came to leave Cairo; our departure was delayed first by engine trouble and again when it suddenly occurred to one of the passengers to ask what had happened to his cobras. Only when these had been located, still safely tucked up in their crate, were we free to take off for Basra. No sooner were we in the air than the pilot came back from the flight deck to tell us that this would be the worst bit of the journey; he aimed to keep above the weather, at which height we would need oxygen. He added that he hoped that the dust storms of the last few days in the Basra area would cease with nightfall. I changed into a thin suit, immediately upset coffee all over it, changed back and began to feel apprehensive.

We arrived over Basra at around eight o'clock, by which time it was dark. As we circled the airfield I was able to see quite clearly ships berthed in the Shatt-el-Arab at the confluence of the Tigris and the Euphrates, even lights in the hold of one of the ships – yet our pilot was unable to find the runway. Every time he attempted to do so, a shower of flares indicated that he was off course. After an hour or so of trying he sent the steward back with the message that, since he could not get down at Basra, he was going to try to land at the RAF airfield at Shaibah. Since I knew that Shaibah had no facilities for night landing, I realized that our safe descent was exceedingly problematical and felt somewhat alarmed. After a short time, however, and rather to my surprise, I seemed to run out of fear. Looking round at my fellow passengers, a mixed lot of Indians and British, I wondered if they were aware of our plight. If they were, they showed no sign of it; they had the same stony, fixed expressions as commuters do when, having endured each other's company for a while, there is nothing to do but wait for arrival and release. It struck me as odd that, having survived the war, this should be my 'bus stop', the place where I got off. I felt sad for my mother and wished I could have told her so.

We took an age to travel the short distance between Basra and Shaibah; then suddenly, and without any warning, we were on the ground with a series of violent bumps. I said to the man sitting opposite me, Jack Brace, an Australian jockey who was on his way to ride in some races in Bombay, 'That's wonderful. I never expected to come down the right way up.' He replied that in his line of business he lived on his nerves and never allowed himself to think of what might happen, and he hadn't done so then. I don't remember and never have been able to remember anything after that until I found myself walking with someone in pitch darkness, I had no idea where.

'Where are we?' I asked.

'At Bosham,' he replied.

I wondered about that, for I couldn't remember arriving there. I asked again.

'At Bosham in Sussex,' he replied.

We stumbled on and, as we did so, a funny feeling came to me that we had had something to do with an aeroplane. I suggested this to my companion.

'You are talking balls,' he said. 'We have been here in Bosham for a fortnight.'

'I don't think I have ever been to Bosham, and I do think we have been involved with an aeroplane and that something has gone wrong.' As I said it I put my hand up to my head, which I found to be in a bit of a mess. I told him of this and suggested that he should have a look round himself. I don't remember his reply, but it turned out later that he had broken, or at least seriously damaged, his neck.

As it began to get light I found that we were quite near the aircraft; we could never have been far away. It was a wreck: the front part, engine, flight deck and wings seemed to have flown straight into the ground. There was no sign of the crew, all of whom had, we later learned, been killed. The rear part, in which the twelve passengers had been seated, had broken off quite neatly from behind the wing and was lying well separated from the rest, flat on the ground without its undercarriage. Seated in the rear of three compartments, I could not have been thrown out; I must have got out under my own steam through the gaping hole in the front, though I had no recollection of doing so.

I was thirsty and wanted to find some water. I was also concerned to see if there was anyone remaining in the body of the aeroplane who needed help. Finally, I had an idea that, if I could find some fuel, I would soak my coat in it and at a safe distance from the aircraft – I was sensible enough for that – start a fire to show where we were. I was, however, totally unable to focus on any one of these. I did manage to get back into the passenger section but in the dark trod on an injured passenger, who groaned. I beat a hasty retreat and then, running to somewhere undefined, collided, or the bridge of my nose did, with the tail fin of the aircraft. Seeing someone who was lying prostrate on the ground with his head on a cushion, I placed my own beside his and passed out.

Around mid-morning a search party of British and Indian troops arrived, picked up the pieces, people, luggage, coats, books and a mass of coins and took the lot to a British military hospital, which, by the grace of God, was nearby and still in full operation. It had been due for closure some six weeks before we got there and was shut down not long afterwards. The hospital had a team of nurses who were like angels and a first-class surgeon from University

College Hospital London who sewed up with amazing skill those who needed it. I had twenty or so stitches in my own head. We were marvellously looked after; our luck in finding them all there was hard to believe – without them we would have been in deep trouble. As it was, the daytime shade temperature of 130 degrees Fahrenheit was more than the rather primitive air conditioning system could take and from time to time it used to pack up and take a rest; the temperature would then rise like a rocket.

We were all of us of one mind: there had been a landing which, though rough, had not ended in a crash, for the aeroplane had been in one piece. We all agreed that the pilot must have, for some reason unknown to us, taken off after that first landing and that the crash had come later and at some distance further on. After a week or so some official persons arrived, headed by a lady from, I think, the Board of Trade, to carry out an enquiry. Our statements, made with confidence, of an earlier touchdown at some point before the final crash were dismissed as hallucinations. Was it not odd, we asked, that all of us agreed and were confident about that first landing? No, they said; it was not in the least unusual for people who had sustained a shock to communicate such notions to each other and thereafter share them. When pressed, however, they agreed with some reluctance and purely to humour us to go back over the flight line and have a look. They were amazed and not a little put out to find, at some distance back in the desert, marks which showed beyond all doubt that the aircraft had landed there previous to the crash and had taken off again. The official mind, having gathered relevant data and arrived at an inescapable conclusion, tends to dig itself in and defend the position it has taken up against all who are perverse enough to doubt. It then feels most put out when it is shown to be wrong and, much worse, when others can fairly say, 'We told you so.'

Leo Cole, manager of the Ottoman Bank in Basra, kindly took me in hand when, after a week, I was on the mend, and introduced me to a few people in the city. I visited the British Club and heard the tale of one of those loud-voiced Americans whose skill lies in winning for their fellow countrymen a reputation which they are far from deserving.

'I hear they call this place the asshole of the world.'

'Aye,' said an old Scotsman sitting at the end of the bar, 'and you're just passing through.'

Having spent ten days or so getting over at least the worst effects of the crash, the problem was how to get away and whether to go back home or on to India. Eventually, after a good deal of talk, a fresh aircraft was sent out to Baghdad from London to take us on to India. Shortly before our departure the desert, normally empty, seemed suddenly to be full of people, columns of them like ants emerging from all directions. They had come, we were told, in order to touch Jagjivan Ran, one of our fellow passengers, who was to be the new Minister of Education – a great man who was one of those helping to save India from the British. It was with mixed feelings of relief and trepidation that we found ourselves in the air again on the next lap of our journey via Karachi to Delhi, myself hairless and with a heavily bandaged head.

On arrival in Delhi I was taken, to my horror, not to the comfortable seclusion of the Hyderabad Guest House but to the busy formality of Viceroy's House, where Walter was staying and I too was booked in. Viceroy's House inevitably had its formal side, but in Wavell's time there had been an atmosphere of friendliness and warmth. People loved and admired him and thought he had been unlucky; his staff gave the impression that they would happily walk over hot coals for him. His huge achievements had left him free of conceit and without a vestige of self-importance. Mountbatten, who had succeeded him, was very different; he was an actor, very conscious of his audience, a man who liked to be centre stage, who was never happy to sit quietly in the wings as Wavell had been when he had nothing particular to do or say. It was a joy to find Martin Gilliat, whom I had not seen since we were together in Eichstätt. He had just become Deputy Military Secretary to the Viceroy, and had transplanted with ease and grace from the squalor of a prison camp to the splendour of Viceroy's House.

It had been on Mountbatten's recommendation that the run-up time to independence had been shortened from two years to one. In that he was certainly right. Once the decision had been made to go, British influence began, slowly at first, to evaporate. It became clear that we could do little more than hold the ring and, as time went on, our ability even to do that would diminish, the risks would grow and the process of exodus would become more hazardous. Partition was an added and severe problem. It wasn't all that simple even to draw the lines on a map; giving those lines meaning on the ground involved both pain and bloodshed. The human consequences, terrible at the time, have lingered; Kashmir, that beautiful paradise, is still torn today by the hatreds and passions generated at that time.

The British rule in India has been harshly judged by many, particularly by Americans, who, perhaps prompted by their own history and with all the clarity of hindsight, have fastened upon every error and been blind to achievement; they have taken no account of Indian soldiers fighting for the Allied cause. Skills and understanding and dedication of a high order had been required to govern and administer this hugely varied sub-continent. The British brought to India the benefit of a language which, though not spoken by all, is spoken everywhere. For all its vast problems, India has remained a democracy; its huge armed forces have never made a bid for political power; its constitution has not been much changed – perhaps it should have been; but as with other countries in the world, not excluding our own, long-term problems are seen by politicians as hazardous and unrewarding and therefore go to the bottom of the heap. It is possible that there are more people in India who have friendly thoughts about the British rule than there are in the rest of the world, including our own country.

I travelled a great deal less in 1947 than I had done in the previous year. There was less reason to do so: the facts had been found and digested, papers written, assessments made and decisions reached. It was a time when there wasn't much alternative but to let events take their course and hope that what happened would not differ too drastically from what was planned. Travel was also less easy in the gap between Empire and self-rule. With Partition in the offing, huge numbers of people were on the move; communal feelings were running high and many took the opportunity to advance their own interests by whatever means were available. Moreover, I had some after-effects of the air crash to contend with.

On a splendid spring day in the previous year, 1946, we had been driving back to lunch when Walter suddenly yelled 'Stop!', leaped out of the car and embraced with warmth a brigadier in the WACI (Women's Army Corps India), Biddy Carlisle. She came back with us for lunch that day and hardly left Walter's side thereafter. Fifteen months later, when affairs in India were just reaching a climax, they were both of them free to get married. Since no one was quite sure when the jurisdiction of the Resident in Hyderabad, a Crown appointee, would expire, the wedding had to take place before 14 August, the day on which power was to be transferred. Anxious to avoid the 13th, they opted at first for 12 August; but, having gone to Delhi in the previous week, first Walter and then Biddy became ill and she was not able to travel until the 13th. I had had a bit of a fever and had stayed in Hyderabad. With telephone contact only possible on the military line and through the ADC's room at Viceroy's House, arrangements were hard to make and requirements fluctuated.

In the end, the wedding was postponed till the 13th and, with more hope than confidence, a Deccan Airways plane with some of the seats taken out to make room for a camp bed was sent up to Delhi to bring them back that morning. They arrived in Hyderabad around midday, both the worse for wear, with Biddy looking particularly frail. Someone commented that she would never get up the Residency steps in the afternoon. I thought that after an hour's rest she would manage them and probably two at a time; she did so, and never looked back. They had some days of honeymoon at a special guest house out in the country at Gandi Pet. I visited them once, returning after dark to Hyderabad through a really memorable electric storm; lightning such as I have never seen flared across the sky, accompanied by explosions of thunder. Outcrops of rock and massive boulders, the monuments of some cosmic disturbance millions of years before, seemed to be on the move again, suggesting that the end of the world might well precede that of British rule in India.

On the evening of 14 August, the day after the wedding, a splendid banquet was held to mark the transfer of power, which was to become effective at midnight. The Nizam himself presided; he wore a white dastur, the headgear of the ruler, a rather untidy black sherwani and a crumpled sash indicating that he was a Knight Grand Cross of the Star of India. The room was ringed with Hyderabad Lancers in full dress. The women, in gorgeous saris, looked breathtaking; the men too were colourful. Walter and I, in ordinary evening dress clothes, were a bit drab, though his stars and ribbons gave him a bit of a lift; I looked and felt like a waiter. For all its splendour, the occasion had about it the haunting sadness of a farewell. There came a moment in that candle-lit room when, aided perhaps by the memories and thoughts of those present, the whole host of those who had made a mark or written a line or so in the history of Hyderabad and India seemed to return to the stage for a curtain call. It was at that moment that HEH the Nizam of Hyderabad and Berar rose and proposed quietly and simply and for the last time the health of the King Emperor. The pageant was over: the curtain fell and the book that they had all written was placed on the shelf.

The aftermath was a sad and shameful one. Lord Mountbatten, by that time Governor General of the new India, wrote as late as 12 August to the Nizam saying that the new Indian Government had agreed to his continuing negotiations with Hyderabad for a further two months; the offer to accede on terms already proposed would remain open during that period. Referring to the Nizam's fear that failure to accede would be treated by the new Indian Government as a hostile act and that Hyderabad might be subjected to a blockade, he added that he was satisfied that 'the leaders of the new Dominion have no intention of applying such pressure'. The Indian Government had, however, other ideas: at the instance of Patel, the Minister responsible for relations with the States, on 13 September, one month and one day after Mountbatten had given that assurance, Indian forces invaded Hyderabad in what was described as a 'police action'. That was a description which those responsible found convenient, in that it covered up an act of perfidy and aggression in which no one participating had ground for pride. Walter was, I recall, deeply shocked and disappointed that the new Government of India should have stooped so low. Many years later I heard how during the action a mob, stirred up doubtless by the invaders, set out to seize and kill Chhatari, still Prime Minister of Hyderabad. His wife, who was in purdah and was not accustomed to appearing in public, walked to the door alone and with the aid of a stick – she was lame as a result of polio. There she confronted the angry crowd and indicated that, if they wanted to kill her husband, they must first kill her. The mob fell silent and, after a moment or two of hesitation, withdrew. Shortly after that incident Hyderabad, having no option, surrendered.

Seen from this distance of time, even if the Nizam had been wise enough to follow the advice which Walter had so patiently given him it is difficult to see how a regime so isolated could have survived for long. The world was changing at a speed which no one could control. Promises which yesterday had seemed to be a matter of honour had become inconvenient, untenable and not all that important; and so, it seems, they have remained.

VI

Neophyte in Politics

Politics is, perhaps, the only profession for which no preparation
is thought necessary.

Robert Louis Stevenson

Those two visits to India in 1946 and 1947 could hardly
have provided a sharper change from the grey discomfort
of existence in the backwater of a prison camp. Suddenly I found
myself caught up by a fast-running stream, a cascade of events.
A background of luxurious living, to which I was by no means
accustomed, and the drama of an air crash had highlighted the
change. Returning to England and becoming immersed in the dull
routine of Lloyd's seemed very much a step backwards. Not long
after my return, however, I persuaded Diana Clunch, whom I had
met a few months earlier, to marry me; she and her father were on
a visit to London from South Africa at the time. Tragically he died
soon afterwards, following an operation which, being a convinced
Christian Scientist, he felt to be something of a betrayal of his
beliefs. Diana returned to Durban; a few months later I followed,
and we were married in December 1947 in Johannesburg.

After a blissful fortnight spent enjoying some of the beautiful
places in South Africa we returned to London. Diana was
marvellously patient and somehow managed the move from a
comfortable home in South Africa to the confused arrangements
of our early married life. She even accepted my departure from
Lloyd's, which, much as I hated it, at least offered a living wage
and prospects; and put up with my decision to enter politics. The
suggestion which I made to my employer, that I might find time
and room for politics in parallel with Lloyd's, met with a negative

93

response: it must be one or other. It was more than my tenuous hold on common sense could stand, and I left without much thought for either the cost or the consequences. Indeed, my timing could hardly have been worse: I was married, we had just had a daughter and I had chucked up a job, albeit one which I hated, and all for the will o' the wisp of politics; it was a thoroughly reprehensible step.

The question 'Why on earth did you become a politician?' is one which I have always found almost impossible to answer. The fascination of something which I thought of and still do as embracing the whole gamut of human affairs, more than a flicker of ambition and a vague desire to be useful were at least contributory causes. One attraction was that politics was something which to an extent I could do on my own, or so I thought.

I don't think I had much difficulty in deciding which party I should support. Innate suspicion of those who promised a brave new world and the plain silliness of the Labour Government in taking over and making themselves responsible for 'the means of production, distribution and exchange' pushed me in the direction of the Conservatives. A respect for the past which did not amount to a desire to live in it, and the fact that the Conservative Party carried less doctrinal baggage, were more enduring reasons. Time, of course, has a way of changing things, and the recent phenomenon of New Labour seeming to dump much of that baggage and collecting some at least of the garments which the Conservative Party have jettisoned must be bewildering for many true believers; it has certainly puzzled me.

The first step of getting my name included in the list of candidates kept by Conservative Central Office presented no great difficulty. I had a brief interview with Jim Thomas, who had, as Vice Chairman of the Party, general responsibility for candidates. He watched over the motley flock gradually being assembled with the patience and care of a shepherd who was well accustomed to the waywardness of sheep. Finding a local association which was prepared to adopt me as its standard-bearer was more difficult and took time; competition for safe or winnable seats was brisk. I also felt what now seems to me a becoming hesitation in claiming that I was a fit and proper person to have a part in the government of the country. Eventually fate led me to Bristol Central, a safe Labour seat, but where none the less there was a quite lively body of Conservatives who helped me to believe that I was much better than I was and that if we all tried very hard we might win the seat. Although my memory of those days is dim, I do remember becoming gradually aware of the defensive screen of disinterest and detachment which people employ to protect themselves from unwelcome intrusions. Those who go about suggesting not only that all is not well in the world, but that they and their party are the ones to put things right, tend to be regarded with the deepest suspicion. The first part of the message is something that most people will go along with; the second they swallow only with difficulty.

To help the beginner and to save him from immediate and total despair, there are in almost every constituency enthusiasts who, for no reward and little thanks, are prepared to shoulder the unending tasks of recruiting members, collecting subscriptions, running functions which bring people together and generally providing the whole thing with something like a human face. Come an election, those same people will be found knocking on doors, delivering cascades of pamphlets, few of which will ever be read, and seeking to persuade those whom they can entice to the doorstep that their party has wise and beneficial policies which will bring them great benefit; that it also has enlightened persons, of whom the candidate is one, to put those policies into effect. It is, of course, something of a ritual, but it offers, or used to offer, at least a meeting point between candidate and voter. Television has, however, changed things, turning the whole process into something of a circus in which teams of selected gladiators, in the course of defending themselves against the inquisitorial lions of the media, seek to attract, entertain, arouse and persuade the public. Meanwhile, candidates spend time and energy calling on people who are not at home and addressing meagre audiences in a selection of bleak, cheerless and almost empty halls.

It was the start of an unending process of education. I had at least a toehold on the bottom-most rung of the ladder; to help and advise me, there was an agent. He oozed respect for well-placed persons, particularly those with double-barrelled names, which he pronounced with greasy homage; he looked on me with an unease so profound as to leave no room for even the slightest display of enthusiasm. Unable, so it seemed, to remember my name, he used to press the tips of his fingers together and gaze upwards in the hope that it might be whispered to him by a passing angel. He was rather jealous of a well-named Miss Pamphlett, the agent for Clifton, Oliver Stanley's constituency and the only one in Bristol held at that time by the Conservatives; her energy and competence showed my own agent up. Happily he moved to Torquay, a safe seat and one to which he was well suited.

There were moments of deep depression; the whole venture began to look like a ghastly error and my feet got colder and colder. Scales seemed to fall from my eyes in layers as I began to realize slowly and fearfully what I had taken on and how difficult it was going to be. Yet there was no retreat, no way out, but forwards, or perhaps downwards, with only Micawber's hope that something would turn up. It was a miserable period, with no one to blame but myself. Robert Lyne, a barrister and an alderman of the city, and his wife Veronica were towers of strength and encouraged me to press on. So too did the bachelor John Gascoigne, a director of Imperial Tobacco, who became a firm friend; he had no part in either politics or Bristol's affairs. John died sadly of cancer. Oliver Stanley, surely one of the sources of light in the Conservative Party, was kind and understanding; he saw me building hopes, false maybe, but necessary, of winning when the election came. He warned that it might not happen and not to expect too much of the worthies of Bristol if it didn't. His death soon afterwards was a huge loss, for it removed from the arena a man whose wit and humour leavened that lump of earnestness which so many hang like millstones round the necks of their speeches.

With the 1950 General Election over, things began to change. Although defeated by a large margin, I had not disgraced myself, and the close overall result meant that another election could not be long postponed. Furthermore, other prospects appeared; two Conservative-held constituencies in Somerset, Wells and Yeovil were needing new candidates. I hoped to get Wells but, faced with the selection committee, made an awful hash of things in a speech the end of which I seemed quite unable to find. Not surprisingly, I was turned down. Having previously gone through the selection process at Yeovil, where I had been less nervous and had performed better, I was in due course selected.

Bill Kingsmill, the sitting Member, and Harold Walker, the Chairman, together gave me an idea of what was expected of a local Member of Parliament. Bill had commanded a battalion of the Grenadier Guards with courage and distinction and was Chairman of the brewers Taylor Walker. Experience in war had led him to believe that he might continue to be of service in peace; but five years in one Parliament and a month or so in the next had convinced him that he could, without any great difficulty, find other and better ways of spending his time. He was from the moment of my selection and for years afterwards helpful, encouraging and generous. He took me everywhere with him in the constituency; he entertained me in the House of Commons and introduced me to many people, including the future Speaker, W. S. Morrison; he even found me accommodation in London on very favourable terms after I had been elected. At his suggestion, I went to sit at the table in the Members' Dining Room waited on by Mrs Goddard.

'Who are you?' she asked on my first appearance, 'and where do you come from?'

I told her my name and that I came from Yeovil.

'What!' she said with horror. 'Instead of my colonel?'

Since Bill had thoughtfully provided me with a chit which would provide her with refreshment at a nearby establishment owned by his company, she forgave me. She even came to look on me with favour as a reminder of 'my colonel' and, indeed, a channel of communication through which welcome messages were delivered from time to time.

A new parliamentary candidate neither knows nor is known; he needs friends who will keep him on the rails and generally clean up after him. In this I was fortunate. Harold Walker was a glove manufacturer, one of those classless people who wherever they go are welcomed, listened to and loved. A Lancastrian, he had fought in the First World War in the Manchester Regiment, for most of the time in the ranks; in peacetime he set up as a glove manufacturer, one of many in the area. He was a friend who never wavered, whatever I did or did not do. Walter Shuldham, who was President of the local Conservative Association, was also stalwart in support. My constituency agent, Geoffrey Hearn, was a marvel; he spoon-fed me, briefed me, kept me out of trouble and planned my life. He went on quite rightly to greater things at Conservative Central Office, but was brought down by illness. Miss Hudson Lewis, known as Hustle, was his dedicated and somewhat authoritarian deputy. Her role was to take care of the ladies who were the backbone of the Association; stronger in candour than tact, she was accustomed to proclaim her views in a stentorian voice. Ill in hospital, she would lament loudly in a crowded ward that there was no one she could talk to. She used at times to speak rather archly of her friendship with the cartoonist H. M. Bateman; he should have been inspired to take her as the model for a series of 'the lady who . . .' cartoons. The Yeovil seat had first been won by the Conservatives in 1910 by Aubrey Herbert, the original of John Buchan's character Sandy Arbuthnot, the hero of *Greenmantle*. Although he had died long before I got to Yeovil, he left a mark which endured for a good deal longer than most. In my earlier years particularly, I used constantly to come across people who had known him and still remembered him thirty years after his death. 'That's just what Aubrey Herbert would have done,' was the greatest compliment they could pay.

In October 1951 I was duly elected, with a modest majority. I remember my alarm on polling day when the *Daily Mirror* produced its 'Whose Finger on the Trigger?' headline, with the suggestion that Churchill was a warmonger. A day or so in the House of Commons sufficed to correct any feeling that I had achieved something. My first impressions of that extraordinary assembly were confused and contradictory. It seemed to have so many different faces and moods: cheap, commonplace and pedestrian at one moment; alarming, like a hysterical and avenging mob, the next; then quite suddenly calm, dignified and having a wisdom of its own, which somehow took hold of those who ordinarily had none. It used to have a collective and instinctive judgement which enabled it to measure people and cut them down to size; it may have it still – I am not sure. Attending my first meeting of the 1922 Committee I experienced considerable unease, as if I had somehow got into the wrong room; it was a feeling which I never entirely lost. The committee, which comprises all the backbench supporters of the Party, is a useful if not very pleasant institution. For the rank and file it provides an opportunity to say in private things which, if uttered in public, would be regarded as treason. For Ministers it is a sounding board, a place where they can give ideas an airing; it can also at times become for them something of a kangaroo court; for the Whips it is an opportunity to detect the first signs that storms or unsettled weather may lie ahead.

For those who are reluctant, as I was, to spend too many of their waking hours entombed at Westminster, a good steady pair is essential; without one there can be little escape from the treadmill. There was, when I first arrived, a list, the product of someone's imagination, which suggested that a pair with some rather grand person like Dick Stokes would cost two dozen oysters and a bottle of champagne, while one with Will Nally could be had for a half of bitter. I was lucky in having three pairs over the years. Percy Morris, a retired railwayman from Swansea who, particularly in the year when he was Lord Mayor, needed to be away from Westminster for much of the time, was a great source of help and comfort. When he left the House of Commons he passed me on to Dai Williams, a retired coal miner from Neath and one of the kindest of men; he would pair with me if I was in some difficulty, even though he himself intended to remain in the precincts. Then, after an unsettled period, I reached a happy arrangement with Renee Short from Wolverhampton which lasted for the rest of my days in the Commons.

A maiden speech is like some tribal initiation ceremony, something you must put behind you before you can claim to belong. It is a nerve-racking occasion, but rather like being sick, you feel better when it is over. You are listened to politely; you are told by the next speaker, who almost invariably comes from the other side, how much the House enjoyed your speech and how much they look forward to hearing you again. The Prime Minister, Mr Churchill himself, was in his place when I rose, which added to the terror of the occasion. His attention was focussed at first on what his neighbour was saying to him; but after a few moments he turned towards me with what then seemed a baleful, even hostile, stare, paused, rose to his feet and left the Chamber, leaving me to continue with a speech which I later realized was one of quite unusual dullness.

Mr Churchill was formidable; I can only remember one occasion in those early days when I summoned up sufficient courage to address him. Two constituents of mine, Sidney Vaux and his son Billy, antique dealers, admired him above all others and wished to give him, in token of their admiration, an ebony walking stick which had a carved ivory lion as its handle. How, they asked me, should they go about it? I had no idea, but said that if the opportunity came my way, which was most unlikely, I would tell the Prime Minister about the stick and ask him if he would accept it. A few days later I was in the Smoking Room alone, and either in or near the chair which he was accustomed to use, when the door opened and in came the great man.

As he approached, I leaped up; 'Good afternoon, sir.'

He said something inaudible but to the same effect.

'Sir, I have two constituents who are antique dealers and who possess a stick which they think well of and which they would like to give to you as token of their admiration.'

'What did you say?' The question came out in a roar.

Miserably I repeated the message.

'A stick,' he said. 'I thought you said that the first time. No one', he spoke the words very slowly, 'has ever offered me a stick before. What kind of a stick is it, anyway?'

I had to confess that I hadn't seen it, but that I was confident, such was their regard for him, that they would not presume to offer him anything which was not of the highest quality.

After what seemed an age, but cannot have been much more than five minutes, someone else came into the room whom he knew and to whom he wished to talk. He turned to me with a charming smile and said, 'Thank you. You may tell them that I would be very glad to accept their stick. And thank you, my dear, for the nice things you have said.'

I brought the stick to London myself, gave it to the private secretary and in due course my constituents received a letter of thanks signed by the Prime Minister. Meanwhile, one which I had drafted for them to send at the same time had somehow been held up and didn't reach Number Ten until some time later. In it they expressed delight that he was willing to accept their gift and said some flowery things about its suitability; the lion which adorned it being the symbol not only of his party and his country, but of his own indomitable spirit. This evoked a warm and splendid response; a Private Secretary wrote to say that the Prime Minister had, before leaving for the United States to see President Eisenhower, directed him to write and say how much he had appreciated all the generous things in the letter. He hoped that Mr Vaux would accept the book which he was sending him, his life of his father, Lord Randolph Churchill.

Sir Winston Churchill, as he soon became, was already a legend. There has certainly been no one in my lifetime who has ever stood for so much or made so many feel that they had within them something extra, something which they had not used before. History will recall, even though now only a few can remember, how in a terrible time he recognized evil for what it was and, in unforgettable language, brought hope to those who had come near to losing it. There were those who thought that he ought not to have come back for that second spell as Prime Minister and that he stayed too long; yet he left behind him not a gap but a void, which no one since has even looked like filling. He was a last link with other times; times in which vision, rather than psephological calculations, lit the way ahead; in which thinking had not become the province of the computer and leadership had not been displaced by management. He was a giant whom lesser men have been tempted to disparage; they could neither match his thought nor frame his language. Writing in 1948 in the Preface to *The Second World War*, he expressed 'the earnest hope that pondering upon the past may give guidance in days to come, enable a new generation to repair some of the errors of former years and thus govern in accordance with the needs and the glory of man the awful unfolding science of the future'. If such language is on the grand side for us today and makes us feel uncomfortable, it is perhaps because we have grown smaller and vision has left us. The last speech which I heard him make was a rather dull, prosaic affair on a Defence White Paper. He ended by saying that he had confined his remarks to the facts and figures contained in it; he had not, he said, dwelt upon 'the great ocean of human destiny on which this little paper floats'. Not many even think in terms of human destiny today.

The Coronation was a splendid occasion, one in which the nation rejoiced in homage and thankfulness. The wonderful ceremony was followed by a triumphal progress through London's crowded streets which even the rain could not spoil. Inevitably it was held to be not only the beginning of a reign, but an era from which much was hoped. It didn't seem possible that such an event, attended by so grand a concourse of people, could ever occur again. Nothing that has happened since, with the rather surprising exception of the celebrations in 1995 of the fiftieth anniversaries of victory first in Europe and then in the Far East, has brought us together in the same way; nothing since has generated an atmosphere so free of the snide comment and vinegary disapproval which are now fed to us daily. That spirit, which took over briefly on those two anniversaries, suggested that at last a change of diet, which helped people to recover their pride, might not be unwelcome.

Viewed from the Government Front Bench or from a ministerial chair in a Department of State, life is usually full of interest; seen from a place on the backbenches, where adulation and sheeplike assent are seen as virtues, it can be and often is both mortifying and dull. It was not long, a year or two, before the rather commonplace thought occurred to me that the Government was unconscionably slow to do the things its supporters wanted and unwilling to pay even minimal attention to their views. Rather boldly one evening I decided to share such thoughts with the Deputy Chief Whip, Ted Heath, and enquired of Tam Galbraith, one of the assistant Whips, if the great man was in. 'Yes,' he responded unforgettably. 'What do you want, a job or an honour?' I explained that I was not seeking either. Ted, in a good mood, extended to me a kindly tolerance that left me feeling that my complaints were not as well founded as I had thought. The role of the Whips is important: in Government their first duty is to ensure that, whatever the business is, it goes through; in Opposition to ensure that their flock vote as and when required. They need to know how to coax, cajole, persuade and bully. It is also their business to identify those worthy of promotion or some other mark of favour. Their efforts will be received with anything from resentment to subservience, with somewhere in the middle a friendly disregard. One distinguished Labour member, Harold Lever, enjoying, to the intense irritation of his Whips, an extended honeymoon, sent to the Chief Whip a postcard: 'Thinking only of you.'

After a time spent wondering why I was there and what I should do, I was invited, much to my surprise, to become a Parliamentary Private Secretary.

'To whom?' I asked.

'Do you not feel equally warmly towards all our colleagues?'

I had to admit that I admired some of them more than others, but was delighted when Ted Heath said Nigel Birch; he was one whom I greatly admired and of whom I stood in some awe. At the time he was Parliamentary Secretary to the Ministry of Defence; later he went on to become Minister of Works and Secretary of State for Air. He explained my not very onerous duties to me, ending up with the instruction, 'Oh, there is another thing: when you are going on a visit with me, particularly to military establishments, for God's sake wear a hat. Edward Boyle (my immediate predecessor) never did – you must have something to take off to people.' He had a first-class mind and judgement to go with it; he saw the difference between right and wrong quicker than most and more clearly; he had wit and a sharp tongue. He enjoyed office, but curried no favours to get it. He was, however, diabetic, with eyesight so poor that in the last years of his life he was not far off being blind. It was an immense handicap, which only his considerable resources of courage and intelligence enabled him to overcome. He played a considerable part in my political education, shedding a good deal of light in the course of it on the merits and defects of his colleagues.

The Ministry of Defence, a combination of the functions of the Admiralty, the War Office and the Air Ministry, was at that time an idea that was taking shape but had not yet put down roots. At the outset the Prime Minister himself had taken the post of Minister of Defence until such time as arrangements had been made for Field Marshal Lord Alexander, then Governor General of Canada, to return to this country and take over. In 1953 it was modestly housed in Storey's Gate, not much more than the Treasury's annex – even its backside; it still had some way to go before it was able to impose its authority upon the three Service Ministries. Sir Harold Parker, then the Permanent Secretary, was not one who left much of a mark on anything, save perhaps the turf on Wimbledon golf course. I used to meet him on my regular visits to the Department, though he never managed to remember who I was when we next met. One day, however, when I was on my way to see Nigel, I was gratified and surprised when he greeted me warmly, said, 'Come with me. I want you to have a word with the Minister', and steered me through into Lord Alexander's office.

I said, 'Good morning, sir.'

He responded with something of the same kind, looked surprised and waited.

I said nothing and, after a long pause, Sir Harold urged, 'Go on, tell the Minister what you were saying to me yesterday.'

I then had to explain that I was Nigel Birch's PPS, that I hadn't said anything to Sir Harold yesterday, nor had I seen him for some weeks, and when we had last met he hadn't known who I was and quite evidently still didn't. Alexander looked amused and relieved and I departed, leaving the Permanent Secretary to explain. He was a rather dull advance copy of Sir Humphrey, but lacking both the urbanity and the humour.

As a backbench MP, I began to realize the extent to which the state machine had come to dominate society: housing, education, pensions, health, national service, publicly owned industries, taxation and planning were all fields in which the state had a major role as employer, provider or sponsor; its tentacles reached deep. One obvious consequence was that a huge volume of complaint, irritation and disappointment became focussed upon the state. A combination of unwillingness and inability on the part of the machine to produce answers that were civil, sensible and comprehensible has led to an ever-increasing postbag for MPs, as well as to multiplication in the number of special-interest pressure groups. It is worth recording that in 1951 the only free postage facilities available to MPs were for letters to Ministers and nationalised industries; the rest and, of course, pay for secretaries had to come from MPs' pockets.

My constituency had special concerns of its own. Westland, producing helicopters, was the largest single employer; glovemaking, an old craft industry with a host of part-time outworkers, had particular problems with purchase tax and something called the 'D scheme', the details of which I have long forgotten. The Fleet Air Arm at Yeovilton and the RAF at Merryfield gave rise to large numbers of complaints about noise and low flying. I learned something from all these, but perhaps more from a prolonged struggle to get a properly equipped modern hospital, the existing eighty-bedded one being entirely inadequate. The doctors, having said they must have one and have it at once, took a year or more to agree amongst themselves what precisely they wanted. Eventually I approached Iain Macleod, then Minister of Health, who told me, 'I can do nothing for you: it is for the Regional Hospital Board to decide. I could, of course appoint you to that body and then you could fight your own corner.' He added a warning that I would be unlikely to enjoy the experience. After some thought, and with little idea of what I was letting myself in for, I agreed.

The Board used to meet in Bristol once a quarter; it spawned committees which in and out of season poured out paper in torrents. Their minutes, all of which required the Board's approval, left nothing out. Of what possible value, I asked, was my opinion on matters of which I couldn't possibly be expected to have knowledge, such as the rate of pay of a needle sharpener in Bodmin or a six months' sabbatical for a doctor from Tewkesbury of whom I had never heard. 'Sir,' replied the Treasurer, 'officials must be protected'; and in that single short sentence he shed a great light upon many of our procedures. It amounted to saying that minor acts of officials, no matter how ill-conceived, once confirmed by a committee, which may or may not have been aware of what it was doing, and then a Board, which certainly wasn't, were made thereby inviolate. As a member of that Board I began to understand the importance of repetition. I saw in a new light the story of the siege of Jericho: if the Israelites had not gone round and round its walls and the priests had not blown again and again on their ram's-horn trumpets those walls would in all probability be standing today with a warlike operation still going on around them. Large organizations are slow-moving, insensitive, sleepy things, skilled in self-defence and given to procrastination. Those who wish to extract concessions or benefits from them should have in mind the old adage: 'The axle that squeaks the loudest gets the most grease.' Yeovil, after a time, did get a new hospital.

The House of Commons is an unusual place; not the least of its virtues has been its ability to attract and accommodate a quota of memorable characters. I suppose it is part of the ageing process to think that there were more of them in my early days than later on. I mention just a few unusuals of whom, for one reason or another, I have a lively memory. Apart from Churchill, who towered over all, there were men and women of different shapes and sizes and in such variety as to provide a remarkably accurate reflection of the electorate. Attlee, as Leader of the Opposition, was perhaps one of the more surprising; insignificant in appearance, he was able without apparent strain to hold together a Party which seemed to relish its divisions. He was a man of few words and no pretences; the explanation offered to one of his Ministers for dismissing him consisted of the words, 'Not up to it, not up to it.' Attlee gave at least the appearance of being able to handle without difficulty the toughs who sat behind him.

Aneurin Bevan was a majestic orator, a master of scorn and one who, like others of his countrymen, understood far better than most English MPs the power of their language; he made it his arsenal. Kenneth Pickthorn, too, was different; didactic, donnish, not much liked by the Labour Party, he used to quote with evident enjoyment a line fom Stephano's drinking song in *The Tempest*, 'Yet a tailor might scratch her where'er she did itch'. Leslie Hale's particular talent lay in his ability to clothe the trivial and the unimportant with huge solemnity. He was the fastest speaker of any that I have ever heard; it was said of him – and I am indebted to Jim Callaghan for this – that he could make a speech in the course of one of Reggie Paget's lengthy pauses. The latter, an Old Etonian and a Master of Hounds, spoke with massive deliberation, as if every word were a fence which was to be carefully measured before being jumped; he was an unusual feature on the Labour benches.

Fitzroy Maclean first became a Member of Parliament in 1941, principally because it made possible his escape from the toils of the Foreign Service and freed him to join the Army. He enlisted in the Cameron Highlanders and embarked upon a dazzling military career in Yugoslavia. Although, when the war was over, he remained an MP for another thirty years and was for a time a junior Minister, he used the House of Commons more as a base than an arena. He needed space into which he could reach, and only the remote corners of the world sufficed. His wife Veronica, whom he described as 'my favourite fellow traveller', said of him that it was his spirit of contradiction which largely dictated his actions. Whatever it was that drove him, his kind is not often repeated.

Gerald Nabarro, an ex-sergeant major with a moustache and a voice to prove it, used both to ensure that he was noticed and heard. He was a man for causes: Schedule A property tax, purchase tax and clean air were three in which he persisted; he didn't mind being awkward or a nuisance so long as he won the argument, and he often did. He was a loner who relished publicity but didn't endear himself to the powers that be; so, sadly, he never held office. Sadder still, there aren't any of his kind around today. Sir William Darling, sometime Lord Provost of Edinburgh, one of the MPs for the city and head of a large firm of drapers, had that rather doubtful asset, a sense of humour. I say 'doubtful', for those who make people laugh are in danger of being dismissed as frivolous; or, even worse, suspected of being disrespectful towards the earnest and the self-important. Immaculate as always in black coat and sponge bag trousers, he stopped in front of me one day in one of those long, high-ceilinged corridors and in his deep bass voice enquired, 'Peyton, what are you doing with your life here?'

'Nothing, Sir William, absolutely nothing,' I replied.

'Ah, so you know that, do you?' He went on, 'Do you know that book *Fortitude* by Hugh Walpole? It ends with the words, "He turned again and faced the long littleness of life."'

It is unimportant that that book doesn't end in that way, but the words have come to mind again and again as I have walked in those corridors and have listened to the pitter-patter of the clay footsteps of those who hurry importantly along them.

Hinch (Viscount Hinchingbrooke), a splendid speaker and a considerable parliamentary performer, was inclined at times to get things wrong; he certainly did so when he renounced his newly inherited earldom in a vain attempt to get back to the House of Commons. Enoch Powell, whose habit of spelling out

107

with piercing clarity the facts of a situation and pointing to the consequences did not always endear him to the leaders of his Party, ended up respected and feared, but alone. He was quick to perceive weakness both in argument and in people, and shared not at all the English penchant for mental cosiness. Iain Macleod's death, just after he had become Chancellor of the Exchequer, still has the look of an irreparable loss. He was the sort of prophet of whom political parties, particularly the Conservatives, stand in need; he had a very welcome lighter side to him. Tony Benn (Anthony Wedgwood-Benn in the beginning) seemed always to speak with the unparallelled earnestness of one who saw things so much more clearly than other people, without ever allowing even a spike of humour to intrude. I wonder what history will make of his tapes; maybe it will see him as the prophet of that political correctness which has become such an easy and useful alternative to the painful business of thinking. Nigel Birch, of whom I have already written, was one of the wittiest speakers in my time, with certainly the sharpest edge to his tongue; 'Never glad confident morning again' was his all-but-epitaph on Harold Macmillan.

I must include Sidney Silverman in this rather short list, as much for his extraordinary persistence as for anything else. Those who persist in and constantly repeat their arguments are in danger of becoming simply boring. Silverman never did; his role in securing the abolition of the death penalty can hardly be exaggerated. It is an argument which has gone on and on. I had myself favoured capital punishment without giving it much thought, until one day after I had become a Member of Parliament I read on the tape, with something of a shock, that a man had been hanged in Pentonville. It then began to dawn upon me that the way I voted on the issue was important; it caused me considerable unease. At first, I harboured the hope that the macabre business of hanging could be replaced with something less brutal and less ceremonious. I came, however, to understand that the State, if it were going to kill a man, could only do so formally; it couldn't just hand him a nasty drink or covertly make one available to him.

The conclusion of the Royal Commission on Capital Punishment that, of all the ways of execution, hanging was the quickest, surest and most humane, was an important factor in my thinking. Sir

Ernest Gower's *A Life for a Life* indicated that, while chairing the Royal Commission, he had himself changed from supporting to opposing capital punishment, and pushed me in the same direction. Harry d'Avigdor Goldsmid, at that time a Conservative MP, told me how shocked he had been by the atmosphere of excitement which had prevailed at an execution which, in some official capacity, he had had to attend. I thought I should seek out a policeman and hear what he had to say. I met by chance Eric St Johnston, the then Inspector General of Constabulary, who replied brusquely, 'We should get rid of the beastly thing as soon as possible.' My conclusion, and it caused me endless difficulties in my constituency, was that the ceremonial which was inevitably involved in the State taking a life was only tolerable if one could be certain of three things: first, that it did in fact deter people from committing murder; second, that juries would continue to convict those whom they thought were guilty, knowing that they would be sending them to the gallows; lastly, that the possibility of error could be eliminated. Those considerations, reinforced by thoughts of the publicity and sensationalism which increasingly would accompany all executions, led me to think that capital punishment did harm rather than good, and thereafter I voted against it.

VII

Suez – an Unlearnt Lesson

The best lack all conviction.
The worst are full of a passionate intensity.
W. B. Yeats

M uch of the time in Parliament is taken up with nuts and bolts and argument, which, though it may echo some popular clamour, will not be long remembered, even by those taking part. Then quite suddenly something happens, or rather irrupts into the familiar, in such a way as to reduce what yesterday seemed important to the level of the humdrum and the trivial. The parliamentary programme, which was so congested as to have no room for more, becomes suddenly flexible; budgetary considerations, sovereign yesterday, become, with equal suddenness, subordinate.

In 1956 Colonel Nasser, the Egyptian dictator, seized the Suez Canal, an essential route for oil supplies. This outraged the British and French Governments, whose interests were enshrined in treaties. The immediate impact of this event in Britain was traumatic, splitting the nation, political parties, the media and even families. In the House of Commons uproar and fury came near to overwhelming debate after debate. The operation itself took so long to get going that, by the time its military objectives had been secured, world opinion had so piled up against us as to render them worthless. It was an astonishing episode, in which events took over and those who might have had hold of the reins seemed to let them drop. A dictator, uninhibited by considerations of good faith, reminded us all how easy it is to throw a spanner in the works and how hard it is to handle the ensuing disturbance. The Opposition were not averse to making what political capital they could out of the awkward position in which the Government found itself. Cooperation with the French was, as always, fraught with difficulty. Colluding with Israel was against the rules but hard in practice to avoid. The American President, Eisenhower, was keen not to become involved in anything that might jeopardize his chances of re-election; his Secretary of State, Dulles, never one to allow friendship to become a burden, offered that least helpful of all commodities, 'moral support'. The Russians stood ready as always to let opportunity get the better of ethics.

The outcome of it all was that in the Middle East the Canal was blocked and Nasser a hero. At home, the Prime Minister was too ill to stay in office and the Foreign Secretary had so lost his nerve that he was for a time unable to cope with the House of Commons in its nastiest mood. Two Ministers, Edward Boyle and Tony Nutting, had resigned; the latter left not only office, but, as I thought unnecessarily, the House of Commons as well. The Government, it seemed, was doomed.

For me, Suez had one interesting aftermath. The oil companies concluded that politicians who understood the rudiments of the oil business and knew something of the Middle East might be less of a nuisance than those who did not: they therefore organized tours by small groups of MPs and they did it very well. A visit to a refugee camp in the Lebanon, full of sad old men who had lost everything and young ones who had never had anything, showed where the grapes of wrath were being stored. Iraq, seething and full of menace, had, we were assured by someone whose pomposity outstripped his perceptiveness, the most secure regime in the Middle East. Not long after our visit the mutilated corpses of the young King, the Regent and Nuri Said, the Chief Minister, were being dragged through the streets to the cheers of the crowd. Kuwait, overflowing with money, was generating substantial development. It was a magnet, drawing in people willing to do jobs which Kuwaitis could not or would not; it was becoming also a focus of envy.

The oil companies, we learned, possess an impressive array of skills. They must first find oil, more often than not in harsh, remote places; then extract, transport and refine it; and finally distribute and market its products. On a different level they must find, care for and train the people (expatriates and locals) capable of carrying out an immensely complex and hazardous operation. Third, they have to understand and come to terms with the Governments and owners of the land beneath which is stored this substance which has become the life blood of what we describe as Western civilization. The rigs, the wells, the flares, the pipelines, the refineries, the tank farms, the loading jetties, the tankers – huge and ungainly – all reflected a great range of technologies which had their source in the mind of man and were kept in operation by his skill, vigilance and guts. The pipelines were not the least striking: a great arterial system carrying oil over thousands of miles of empty desert to a loading port or refinery; strong enough to survive a fierce climate, designed to hold and carry a volatile and hazardous material; but not easily defended and dependent for its survival upon a wide range of consents which might at some time be withdrawn. That intricate network of pipelines reflects to a degree the structure of human society, at once robust and fragile. In the harsh light of the Middle East, it would be hard not to perceive the haphazard distribution of wealth between both individuals and nations and not to be disturbed by it.

What is less arresting, but at least as real, is the unquestioning reliance placed by the rest of the world upon the great network of arrangements which sustain the supply of a crucial raw material. That network, like a cobweb, is complex and, like a cobweb, is both strong and delicate. It is a matter for surprise that the ruptures which occur from time to time have not been more frequent and their effects more dire in a world which, despite the yearnings of many to preserve national entities, is being remorselessly pressed together. As the number of people in the world continues to rise, so the pressures upon vital arrangements and upon those who make them will surely mount. Moreover, it is to be expected that a combination of fundamentalism and advances in communication technology will ensure a growing awareness of the imperfections in the scheme of things and of the suffering they cause. Handling so explosive a mixture is likely to prove well beyond the capacity of institutions which events will cause to look more and more inept. We could well find ourselves drifting to a point at which, in Yeats's grim words,

Things fall apart, the centre cannot hold,
Mere anarchy is loosed upon the world.
The blood dimmed tide is loosed and everywhere
The ceremony of innocence is drowned.
The best lack all conviction and
The worst are full of a passionate intensity.

That 'passionate intensity' of which the worst are full is something
we can never bring ourselves to believe until we meet it face to
face, and afterwards we do not long remember it. It seemed to
me, when the Suez venture ended in failure and humiliation,
that nothing could save the Government from falling apart. At
that stage, however, Macmillan replaced Eden as Prime Minister.
Having been first a hawk, he had moved over to join the doves as
the pressures on sterling mounted; he was probably the only one
who could at that time have massaged and coaxed his Party back
into some semblance of unity and calm. Over the next two years
he saw it through convalescence to recovery, turning himself in
the process into 'Super Mac'. He was even able, on the eve of
a Commonwealth tour in that year, to shrug off the resignation
of all three Treasury Ministers as 'a little local difficulty'.

A year later he led his party to victory in the polls with a
majority which was nearly double – an astonishing achievement
by any measure. It took us, however, back into our dreams, where
I suppose many were happy to be, not forward into a new and
difficult world. What had been a calamity had been excised from
the memory, its lessons unlearned. It was a supreme example of
our ability to put completely out of our minds what we find
uncomfortable to remember, to hide from ourselves what had
become obvious to others. We had got stuck in time; cocooned
in the memory of the victory of ten years before; unaware of the
extent to which power and influence had been ebbing away.

Although that process of debilitation has continued, the embers
of tradition have kept alive in us a feeling that we ought to sustain
a capacity to defend ourselves. We have not, however, understood
that in the modern world military capacity tends to impose duties
without conferring influence; moreover, faced with demands which
we see as more popular and therefore more pressing, we have come

to regard defence expenditure as an area in which savings can be made without present pain. Despite that, we have not lost the urge to play our old role in world affairs, and we look to our depleted armed forces to meet commitments which have not changed. In Northern Ireland we have little choice; in the Falklands we had not much more, though I don't believe for one moment we could mount that astonishing operation again. We saw it as our duty and our interest to fight in the Gulf War; we saw it as our duty to go into Bosnia in an attempt to keep apart peoples moved by ancient hatreds into fighting one another. Recently, we have been so shocked by the television pictures of horrendous events in Africa that we have even contemplated a sortie into Rwanda and Zaire. The fact that we have had troops stuck in Bosnia for years has not taught us to face and answer daunting questions. How many troops may eventually be required, and for how long? What will they be there to do? How welcome will they be? How sure can we be that we will be able to get them out? Who will replace them? Lastly, how, when it is all over, can anyone stop the same ghastly thing happening again? Such grim questions are not answered by bland statements that we are a civilized country.

I understood, of course, when I began to write this book that, if the story was to have any coherence, I would need to separate the strands and tell of each in turn. What I did not appreciate was, having done so, how hard it would be to recapture their relationship to each other; nor did I realize that it is at least as hard for the mind as it is for the eye to focus upon something which is so close as virtually to shut out all else. I therefore hoped to leave out altogether those things of which I found it all but impossible to write. Suez was colossal, but being at some distance from me did not shut out the light; what follows now, though tiny on the world stage, did so entirely. I thought at first and very much hoped that it would be possible to gloss over, even to leave out altogether, the times of sadness and failure and getting things wrong. Slowly, however, it became clear to me that to do so would be like tearing a piece out of a picture: the attention of anyone looking at it would be attracted to and absorbed by the hole and the jagged edges around it. I began to understand that, since I was describing a journey, it made no sense to tell of coming to a river and then of being on the other side without making some mention of crossing it. Doing so has been hard beyond anything I had imagined.

It is easy now to see how politics may or may not be something of an adventure for those immediately involved in them; what was much less obvious to me at the time was the profoundly disturbing impact they can have on others and particularly upon a marriage. Looking back now on the middle years of my life, it would not be possible either to overlook the confusion or to explain it, much less to excuse it, without a purposeless descent into despair. Suffice it to say that, having been married at the end of 1947, it was not until 1950, two and a half years later, following my adoption as Conservative candidate for Yeovil, that we really got settled in a long-term home at Odcombe in Somerset. I had much to be grateful for: Diana and our three children, Sarah, Tom and Charlie, born in 1948, 1950 and 1955, made it impossible to continue merely to meander; gradually a degree of focus and aim began to emerge in my life.

In the autumn of 1960 a terrible thing occurred. It took me back to those days of overwhelming despair of exactly twenty years before, when the world had seemed on the edge of disintegration; but this time the grief and the anguish belonged only to us. Our son Charlie, aged five, died in the course of a minor operation on his eye in Yeovil Hospital. The operation, which should have been quite a short, simple affair, free of all complications, took place on a Sunday morning, All Saints' Day. Diana and I waited for a telephone call. Unworried at first, we became anxious; I telephoned to the hospital and was surprised to be put through to a friend, John Nicol, a surgeon who had not been involved beforehand but who had been called in. 'Something terrible has happened,' he said. 'You had better come' – words I shall never forget.

Miserably we drove the two or three miles to Yeovil and there learned that a lung had collapsed, that the little boy was dead. We returned home shattered, unable to absorb what had happened, searching for something which would tell us that it was a nightmare from which we would awake. There it was, a cup from which one couldn't possibly drink, but from which there was no turning away. Somehow we both stumbled through the days and nights that followed. Now only a few incidents pick themselves out from the anguish, which many years later can still come at one afresh: the distress of the anaesthetist; the dry procedure of an inquest; talking with an undertaker about the arrangements for the funeral, with a clergyman about the service; being called on the telephone not long before midnight by a *Daily Herald* reporter who wanted to know if we were going to sue the hospital; anger might have been a relief, but all I could manage was, 'No, it wouldn't bring him back.' Cora and Ian Bullen, two of the kindest people I have ever known, asked us to join them for a few days at a hotel at Versailles. We went and recovered at least an appearance of balance and we started to learn, or try to learn, the impossible lesson of how to live without our son.

Christopher Holland-Martin, who was one of Charlie's god-fathers and whom I first met in 1951 when we both entered the House of Commons, had died not long before. He had been playing tennis in Salisbury, Southern Rhodesia, when he had a heart attack. He had seemed to recover, but a second attack after his return home had killed him. Life seemed empty without him and the House of Commons a lonelier place. He had become my closest, perhaps my only close, friend in the House at that time. One day in our garden at Odcombe I came as near as I have ever done to seeing something which wasn't there, Christopher's face, and to hearing him say in his familiar voice, with an urgency which he used to impart into his speaking, 'Don't worry – he is all right.' Charlie's death left no room in my mind or heart for much else; there just wasn't anything to put by the side of it. I have a dim recollection of going to South Africa, where I stayed briefly with my mother-in-law and Diana's sister and brother-in-law, Monica and Ian Gwynne-Evans, in Johannesburg, and of being in Swaziland and Lourenço Marques. For the best part of two years I stumbled along, somewhere near the outside edge of sanity. There was, I found, comfort to be had from understanding just how close to each other joy and sorrow are; from knowing that even if I had been given the chance to wipe out both the memory of that small boy and the anguish of his death, I would still have wished to keep what I could of him.

In the autumn of 1962, by which time I had become a junior Minister, I met Mary again, and the feeling of earlier years, of the time in York, in London and elsewhere, came back with overwhelming force. I thought at first it might be possible to live two lives; it wasn't, and in 1966 my marriage to Diana ended. The failure and the fault were mine. Divorce has become easy and frequent; while there may or may not be financial penalties, others, once imposed by the outside world and at least as painful, have been eroded to nothing. There remains, however, the memory of failure, ineradicable, of having done someone who least deserved it a grievous injury.

VIII

Junior Minister: 1962–1964

Drest in a little brief authority.
William Shakespeare, *Measure for Measure*

In the summer of 1962, when I had just got back from a
visit to America, I received a letter in his own handwriting
from the Chief Whip, Martin Redmayne, saying that the Prime
Minister, Harold Macmillan, was minded to offer me the post of
Parliamentary Secretary to the Ministry of Power and advising me
to accept it: 'Worse things could happen to you at your age.' I
could hardly do other than say 'Yes.'

Number Ten Downing Street in the summer of 1962, having
been seized with every kind of rot, was undergoing repair. Its
illustrious tenant had moved for the time being to Admiralty
House, to which I was summoned for the laying on of hands.
Before the hour appointed I spent some time at the National
Gallery, looking for most of it at the Leonardo cartoon of the
Madonna and Child: it calmed me down. The Prime Minister
looked as if he had just got up, immaculate, comfortable, relaxed.
'Now that we are colleagues,' he said, 'I can talk to you openly.
Poor old Treasury, they will plunge us all into a slump.' I was so
deeply immersed in what was happening to me that, although the
words stuck, I failed to digest that he was talking of what was in
his mind at the time, as much to himself as to me, and showing
something of his intentions. I went on my way with instructions
to tell no one, save my wife and my mother, that I had become
one of her Ministers until the Queen had been informed; the
likelihood of her being particularly interested had not previously
crossed my mind.

...y brother Tommy, my mother, my father, Tony Stevenson, Teddy Stevenson,
...a Stevenson (my first cousin)

Tommy, 2nd Lieutenant, 60th Rifles

Lionel Massey, 1946

Air crash at Shaibah near Basra, 1947

Left to right:
Bill Kingsmill, then MP for
Yeovil, Macmillan, JP, then
the candidate for Yeovil

Electioneering in Yeovil

First election to Parliament, Yeovil 1951

Walter Monckton

Linby, 1962

Wedding Day, 1966

ories in opposition to steel nationalisation, 1966

out to take off in a Phantom, 1970

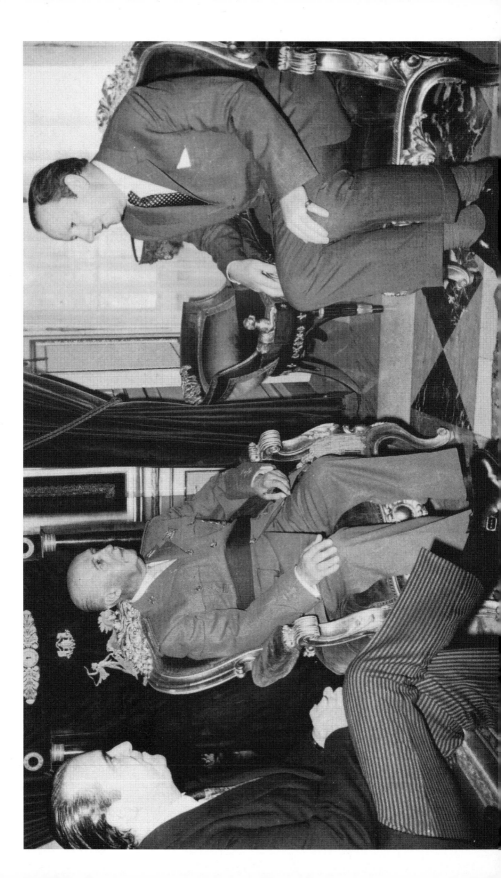

hannel Tunnel Press Conference, 1973

ith John Betjeman visiting British Rail, 1973

A winner between the French Ambassador and JP at Newbury, 1973

otor-cyclists opposed to
ash helmets, General
ection 1974

Jack Hamson and Mary,
Hinton St George, 1982

Introduction to the House of Lords, sponsored by Lord Zuckerman and Lord Home, 1983

With Margaret Thatcher visiting Alcan, 1985

th Gosh and Dick Troughton, 1989

th Mary and Sir Fitzroy Maclean

ck Jones's 80th birthday, 1995, with mace (see page 153)

ith David and John Leach

Variations by William Walton

Henry Coombe Tennant　Grandchildren

So in June 1962, after nearly eleven years in the House of Commons, I became a Minister, albeit a junior one. It was a new world, fenced in with rules, routines, procedures and precedents, kept on the move by an unending flow of paper which required attention if not action. Civil servants, for the most part benign and helpful, tend to see Ministers, particularly new and young ones, as creators rather than solvers of problems and in urgent need of guidance. One lady Under Secretary, fearful as to what I might do or say when on the loose, ended her briefing to me with this caution, which I preserved, 'If the Parliamentary Secretary is asked whether or not a public inquiry into the present application is likely, he may wish to say no more than that it is not at present possible to say, although it is true that the objections received do not appear to be insuperable.'

Not long after I arrived at the Ministry of Power, and I had begun to feel that I knew what it was all about, I questioned some advice which I had received; it concerned, I think, the price of coal going to Northern Ireland. I expected an answer from some lowly official who could be expected to appreciate just how important I was. Instead I was confronted with the Deputy Secretary, Matthew Stevenson, a tall, angular, somewhat austere Scot of whom I stood in considerable awe. He sat down in front of me, stretched out his arm across the desk and examined carefully the back of his open hand.

'I hear, Parliamentary Secretary, that you don't like your brief.'

'No,' I replied, 'you could say that.'

'May I put it to you like this' – with great emphasis – 'you have no business to incur the odium of senior Ministers in this way.'

'But I have been doing so for years and have survived.'

'That may be, but you ought not to do so now on behalf of this Minister and this Department.' I don't remember the rest of that exchange, and it wasn't important. What was important was that, after an hour of it, we went out to lunch together and began a friendship which lasted until his death nearly twenty years later.

Matthew Stevenson started life in the Inland Revenue, moved first to the Treasury and then to the Ministry of Power. When, during the war, he was offered an important post by one of the oil companies, at I do not doubt a salary four or five times what he was then getting, he turned it down on the grounds that he was and intended to remain a public servant. At a later stage in his career, in 1964, when he had become the Permanent Secretary, there occurred one of those minor incidents which shed light upon the way in which, on occasion, irrelevancy is preferred to common sense. Dick Crossman, Labour's Minister of Housing and Local Government, wished to replace Evelyn Sharp as his Permanent Secretary: told by the then Prime Minister, Harold Wilson, that he could help himself to any Permanent Secretary he fancied, he came upon Stevenson, was impressed, offered him the job and, when Stevenson at first declined, insisted upon having him. The result was that Stevenson was moved from an area of government in which he had acquired great knowledge of the power industries, their problems and the men who managed them. He had been more responsible, though he never got the credit, than anyone else for getting the UK to move into the North Sea. The move looked even more futile when, some weeks later, Crossman, who had demanded the change, became Leader of the House and left the Department. A Minister's whim had been decisive, and the arguments against had not even been considered. Steve was a lowland Scot, something of a puritan, in whom there was no trace of self-seeking and who had a clear view of what was right. There were amongst his contemporaries some who gained greater eminence; there were none who were more devoted to the public interest.

On arrival at the Ministry of Power in the summer of 1962, I expressed a wish to take a tour of the Department. That, I was told, was unusual and unnecessary: officials whom I needed to see would and should come to me, not the other way round. I protested that it was just those others who would not come to see me that I wished to meet; it was possible that they might even like to see me. After I had done one floor, the attitude changed and I was encouraged to finish what I had started. Years later a lady came up to me in the street and, having first assured herself that I was who she thought I was, said that in the thirty years she had spent in the Civil Service, the only occasion on which she had ever met a Minister was during that small tour of mine.

Soon after this unexpected turn of events I was invited by Pud Grosvenor, then MP for Fermanagh, to visit Northern Ireland and take part in celebrating King Billy's victory at the Boyne some three centuries earlier. It was an extraordinary experience. The night of my arrival was made hideous by people with huge drums which they didn't merely beat but thrashed: it came near to psychological warfare. Lord Brookeborough, then Prime Minister of Northern Ireland, came to lunch; he was to make the main speech of the afternoon, then Pud and finally myself. I was not at all clear as to what was expected of me or what on earth I should say to the great multitude of people who would be present, eager, so I was told, to hear every word of the speeches.

Having arrived at the village which was the centre of operations, the three speakers were placed at the head of a huge column which contained some eighteen bands and a vast concourse of people. We then processed round the village to a large field, in the middle of which was a farm cart, a first aid tent and some rather primitive broadcasting arrangements: the latter being largely ineffective caused inconvenience only to a few within a small circle; the great majority, having arranged themselves round the edge of the field where they could hear nothing, were free to refresh themselves until they either felt better or nothing at all. Lord Brookeborough made a long speech to which the limited number who could hear listened respectfully. Pud Grosvenor followed with a much shorter one during which a nurse fainted. I don't think, when my turn eventually came, that I said much more than 'Hello' and 'Goodbye'. So far as I remember, no mention was made of the victory which we were supposed to be celebrating. If anyone did think of it, they took immediate steps to deaden the memory.

Back in London next morning, a Friday, I was summoned by the Chief Whip to his office and told that there had been changes in the Government. Selwyn Lloyd was no longer Chancellor of the Exchequer; he would not, therefore, be coming that evening to speak at a meeting in my constituency. Did I want a substitute? Fearing what I might get, I said I would rather perform on my own. Back in my own office, I found a message that Selwyn wished to see me at the Treasury. I found him on the verge of tears, with Nigel Birch and Edward Boyle both looking miserable.

'I wanted to tell you myself that I am no longer Chancellor of the Exchequer and that I cannot come to your constituency tonight.'

'Do you mean that you are out of the Government altogether?'

'I am nothing. I am out.'

That was the first I heard of 'the night of the long knives'. It was characteristic of Selwyn that he should, at a moment of anguish, have thought to invite me round to explain. I recalled then what the Prime Minister had said to me only two weeks before about 'the poor old Treasury', and reflected upon the odd way in which we conduct our affairs and how thin is the veil of sophistication which serves to conceal for most of the time the strangeness of our actions.

My knowledge of the fuel industries – coal, gas, electricity and oil – was meagre; it consisted of the smattering which I had picked up as a member of the Nationalized Industries Select Committee and during a brief tour of the Middle East. Since both sides knew exactly where they stood, relations between the Department and the oil companies were reasonably smooth; the frontiers separating them, being well defined, did not need to be defended. Moreover, those responsible for the oil industry were familiar with Governments and knew very well how to handle Ministers.

Between the Department and the nationalized industries, things were rather different. Ministers had a great battery of powers: they appointed chairmen and board members and fixed their salaries; the fact that these had to be at rates which would not upset MPs made for considerable difficulties. Ministers could direct and, with Treasury guidance, were the sole bankers, controlling all capital investment; this also was a source of trouble, since Treasury concern with the Budget as often as not clashed head on with the needs of the industries. Ministers were constrained from interfering in what was known as day-to-day management, but which proved to be incapable of definition. The Government, despite its obvious interest in the outcome, was stood firmly on the sidelines during the annual ritual of wage negotiation, permitted only a few audible grunts of dismay and disapproval. The unions, with their own fish to fry, showed little inclination to modify

Stone Age attitudes. Management, meanwhile, were condemned to occupy a hopeless pig-in-the-middle position, belaboured and abused by all.

It was a system born perhaps of our love of checks and balances, brilliantly designed to accommodate unceasing trench warfare, to ensure stalemate and to provide an excuse for every error. In paying due deference to the sovereignty of Parliament, it fettered and frustrated management; gave politicians the opportunity not to control but to harass; and put Ministers in between as a kind of flimsy partition.

The different chairmen had their own ways of handling things. Alf Robens, having been himself a politician, was sharply aware that politicians are never so happy as when they are telling other people what to do and at the same time off-loading responsibility. Management, he realized, would be completely undermined once it was seen that political considerations had precedence over industrial ones. He made it absolutely clear, as Chairman of the National Coal Board, that while he welcomed the friendly interest and understanding of Ministers and would tell them of his plans, he would not put up with constant interference by those who were a long way from the coal face. Henry Jones, a gas man all his life from the old Gas, Light and Coke Company, defended his patch with skill, resented anything said or done by Ministers which challenged his independence, kept them at bay and was friendly so long as they stayed on their side of the line. Ronnie Edwards, Chairman of the Electricity Council, an academic of great wisdom and charm, understood everyone's point of view, kept close to Ministers, but assumed always that they would not be so silly as to take on the task that they had specifically given to him.

The Minister of Power during my first year in the Department was Richard Wood. He is one of those people whom it is impossible not to like and admire. Unworried, so it seemed, by the fact that he had lost both legs in the desert during the war, he listened to people, was courteous to those who had business with him and concerned for those who worked for him. Perhaps the most noticeable thing about him was the ease with which he won and held the trust of others. Younger than I was, he behaved towards me in a kindly, almost paternal way, mixing restraint with encouragement. Freddy Erroll, who succeeded him, was also easy to work for. Whereas Richard had been pleased to be the Minister of Power, Freddy, who had been President of the Board of Trade, felt he had come down in the world and was less so. Moreover, he was for a time ill and away from the office. He was cheerful, good-natured and wonderfully patient. On one occasion, during an electricity dispute, he was hauled out of bed well after midnight by the press. It was too cold, he said, for them to stand outside; he asked them in, gave them drinks, answered questions and was photographed in his dressing gown. The resultant pictures showed him in one paper as having six toes, the toucher-up having sought to improve on nature. For that, he received a profound apology; for the midnight disturbance, no trace of one.

I had only once in my life been down a coal mine and was anxious that the charge, 'They neither know nor care about us', should not be applied to me. I aimed to do so, if at all possible, once a month. Although I fell short of the target, those visits taught me something about the industry: underground working, its hazards to life, limb and health, and its isolation. Returning to the surface one day after going down a pit on the borders of Northumberland and Durham, I was delighted to be presented with a miner's lamp. I made a short speech in front of a TV camera, thanking the man who gave it to me and telling him that I would keep it, cherish it and remember the day I received it and the man who gave it to me long after he had forgotten. Later, I saw him again and said, 'Mr Hough, I would like you to know that I meant what I said just now.'

'Sir,' he said, 'I never expected to meet anyone like you, let alone talk to him.'

'What on earth,' I wondered, 'have we done to one another?' It wasn't a question which called for an answer, and we didn't have one anyhow.

On a visit to South Wales, I asked the local division of the Coal Board to invite my faithful pair, Dai Williams, to dinner; we were due to go down a pit in the Vale of Neath in his constituency the following morning. After dinner this rather shy, quiet-spoken man took over the evening; he told of his father, who had been a smallholder who worked 'in the anthracite' two or three days a week for a small company which could handle flexible arrangements. Then the amalgamations had come: the men who dug the coal expected to go on as before; but the companies required whole-time working and were not disposed to accept anything else or even to listen, and so misunderstandings arose and endured. The pit which we visited in the morning was a small drift mine in which new equipment was being installed; this involved even more talk than is usual in Wales and a degree of confusion as to how the new system fitted together. Asked, when we got back to the surface, what I thought of the pit, I said that I didn't think that as a visitor I ought to express an opinion; it might be misunderstood. They protested that I couldn't come to their pit and say nothing. When I told them that they were such good talkers that I would be surprised if they ever found time to mine coal, they laughed. 'We don't talk – we sing.'

The Chief Inspector of Mines told me of a mining company in the Lowlands of Scotland which, in the years between the wars, had provided its workers with rented accommodation in two rows of terraced houses; a few yards behind there were earth closets, one to every four houses. The company had a shop which the wives, if they valued their husbands' jobs, were expected to use. Profits were, of course, important, but such concentration on them to the exclusion of all else was not only wrong but self-defeating. It did much to bring about the 'them and us' attitudes, which lived on and which public ownership did little to dispel. A coal mine is a community of its own, and on its own. Life revolves round the pit for those who work in it, for those who have done so, for those who will and, at least as important, for their wives and mothers. They are separate, different from the outside world, which beyond a vague sympathy for those who do a dirty and dangerous job is remote and ill-informed. Such isolation enhances differences, enshrining them in tradition and making mere demagogues seem like champions. As so often happens in human affairs, measures intended to improve create at least as many problems as they solve. It made little sense to transfer the ownership of the whole of the coal industry, large pits and small ones, wherever situated, to the Government, even less to put the management of it in the hands of one large, centralized, bureaucratic organization, closer in its thinking as well as in distance to Whitehall and Westminster than it was to the pits. It is hard to see that either the nation or the industry or the miners gained anything as a result of putting coal within Whitehall's bailiwick and giving it the Treasury for a banker. Nor can it be said that the ending of it was anything but insensitive and messy; the handing of the whole of the English coalfield to one man savoured of a wish to cut and run for the highest price they could get, rather than ensure competition. It was a rather shameful end to a long, sad story.

In 1963 there occurred one of those incidents, not themselves of earth-shaking importance, but which in this country are seized upon, relished and enlarged to something far beyond life size. The twin ingredients of sex and national security can be relied upon to make quite a modest firework seem more like a nuclear explosion. Jack Profumo was and is a character, kindly, amusing and keen to be amused. He became Secretary of State for War. As is well known and as he has never been allowed to forget, he became involved with an exceptionally pretty girl, whom the Russian Naval Attaché also found attractive. It got out, as these things do, and came particularly to the ears of Colonel George Wigg MP, who at that time was a sort of self-appointed Cerberus, keeping a sleepless watch over all that might concern national security. The matter became the focus of attention in Parliament and in the press and even the subject of a special inquiry by the Master of the Rolls. Solemn briefings were given to junior Ministers by the Lord Chancellor. Colonel Wigg, with one or two of his colleagues baying for ministerial blood, made it their business literally to hunt Jack, in order to protect not so much the nation's morals as its security, which they suggested was imperilled. Under pressure at the despatch box – a piece of furniture hardly designed for the carriage of despatches, but which has become invested with the aura of a sacred vessel – Jack denied what was alleged. His pursuers then moved in for the kill, not because he had betrayed any secrets (he hadn't) but because he had in a phrase lied to the House of Commons. He had, of course, erred, but it is permissible to wonder how many people, least of all his pursuers, could confidently say that under such pressure they would not have sought to avoid the consequences, embarrassment for their colleagues, distress for their friends, pain for their families and unending anguish for themselves. Finally cornered, Jack admitted it all and left the stage almost a broken man. With the support, however, of a devoted wife and family he not only survived, but made during the years that followed full and splendid amends in his work for Toynbee Hall in the East End of London; those for whom it has cared have reason to be grateful to him.

The Prime Minister had been much battered by events. The days of 'Super Mac' were over. Large matters could no longer be dismissed as 'little local difficulties'; the winds of change were blowing nearer home than Africa. Tired and ill, Macmillan had a prostate gland operation and resigned office. Soon after coming round from the anaesthetic he found in his room a white-coated man whom he assumed to be a doctor. It was, in fact, the man who had come to remove the official scrambler telephone. His comment, 'They soon roll up the red carpet', could not be improved upon; the gap between adulation and rejection is often quite short.

By chance the legions of the Conservative Party were at the time, early October 1963, gathering at Blackpool for the annual Party Conference. It is the custom on such occasions for Ministers and other Party grandees to hand down, as if from Sinai, not quite the tablets of the law, but statements of the great things which they have done and what they have in mind for the future. Depending on whether the Party is in office or opposition, the people are declared to be better or worse off than ever before, healthier or sicker, happier or more miserable. After four days of speeches and applause they go home. Those Ministers, to whom applause is as necessary as watering is to a row of lettuces in a spell of hot, dry weather, will have succumbed to temptation and pledged themselves to do great things. Later it becomes clear that what, in the exhilarating sea air and before audiences longing to rise to their feet and cheer, seemed inspired, proves in practice to be impracticable or even silly. Such demonstrations are put on to extract applause from the immediate audience, who act as a chorus, and thereby impress the media. The latter come, however, clad in the armour of scepticism, knowing what to expect and rendered somewhat unfresh by three such affairs (TUC, Liberal and Labour) in as many weeks; their purpose being not to praise Caesar, but to bury him if the chance comes along.

The 1963 Conference was unusual. Harold Macmillan had gone; he had served the Party and the country well and had earned their thanks. Now he had to be faded out – always an easier task than expected and usually performed with some relish. There remained the question of who should replace him, and the delegates were in a position not just to pass or reject motions but to give a clear indication as to who they would prefer. The potential successors were all there, not just on a television screen but in front of them, on the platform, on the seafront, in the foyer of the Imperial Hotel, at fringe meetings, at receptions, some of them even on the dance floor.

Rab Butler was Harold's deputy; he had played an immense part in bringing the Conservative Party to life again after the shattering defeat of 1945; he had long experience of high office; he was the party's leading thinker and the framer of its policies; he was surely the obvious successor. I wondered, however, at the time, and do so still, how determined he was to win the prize, how much in his heart he really wanted it. I didn't know him well and was certainly not in his confidence, but I felt that in those few days at Blackpool the ball was at his feet; all that he had to do was to pick it up and run with it. He had the Party faithful gathered before him and the opportunity to assert his claim over the heads of MPs, most of whom at least saw him as the likely successor. A resolute assertion by him, as Deputy Prime Minister, to that audience of his entitlement to their support would, I thought, have made his success certain; but he didn't make it, and the Conference ended and the delegates departed without expressing a preference, or having a clear opportunity to do so.

There was at that time no established procedure for choosing a new leader, but a widespread process of consultation ensured that everyone had ample opportunity to express opinions, to be aware of those of others and generally to reflect. The press didn't like it, for they couldn't be sure exactly what was going on. It was, nevertheless, a painstaking and exhaustive process which to my mind was infinitely preferable to the new one, designed by Humphrey Berkeley, then Conservative MP for Lancaster. It was strange that he should have had such influence, for his links with the Party proved to be far from durable. The old system made allowances for the fact that few of us are so wise, so perceptive and so well informed that we can be sure of reaching right decisions tidily, quickly and without need for reflection and second thoughts; it also took account of a wider range of opinions outside the ranks of professional politicians. The new one put the decision in the hands of Conservative MPs alone; it conferred upon them a power in government which they ought not to have and which they were and are certain to misuse.

In the event Alec Home, who was my preference, emerged as the one who was most widely acceptable. As a hereditary peer he had a difficult start: he was, as Mr Wilson pointed out, the 14th Earl of Home. He therefore had first to renounce his peerage and then move from Lords to Commons, and to do so as Prime Minister, something which no one had done before. It involved finding a seat and fighting and winning a by-election, and meant that for a time he was head of the Government, but without a seat in either House. His Party had been in office for twelve years and was still suffering from the shock of the Profumo affair. Iain Macleod and Enoch Powell were unwilling to serve under him and, with an ageing Parliament already into its fifth year, he had little time in which to dig himself in. Despite all that, the 14th Earl of Home managed to cope with the fourteenth Mr Wilson.

To lose an election in those circumstances, after less than a year in office and by only a narrow margin, was no small achievement. Despite that, the Conservative Party, or rather a sufficient number of Conservative MPs, persuaded themselves that a change of leader was necessary, just as they have done on other occasions since. Alec himself, having first accepted with grace – and there isn't a lot of that around – the mantle which had been thrust upon him, was then prepared not only to step aside but to put in place a procedure for choosing his successor. In 1965, under the new rules, Ted Heath became the new leader, defeating Reggie Maudling, who had shone so in the fifties but whose stature had sadly diminished.

Harold Wilson's first Government, which just scraped into office in 1964 with a majority of only three or four overall, couldn't do much more than mark time and wait. George Brown, ever an enthusiast, made use of the interval to produce, with a fanfare of trumpets, a National Plan, which withered, however, almost before the ink was dry and was soon rotted down into the compost of history. In 1966, after eighteen months of preparation, the Prime Minister judged it to be the time for an appeal to the country and turned his slender majority into one of ninety-seven.

Having been on the Opposition front bench as spokesman for Power matters, I hoped to remain there. A few days after the new Parliament had met, I was on my way to Epsom for a day's racing when I received a message to ring Willie Whitelaw and was told by him that Ted Heath wished to see me that afternoon. I groaned and asked if it was necessary, since I did have other and more enjoyable things in mind. 'No,' he said, 'it isn't. All he wants to tell you is that you are not going to be on the front bench, and he can do that another time.' I was rather upset but went off to Epsom, where my host was Edwin McAlpine, head at the time of Sir Robert McAlpine, the contractors; he used to say that contracting was about people. I cannot easily call to mind anyone who knew so many whom he could call his friends, nor anyone who remained so invincibly cheerful; he laughed a lot, enjoyed the good things of life and liked to share them. I began to learn that afternoon that what had seemed a terrible setback might not be all that much of a reverse; it proved to be a release. Life on the Opposition front bench for those low in the pecking order is not unlike that of a galley slave, spent below decks without sight of where you are or any clue about where you are going.

With Harold Wilson's second administration, we faced an avalanche of words. The white heat of the technological revolution was upon us; we were entering a new world and the old fuddy-duddy ways would go. But somehow or other they didn't, and things remained much as they had been. The pound was devalued, though 'the one in your pocket', we were assured in a famous phrase, would not be affected; taxes and prices went up; new laws poured through Parliament; the iron and steel industry was taken back into public ownership. There was the same old conviction, which remains with us, that we had nothing to learn from other countries, who, we easily persuade ourselves, admire our institutions, envy us our Civil Service and wish very much that the BBC was theirs. I used to amuse myself, and now and again a few others, at the bi-weekly circus event of Prime Minister's questions.

Once, when Mr Wilson had been to the USA and had come back with not very much, he made a statement in the Commons in the course of which he made much of a musical evening at the White House. The usual rather serious questions followed until my turn came and I asked him if the repertoire had included 'Run Rabbit Run'; the House laughed and he seemed put out. The occasion of Prime Minister's questions was something of a game then; it has since degenerated into a farce, having more in common with a darts tournament than with a serious inquisition.

IX

Minister of Transport

There's one thing about Englishmen. You couldn't get the English to fix anything at the start. No! They like to sit and watch it grow worse.

Will Rogers

In July 1966, Mary and I were married in a Registry Office in Kensington; it was a drab little ceremony, not unlike cashing a cheque at a bank or buying a ticket for a film show. We spent the first week of our honeymoon in Ischia with William and Su Walton and afterwards used to see them regularly, both in London and in Ischia. He was an unforgettable, whose friendship was pure joy. Born in Oldham in 1902, he went up to Oxford as a chorister and scholar at Christ Church. Quite early on, at the age of nineteen, he was taken up and cherished by the discerning Sitwells, who, as he said himself, made the whole difference to his life. Many years later Sacheverell Sitwell, looking back at his protégé's youthful brilliance, wrote of him that 'what might have been the flash of a meteor has become a fixed star and something more lasting in the firmament'. William wrote marvellous and stirring music; he had strong opinions about people and about music; he regarded Schoenberg with hostility and the Beatles with vague disapproval, as if they had done something rather mischievous.

Belshazzar's Feast has, for me, something of the essence of Walton; I remember him conducting it with relish at a concert in the Festival Hall to celebrate his seventieth birthday and, rather sadly, seeing him watch André Previn do so ten years later in the same place on his eightieth birthday. Two powerful and almost shattering monosyllables stand out from the whole piece; the single word 'wept' encapsulates the misery of the Israelites as, mourning

132

for Jerusalem, they gaze without hope on the waters of Babylon. At the end of a passage which tells of feasting in honour of the gods, the story goes on to tell how the fingers of a man's hand had appeared and had written on the wall that Belshazzar had been weighed and found wanting and that in the night he had been 'slain'; a short pause is followed by a great outburst of rejoicing.

Against much expert advice, but using the skill and ingenuity of a local architect, William and Su had built themselves a house, La Mortella, which was somehow stitched into the rock of the mountain behind. High above the road and the sea, it looks out towards Epomeo, a volcano no longer active but still imposing. Su, with advice from Russell Page and others, made a marvellous sub-tropical garden. A gardener whose singing distracted William from his own music brought forth yells of '*Basta musica!*' There was a constant flow of visitors, including particularly Larry and Joan Olivier – talent fountained out of them; John Ogdon, gifted pianist and winner of the Leningrad Prize, humble, shy, hardly strong enough to contain what was in him; Lord Goodman, who seemed always to be sitting like a spider at the centre of a web; Peter Sellers, who, without a script, proved disappointingly unfunny and dull; and, by way of contrast, a rogue property developer, very rich, rather nasty and not interested in anything unless he could possess it.

One evening there was a caller, both unusual and unexpected. We had been bathing in the pool above the house and had come down to change, when from our bedroom window I saw a car drive up and out of it emerging an old gentleman with white hair and a silver-knobbed cane to match. 'That,' I said, 'is a truly odious Kraut. I can smell him and his scent from here.' Mary rebuked me for such intolerance and unreason – how could I say such a thing about a nice harmless old gentleman? He turned out not to be a nice old gentleman at all, but Baldur von Schirach, sometime head of the Hitler Youth and ex-Gauleiter of Vienna, who had just completed his prison sentence in Spandau and had come to the Walton house by mistake. The German composer Hans Werner Henze was there at the time and, hearing that this awful man had been so near, took to his bed. 'That man,' he said, 'ruined my youth.'

La Mortella was a haven of peace, even in the summer when the island was filled with Italians on holiday, who regarded silence as an enemy against which it was their duty to wage unceasing war. Something of a problem for William was his mother-in-law, who came to visit for a month and stayed for two years. We had just sat down one evening for a meal in a local restaurant when William seized a pepper mill and, prompted perhaps by its resemblance to a truncheon, struck her firmly and audibly on the head, reducing her to an unaccustomed silence for at least ten minutes. Su, uncertain whether to cry or laugh, yelled, 'Oh, William!' He responded in a tone of great satisfaction, 'I have been wanting to do that for quite a long time.' On another occasion, having arrived at our table for dinner, he set off for the distant lavatory, just beating his mother-in-law to the break. She, having waited with all the patience she could manage, sprang to her feet as soon as he emerged and, determined not to be thwarted again, made for the same destination. They passed each other at the halfway point without a sign of recognition; only when he had got back to the table and she had reached the lavatory door did he deign to notice her. Then, cupping his hands, he shouted the warning, 'Don't sit down, Momma.' I suggested the words would do well as a title for a musical, but he would have none of it; it would involve too much hard work. He also turned down my other suggestion that he should write a *Gadarene Symphony* to express his view of the modern world and its likely end; again too much hard work – too many notes would be required to tell of the pigs hitting the rocks.

Since being turfed off the Front Bench in 1966 I had not moved much in such circles, and was more than a little surprised to be invited by Ted Heath to dine with him one evening in 1969. Having drunk sufficient champagne to extinguish all caution, I accepted his invitation to chair a small committee to produce a policy for the West Country for the General Election; the committee, he assured me, would be composed of helpful, unawkward people. We had little difficulty, in the event, in concluding that the West Country's pressing need was better communications; without them it would become impossible either to move people and goods into and out of the region or to accommodate the growing weight of holiday traffic. We kept our report short and got it in quickly, with the result that it was accepted by the Shadow Cabinet and, in due course, published with the Leader's picture on the front.

The Labour Government had, meanwhile, got itself into difficulties with the unions. Mrs Castle, as Secretary of State for Employment, had rather bravely brought out a White Paper, *In Place of Strife*, which proved to be altogether too near the bone for the unions to live with. Although it was dropped, it had cooled down trade union enthusiasm for the Labour Party. The 1970 General Election produced, to many people's surprise, a Tory victory, with Ted Heath as Prime Minister. As I left home on the following Monday morning it occurred to me to tell Mary where I would be, just in case the unlikely occurred and a call came from Number Ten; I was amazed when she rang me up to say that I was to go there at three o'clock. Selwyn Lloyd, whom I met on the way, asked where I was going and then told me that I should accept whatever was on offer. I told him that at the age of fifty-plus I would certainly not wish to be a Parliamentary Secretary again. Ten minutes later I was in the Cabinet Room, being invited to become Minister of Transport; I drove home in a daze and was only with difficulty able to explain to Mary what had occurred.

I had first met Ted Heath at Oxford, just before the war, when he had been the organ scholar at Balliol and President of the Union, but had lost sight of him until 1951 when he became Deputy Chief Whip in the new Government. He possesses great and diverse abilities, places little reliance upon airs and graces, and gives at times an impression of not being much bothered with personal relations. His determination and his disregard of the odd breezes of supposed public opinion enabled him to change things in his time in a way which others have only seemed to do. Believing that Europe must not again be allowed to become the cauldron in which were generated forces of conflict and catastrophe, he saw it as our duty and our interest to be there and to wield influence. Having secured the agreement of the six existing members to our joining the then European Economic Community, he contrived with a modest majority in the House of Commons to get through the necessary legislation. When, in

1974, a Labour Government came in, they held a referendum, with the result that our membership was confirmed. Five years later Mrs Thatcher, leading a Conservative Government, found herself faced with the problem of Britain's excessive contribution to the Community. She then won a considerable victory, but thereafter gave the impression of being out of sympathy with the forces which had brought the nations together; she became an uncomfortable and protesting passenger.

Ted Heath must be high on the list of those whom it is easy to misunderstand. I invited him to lunch one day when we were still in opposition, principally because William Walton, who was staying with us, seemed seriously to under-rate him, expressing doubts about his ability ever to win a General Election. He was won over when Ted – who was at least his equal when it came to the laconic – recited almost word for word a broadcast interview which William had once given and in which his replies had consisted almost entirely of monosyllables, causing a somewhat abrasive interviewer to run out of material long before the time was up.

There are other sides to Ted not usually found in Prime Ministers. They show up in his books on music and sailing: no other Prime Minister in our history could have written either, let alone both. Nor could any of them have conducted the London Symphony Orchestra – nor, having taken up sailing, won a race like that from Sydney to Hobart in one of the smallest of the boats taking part. My regard for him does not, however, carry to a point at which I am able to share his enthusiasm for madrigals, which he was inclined to offer at the end of dinner. At one such dinner to which I had been invited and madrigals were on offer, my attention had wandered somewhat when I suddenly heard him say, 'Here is one for the Minister of Transport.' The first line was, 'I feign not friendship where I hate.'

Celebration of William Walton's seventieth birthday showed something of Ted Heath which is not always on view. Mary and I had arranged a small dinner party with a dozen or so of his friends and I had, as an afterthought, written to the Prime Minister expressing the hope that he might be able to put in an appearance. Some weeks later he telephoned.

'I've been thinking about your invitation' – he said it several times – 'William Walton is our premier composer' – and he said that more than once. How, he asked, would William react to the idea that the party should be moved to Number Ten?

I said I was sure he would be delighted.

'How about you and Mary?'

'We only wanted to do something for William. It would be wonderful.'

It was a joyous occasion to which he had clearly given much thought. He himself proposed William's health in a speech which was short, generous and amusing, a model for the occasion. Alvar Liddell recited *Façade*; members of the London Symphony Orchestra played a Schubert quintet which Ted had once heard William say he would love to have composed; Sir Arthur Bliss, Master of the Queen's Musick, had written something for the occasion; the Queen Mother came, and fifty or sixty of William's friends. Ted Heath has, of course, his faults and, as is the habit of our time, they have been made much of. There will, I am sure, come a time when they will seem small when measured against what he achieved.

My joy at becoming a Minister was, at that stage, only slightly diminished by the warning that my new Department would at a time uncertain be sucked into the huge and hideous pile which had been erected in Marsham Street and was to be the home of the new Department of the Environment. A number of motoring correspondents telephoned during the evening following my appointment, in a state of some confusion. They had never, one of them said, heard of me. Did I drive a car? Was I like Mrs Castle? I answered 'Yes' to the first question and 'No' to the second, adding to one that I wasn't nearly as pretty. In the morning an immaculate ministerial car took me to the Ministry of Transport at St Christopher House. Elphick, who drove it, must have been the doyen of government drivers. He had turned down the chance of driving one of the more eminent of my colleagues because, he said, it would involve leaving the car outside Number Ten or some other similar place where there would be crowds and people who might touch it. I once asked him if we ought not to be grand and have a flag. 'Sir,' he said with huge distaste,

'Mr Barnes had a flag.' He had driven Alfred Barnes, who had been Minister of Transport in earlier days, and for some reason I never understood had taken against him. Elphick drove with stateliness, always joining the longest line of vehicles in any traffic jam. To hurry was vulgar and he eschewed vulgarity. When after a year he retired, I was able to assemble for a farewell drink as many as six Ministers whom he had driven.

My Private Secretary, David Holmes, took me in hand; for a start telling the Post Office to make me ex-Directory. When I said I didn't want that, he attempted to catch up with the instruction and cancel it, but was never able to do so. He hoped that, so far as possible, I would avoid talking to MPs: it always, he said, led to trouble. I pointed out that I was myself a Member of Parliament and as such obliged to go there from time to time; I couldn't very well refuse to talk to anyone. He admitted that it might be difficult to be totally silent, but stressed the need for care. He had become fond of my predecessor, Fred Mulley, and felt sad for him at his loss of office; would I not ask him out to lunch? I did. Fred at that time was feeling very sorry for himself. He was sure that he would never hold office again; in fact he did, going on to things greater than Transport. Michael Heseltine, who was the Parliamentary Secretary for the first few months, seemed to think that the Prime Minister, in handing out jobs, had somehow got things muddled up and put me where he should have been: We got on well enough, however, and on one occasion, simply by keeping our answers short, got through a record number of Parliamentary Questions in a matter of half an hour.

It was my immense good fortune to find David Serpell as the Permanent Secretary of my Department. He had had a long experience in 'handling' Ministers: Gwilym Lloyd-George and Harold Macmillan had, I think, been his favourites. He nursed me tenderly through the first few weeks; by the autumn, he had become a friend and has remained one. Although himself an advocate of the new Department of the Environment – he became its first Permanent Secretary – he understood how much I disliked the idea of moving into that great spongy heap. He brought to the task a first-rate mind and contrived somehow to create in the Department an atmosphere, not always to be found in Whitehall, of humanity. He wrote to me in the autumn of 1970, just before the move, saying that he was sure that one of his functions would be 'to be available to all, like a bathroom'. I cannot immediately think of any other mandarin who has ever seen himself in such a role.

David was, I think, also the only one of his kind ever to compose a letter to *Private Eye*. That journal, full as always of a benign interest in what goes on, had reported on a meeting with someone who had so entirely devoted himself to the cause of noise abatement that he could not stop talking about it. The official, who was there to give advice on any technical aspect which might arise, interrupted in the hope of bringing the meeting to an end. It had the reverse effect and wound him up again like a clock. I said that I thought it best to let our visitor go on until he had said what he had come to say. In its report of this epic meeting *Private Eye* wrongly named the official as 'Ministry of Transport Mandarin Dale'. David drafted this rejoinder, in verse, which *Private Eye* later published:

> You publish (page 4, column 2)
> A tale which can scarcely be true
> For Mandarin Dale
> (About whom your tale)
> Was not even there. Nor were you.
>   signed L. E. DALE

He was, and still is, particularly good at kindly, unexpected gestures. He possesses a seemingly inexhaustible supply of antique postcards, from which he selects those which have some bearing on the present day. One showed the High Street of Hinton St George, the Somerset village in which I live, in the days before the motor vehicle had begun to clutter up our streets and generally make them unnavigable. David's comment on the back was, 'First results of the new Peyton parking policy'; it was a commentary on my pipe dream that streets and highways should be used for travel and movement, not parking lots. Lack both of the necessary powers and of support from any quarter, coupled with his warnings, saved me from attempting to turn that pipe-dream into reality.

In later times he has always remembered my birthday. When I

reached seventy, long after we had both left the Department, he sent me a bottle of vintage port – Dow 1970 – with a message, 'Berry's note on the Dow makes it exactly right for its present recipient – "superb quality, rich, full and drier in style. Drinking well now and for some years to come."' On another occasion he sent me a shrub which was described as being 'tough and prickly, to be handled with care'. His principal lieutenant, Ian Bancroft, then the Establishment Officer, in due course succeeded him as Permanent Secretary and later went on to become Head of the Civil Service. He gave the impression of having an unusually clear understanding of the worth and merits of his political masters; or, to put it in another way, he was certainly not blind to their imperfections.

During my first weeks I made a tour of the Department, then situated in a rather low-grade building in Southwark. It has long seemed to me that the gulf which exists between Ministers and their official advisers was altogether too wide for the good of either; I have the impression that in recent years it has grown wider still. I wanted to see if I could in a small way narrow the gulf and, in so far as I was successful, I believe it was immensely to my advantage. Some Ministers seem to regard their Departments as if they were rather grand hotels and their officials as waiters or floor staff, the Permanent Secretary being set apart as a kind of maître d'hôtel. Paper, if it were liquid, could according to one's mood or experience be described as either the life blood or the waste product of a Government Department; it flows in a ceaseless, unebbing tide, filling any vacant space that it can find, demanding to be read, or at least initialled, as it passes. It was depressing to find that, on each of the ten floors, no fewer than seven people were needed to sort, distribute, collect and dispatch. I used to reflect how wonderful it would be if anyone who put paper into orbit was obliged to put a pound note (we had such things in those days) on every page, copies included, after the first. The addressee or recipient would keep the money, with no obligation to do more than acknowledge receipt. It would make for brevity and cause people to think before they put paper into orbit or made use of the copying machine.

It was not long after my arrival that I bumped into one of

those barriers which only the old hands know are there. I asked my private office to ring up the Transport and General Workers' Union and say that I would like to meet the General Secretary, Mr Jack Jones. Would he care to call round for a drink or a cup of tea? A few minutes elapsed before first one, then another official in gradually ascending rank arrived in turn and pointed out how unusual this would be. It would be starting something; it was for the Minister of Labour, Robert Carr, to talk to such people; it would be misunderstood both by Mr Jones and by my colleagues. Eventually, however, the telephone call was made. Jack Jones came round for a cup of tea a few days later; it was an interesting occasion, mildly helpful, certainly not harmful, and I learned from him that the post of General Secretary of the Transport and General was not a bed of roses. Jack and I became and have remained friends.

From time to time I was called upon to attend meetings of the Cabinet. I can remember the mixed feelings of regret that I was not a member and relief that, as soon as my item was over, I was free to leave. It was as often as not a strike, or the threat of one, on the railways or in the docks that was responsible for my presence. It then fell to me to explain what the prospects were of cargoes of bananas being unloaded, usually in the port of Barry, before they started to rot and smell abominably. It was clear always that I had failed miserably in my duties if I had not given a full explanation of the situation at peak TV viewing time on the previous evening. My excuse that no one had invited me to do so was regarded as lame. I remember sitting next to Peter Rawlinson, then the Attorney General, on one such occasion and receiving from him welcome encouragement, which was far from being echoed round the table. He and his gorgeous wife Elaine, as beautiful as she is charming, have been friends for many years.

The changeover from one Minister to the next is well handled by the Civil Service, who, like a firm of contract cleaners, descend upon the private office with their cleansing equipment, remove all trace of the former incumbent and generally make things ready for the successor. This applies particularly if a change of Government is involved. Some loose ends are, however, inevitable; one such which I inherited was whether or not the electrification of the main line between London and Glasgow should be completed. Since the section between London and Crewe had already been electrified and the existence of two systems of locomotion on the same route was expensive and inefficient, the argument of the Treasury, which was, in accordance with ritual, against the proposal, was a hard one to follow, and I did not. From time to time Ministers are accorded the privilege of initiating something; it fell to me to open what must be one of the best-designed and best-engineered sections of motorway in the country, that between Eden and Shap on the M6. There was a demonstration by road workers and others seeking a pay rise – I think it was for 'fifty shillings now'. One of the demonstrators, who seemed rather fierce, held up immediately in front of me during my speech a large notice saying: 'We want 50/- and we want it now'. I congratulated him on the way in which he managed unaided to hold up his arms throughout the proceedings, whereas Moses, required to do the same during the course of a battle, had required and been given help. The following week I received this letter from him on Cumberland County Council notepaper.

Dear Mr Peyton,
  You may recall meeting me at Tebay last Thursday. I was delighted to shake hands with you Sir. You may also remember, in your speech, you referred to Moses. He too was a Road Maker in the Wilderness, while you are Transport Minister of the Highways – perhaps, like Moses, sometimes in difficulties.
  Tebay was in the Hills – in the North we call them Fells. But the Mount of Olives was also a hill – a Fell.
  Take courage Minister, the Road you are on now leads to success, or Disaster. Thank you for Listening to us at Eden or was it Tebay?
  Your humble Roadman,
  W. Langley

I liked the line, 'perhaps, like Moses, sometimes in difficulties'. I also liked Mr Langley.
  After a few months the Ministry of Transport, together with those of Housing and Local Government and Works, were sucked into the new Department of the Environment under Peter Walker

142

as Secretary of State. I was to be known in future as 'the Minister for Transport Industries in the Department of the Environment', a rather elaborate mouthful which was intended to explain but served only to confuse. My role in the new set-up was, in Peter Walker's words, 'my Junior Minister in charge of Transport'. This new palace of ministerial varieties was and still is housed in a hideous building composed of three graceless towers – a blot on the otherwise elegant landscape of Westminster. No independent property developer, even the most philistine, would have had the gall to propose such an eyesore. The aim of the Government, both simple and commendable, was to ensure that the claims of the environment were not overlooked when policies which affected it were being formulated. Even allowing my own bias in the 'small is beautiful' direction, I don't believe that large super-departments make for either efficiency or good public relations. They are not easily led or managed, nor do their staffs welcome shotgun weddings.

Plans were soon made for integrating the three Departments and shuffling and redistributing the various functions amongst the Ministers involved. I suspect that the details were settled with the aid of a tombola. At the actual moment chosen by the Secretary of State to reveal his plans to his subordinates I happened to be in a signal box in Derby on a visit to the Railway Research Centre, and received his telephone call there. So far as I was concerned, road planning and construction were to move from Transport to Local Government; the research establishments of the Department would come under me, as would London Planning. I was beginning to feel some surprise when he added, almost as an afterthought, 'Oh yes, you are going to do Sport.' I didn't even have time to ask if he was joking, for at that moment Providence intervened in the shape of a long goods train which crashed, rattled and thundered its way across some rather rough points immediately below the signal box; the noise removed all possibility of thought or hearing. The minute or so which passed before the din ceased was sufficient, however, for me to realize that protest would achieve nothing and that it would be better just to say goodbye.

I could not, however, even begin to see myself as Minister of Sport, which I regarded as something of a non-job, not far removed from farce. On my return to London Eldon Griffiths, the Parliamentary Secretary, who as an ex-rugger Blue had far better credentials than I had, told me that I was due to attend in an hour or so a reception for the Australian cricket team, who had just arrived. I said he would fit in much better and that, since it was he who had first been invited, he should go. To my great relief the appointment went almost unnoticed, though Tony Crosland, speaking from the Opposition Front Bench, did mention it in the House of Commons with mild irony, saying, generously, that while he had been aware at Oxford of my intellectual ability, he had not known of my skill or even interest in any sport. The new arrangement didn't seem to change things and it came as no great surprise when Geoffrey Rippon, having replaced Peter Walker, concluded that we should all go back to where we had been before. There was, however, nothing that he or anyone else could do to improve the building itself or even to arrest the process of its decay. Now, a mere twenty-five years after its completion, it is adorned with fishing nets to catch the bits which fall off and might otherwise injure passers by: an alternative explanation, currently in circulation, is that they are there to catch Ministers who, overcome by despair, may be seeking release. Not long ago, I secured in answer to a question in the House of Lords the assurance that the building would be emptied out in 1997 and subsequently demolished; we shall see.

It wasn't at all difficult to conclude that our transport arrangements left quite a lot to be desired. Two things dawned on me quite soon: first, that those who regularly suffer delays in the course of their journeys have ample opportunity to wonder whether those responsible for our transport arrangements are mad, malevolent or simply inept. Second, given the prevailing attitudes of those who use the system, notions of an integrated network are pie in the sky, to be consumed only by those who have no present responsibility for creating one. I then made a series of discoveries of things which, though blindingly obvious, are often lost sight of: that at the times and in the places where the need for movement is greatest, there is not enough room; that the streets of our towns and villages could not be stretched to accommodate the traffic; that there is a limit to the amount of land in the countryside which can be taken to do so;

that the use of the system is cyclical round the clock, the week and the year, and that the peaks which result refuse to be ironed out; that the cost of providing what is necessary is horrendous, and that of failing to do so is incalculable. To those irremovable difficulties there can be added for good measure certain human attitudes and beliefs which Governments are shy of challenging. These amount to an expectation, first, that public transport ought to be available, no matter how little used; second, that everyone has a right to have a car and be free to go anywhere and at any time; third, that there is some kind of inalienable right to use roads and streets as parking lots.

My major problems, all surrounded by layers of tradition and highly resistant to common-sense solutions, boiled down to a dilapidated railway system; an inadequate road network which not only caused delays and inefficiency but also brought an unacceptable toll of death and injury in its wake; a port network which lost money and which Stone Age attitudes could always bring to a standstill; a bus industry which was a conglomeration of groups and companies of different shapes and sizes in different ownerships; canals too narrow to be commercially useful; and, last but not least, a possible Channel Tunnel. Since civil aviation was not in my time thought of as being related to transport, I had only its backwash to deal with: the provision of road access to airports.

I learned gradually the extent of the handicaps under which our railway system languished: state-owned, conservative in outlook, worn down and starved of capital investment in five years of war; subjected to Treasury thraldom thereafter; unable to earn or borrow enough to modernize itself; incomprehensible accounting; obliged to preserve what was unprofitable; a staff oversized and underpaid; three unions whose concern lay in preserving each its own territory and sustaining its membership; a staff grading system of Byzantine complexity; and working practices of a bygone age. It was a real arsenal of constraints, from which no conceivable fetter had been left out. Only the British, I felt, could have developed it; only the British would have put up with it for so long. Once a year the unions joined together in a ritual dance, seeking a pay rise. Management suspected of being government stooges made a counter-offer. The Government coughed, spluttered and nudged like disapproving chaperones at a ball who, though paying the bill, were inhibited by the rules from joining in.

Finding a new Chairman to succeed Bill Johnson, a lifelong railwayman, was not easy. No established industrialist of merit was willing to take a position in which politics played so large a part for such meagre reward as was on offer. With the approval of my superiors I invited Dick Marsh, who had been a Minister in the Labour Government, to take it on. I told him that I thought the job I was offering was difficult; I already knew mine was impossible. Life in the House of Commons having by that time become, to put it mildly, less than totally absorbing for him, he accepted. I promised him my support, both in public and in private, until and unless I told him otherwise. I asked in return that he would never, if it was in his power to avoid it, allow me to be surprised. On that basis we got along quite well together.

One man with great enthusiasm for the railways and for the Victorian architecture which so often went with them was the Poet Laureate, John Betjeman. He wrote to me saying what vandalism it was to go on building roads – the money should go instead to more civilized means of travel. I persuaded him to pay a visit to the DOE and meet and listen to the supposed vandals who were responsible for the road-building programme. British Rail prepared him for the ordeal by asking him to lunch at the Charing Cross Hotel; they even had his poem 'Phone for the fish knives, Norman' printed on the back of the menu. This put him in a receptive mood for his visit to what he described as 'your gem of architecture on the Horseferry Road'. His letter of thanks was a model.

Dear John,
    Once again I am in your debt for a marvellous day yesterday – the noble classic interior of Barry's SE & CR Hotel at Charing Cross, the stately passages and stairs, the view-commanding suite, the dry champagne, our relaxed and happy selves. Then what fun it was to see my old dog-fancier friend John Scholes, the least museumy of great museum men, in the last moments of his career, though I do not share his happiness in going to York. He will do well with the museum

there. I was enchanted, as always, with the good company you provide. Thoughtfully you bring congenial people together and bring out the best in all of us.

Thank you oh thank you

from

Yours ever, John B.

He gave me a copy of his book *London's Historic Stations*. 'They are part of the lives of the nation,' he wrote in the Preface, 'they witness the smiles of welcome, the sadness of goodbye.' He thought particularly well of St Pancras; the foyer of its hotel was, he said, worthy of King Arthur's Knights. It is sad that its magnificent interior should now be so totally dilapidated; waiting, in the expectation of the Government, to be restored to life and beauty by the kiss of a new operator of the Channel rail-link, who, so the pipe dream goes, will have both the taste and the cash needed. He inscribed the book with the line, halfway between prayer and protest, 'down with long distance lorries, up with the canals'. He was a lovely man who, with all his talents, never took himself over-seriously, describing himself as 'an old fraud like me'. We are most of us, I suppose, forced into wearing the garments of pretence; greater eminence seems to require layers of such clothing.

Sid Greene, now Lord Greene of Harrow Weald, then General Secretary of the National Union of Railwaymen, became a firm friend. He once invited me to address a session of his executive's annual conference in Exmouth. After a cheerful lunch we went to the conference, a cheerless affair in a hall of almost unparalleled gloom. Some seventy or eighty delegates spent a week or more examining in minute detail all that had been done in the union's name during the past year. Their faces indicated quite clearly, first, that they had not in any way been softened up by lunch and, second, that their feelings towards me varied from distaste to detestation. I embarked upon my carefully prepared speech and was heard in much the same way as a climber in distress would be by a bare and rocky mountain. After something less than five minutes it became clear beyond doubt, and I told them so, that it was most unlikely that they would find any interest in anything I had to say. I therefore suggested that, by way of a change, they might ask questions which I would do my best to answer. After what seemed a vey long pause the first questioner came up and was, in due course, followed by others. Sid assisted in the process by providing, from behind his hand, a few gritty comments on each of the questioners and advice as to how they should be handled.

Opportunities to escape from the confines of the Department were always welcome and generally useful. A day or so travelling in a General Manager's coach round some part of the railways with those who ran them was usually more informative than a mass of official paper. Many interesting fragments of knowledge came my way. One of the tunnels outside King's Cross had long been thought to be a dog-leg, since no light could be seen at the end until a certain point was reached. Only after steam had been superseded and the murk which it caused had dispersed was it seen to be straight after all. At the end of one of those tunnels and in a very deep cutting it was possible from the observation window at the rear of the coach to see, laboriously worked in the earth above the entrance, the legend 'Kropotkin Lives'. Who on earth, I wondered, had risked life and limb to make that steep and perilous descent in order to assert to an exceedingly limited audience the immortality of Kropotkin – a Russian aristocrat who in the early years of the century had joined the Bolsheviks. In a new signal 'box' in Leeds, windowless, silent and remote, manned by a new generation of people who did it all with diagrams and lights and wires, I met a relief signalman, one of the old school who had spent his life pulling levers in a box with windows, seeing trains go by, even perhaps waving to the men on the footplate and the guards. I asked him how he was getting on. 'Oh,' he said, sounding near to tears, 'I do miss the trains, sir.' Marshalling yards never failed to fascinate railwaymen of all levels; the top brass would get down from the train and with a mixture of locals engage with real joy in playing trains; they pointed to the computer as evidence that they were fully up-to-date.

The ports, as they were at that time, afforded a remarkable example of the way in which we run our affairs; they were, so I was advised, the responsibility of my Department. Conditions of employment, however, which were at least three-quarters of the problem, were a matter for the Department of Employment;

shipping and shipbuilding for Trade and Industry; navigation for the Admiralty, and so on. The Transport and General Workers' Union had, in one respect at least, more power than anyone else in that it could, if it were so minded, bring things to a standstill; but that vast organization, with its huge membership, was altogether too diverse and cumbersome either to be amenable to central control or to accommodate notions of change. Only in the face of disputes which needed to be made national, if one port were not to grab the traffic of others, did it even appear to coalesce. A High Court judge, Mr Justice Devlin, taking more account of past malpractices and old grievances than of the need, particularly in an island, for efficient ports, had succeeded in making what was already awful that much worse. His recommendation of a National Dock Labour Scheme with a Board on which employers and dockers would be equally represented preserved inviolate an unworkable status quo. British ports, London, Liverpool and the Clyde, lost traffic: Rotterdam, Antwerp, Hamburg, Dunkirk and others, adapting themselves to the massive changes which were taking place in the movement and handling of freight, absorbed what we lost.

The National Bus Company was an odd one; it was a receptacle into which were cast all those bus undertakings which, though publicly owned, had no other obvious home. It was a far from ideal arrangement, satisfying perhaps the doctrinal tastes of its creators, who couldn't think of anything else to do with it. I chiefly remember it because of Tom Beagley, an Under Secretary in the Department, who had it in his care. I have fond memories of him sitting with his head in his hands, saying to me, 'Minister, I worry. You could end up in great difficulties.' He was always concerned to keep me out of trouble and, though a very competent civil servant, was far removed from the popular version of one. The Canals and Inland Waterways, which also fell within the Department's orbit, were a leisure amenity rather than a transport operation, generating enthusiasm rather than earnings; too narrow by far to carry the traffic which the far larger waterways of the Continent could handle.

The Channel Tunnel, having been long a prospect, began to become a problem. Although we were far from sharing the enthusiasm of the French, it was going to be difficult to insist upon continued physical separation from the Continent and at the same time seek to become part of it in other ways. Moreover, there was a real need to accommodate the growing movement of people and freight. While the actual construction of a Tunnel would be a relatively simple matter, there would be other problems which would be severe: the huge grab of land in the area of the terminal, the provision of an adequate rail link between London and the coast, and the massive disturbance to people and property. The French were anxious to know our intentions and I went to Paris for an exploratory meeting. The Minister was pleasant enough, but plainly ill: he died not long afterwards. His Chef de Cabinet, who did most of the talking, was odious: the British, in his view, were approaching the project with a lack of commitment that amounted to bad faith; he said so repeatedly and with such vigour that I thought there wasn't much point in going on and said that we had better go home. The Minister then intervened and the meeting continued more harmoniously, but without achieving much.

His successor understood our difficulties and recognized that, whereas the Tunnel was welcome in the Pas de Calais, it was anathema in Kent and Surrey. He told me that President Pompidou, with whom he lunched every Wednesday, was determined to have a Tunnel. I had to tell him that I didn't lunch once a week with the Prime Minister and that those of my colleagues to whom I had mentioned the matter had shown no trace of enthusiasm. Eventually I sought an opportunity to raise the matter with the Prime Minister, whose mind was on possible institutional links with Europe rather than a physical one. His response to my question, 'Do you want a Tunnel?' was short and direct; 'I don't know. Do we?' I explained my reasons for believing that we did and told him the views of the French. I added that I thought we had reached a stage where we could no longer just go on talking. We had either to say yes to the idea in principle and mean it or no and wring its neck quite openly: the French were asking the question and were entitled to an answer. The Prime Minister agreed that we should proceed and things at once became easier, the scowls of colleagues turning into smiles, hostility into helpfulness. It became established policy that we were going to have a Tunnel, though opposition in the areas most affected understandably increased, particularly in Folkestone.

A Green Paper in March 1973 set out the case for a Tunnel and was followed in due course by an agreement and a treaty. The former was signed at Lancaster House by the French Minister and myself, and by Lord Harcourt and General Maurin as joint Chairmen of the Private Group; the latter with rather more ceremony at Chequers by the President, the Prime Minister and the two Foreign Ministers. The Prime Minister explained beforehand that, since he would be having a small working lunch with the President, it would not be possible to include the four of us, but we should arrive after lunch to witness the signing of the treaty. Having lunched together at a pub on the way down, we found on arrival that the small working lunch had developed into a large and rather grand social affair which had little or nothing to do with the Tunnel; nor did those attending seem to be likely participants in an intimate exchange between the two heads of Government. The tinkles of merry laughter which reached us while we waited rendered my explanations somewhat unconvincing to the two Frenchmen, who were surprised, and to Bill Harcourt, who was furious.

The Tunnel involved frequent meetings with the French in London and Paris; we took it in turns. Christopher Soames, then our Ambassador in Paris, had written in warm and friendly terms at the time of my appointment, welcoming it and saying that it would be necessary for me to come often to Paris and that whenever I did so I should stay at the Embassy. Feeling that the Paris Embassy was a happy hunting ground for a host of visitors I rather hung back, but Christopher would have none of it. He and his wife Mary were kindness itself, with the result that we became regulars, testing their friendship, but enjoying to the full every moment we spent in that beautiful house which she ran so well. They were wonderful hosts; their children at disparate ages, but still young, with more than mere walk-on parts, helped to make the place a home as well as an Embassy. It would be hard to imagine a more inspired appointment than that of Harold Wilson in sending Christopher to Paris at that time. Of generous proportions, he seemed always to be just that bit larger than life; you couldn't miss seeing him, still less hearing him; I don't think he ever even tried to whisper. He gave the impression of real alarm at the possibility of missing someone or something of interest. His huge enjoyment of life and the people and things it contained and his appreciation of all things French ensured his success. Mary was the perfect partner; she even managed to get on terms with General de Gaulle, from whom she received expert advice as to the best places in Paris in which to walk her dogs. Their departure from Paris was a blow which their delightful successors, Edward and Jill Tomkins, succeeded in softening.

While Paris had its lighter and very enjoyable side, Brussels did not. The French Minister who dealt with other transport matters and who attended, as I did, the Council of Ministers, was as unlike his colleague who dealt with the Tunnel as it was possible to be. He troubled himself not at all with such trifles as civility and regarded anyone and anything not French at least with distaste, if not hostility. Meetings of the Council of Ministers were protracted and unfruitful, more of a ritual dance than a useful discussion. Each Minister in turn would read a speech setting out the position of his country and then sit back, leaving it to one of his minions to listen to anything which might be said in reply on behalf of other countries. I used to dread my visits to Brussels: the hotels were good, the food and drink excellent; but in general the place was dull and unwelcoming, the memory of my earlier visit to the city in 1940 still very much alive.

Occasionally, and it was only occasionally, something useful was done. We actually sold Thomas Cook's; the news that we contemplated such a violation of the sacred territory of the public sector caused uproar and indignation on the Labour benches. Tom Bradley, who spoke for the Opposition with his tongue somewhere in the neighbourhood of his cheek, denounced the move with impressive eloquence. Cook's, originally a Belgian company, had been acquired after the German invasion of that country by the Trustee for the property of enemy aliens. Not by any stretch of the imagination had it been one of the 'commanding heights of the economy'; it had been transferred to the British Transport Commission. There it had languished, doing pretty well what it had always done and showing no inclination to follow the example of American Express on which, at one time, it had more than a head start.

Making motorcyclists wear helmets also caused a bit of a stir.

One of them was particularly annoyed and wrote me a letter, of which the 'Dear Sir' at the start was the only polite bit. It went on, 'Because of you and all that bollock-brained f——ing scum who supported you, I am now, for the second year in a row, unable to take a holiday as I always go on my motorcycle. I hope the IRA blow the shit out of you.' I had that one framed. Such letters at least made a welcome change from the mass of long-winded and obscure material which was constantly in circulation and which took time to read, longer to understand, but could not with safety be ignored. A German gentleman once wrote me a polite letter asking for my autograph, addressing it to 'The Minister for Intercourse', without explaining to me what my duties in such an office would be. I tried but failed to persuade my colleagues that wearing seat-belts should be compulsory. I wrote to some forty of those who had charge of hospital casualty wards to seek their opinions; their replies left me in no doubt that seat-belts would certainly save many people from horrific injuries suffered as a result of being projected through their own windscreens. The Cabinet, however, took the view that my proposal involved an unacceptable infringement of personal freedom; the Labour Government which followed had no such inhibitions.

One evening, Jack Jones kindly invited me to be the guest of his London Docks officers. He first showed me round Transport House. In one corner of his office in a glass case was a fearsome object – the mace which Ben Tillett had carried in the Greater London Dock Strike of 1889. I asked Jack if he would lend it to me; the presence of so formidable a weapon – five or six feet in length, with sharp brass studs embedded in its weighted head – on my table would give added weight to my wishes and opinions. He couldn't do that, but he did the next best thing by giving me a replica, still something of a lethal weapon, which I cherish. I introduced him later to Toby Aldington, who was at that time Chairman of the Port of London Authority. This was thought by some to be a mistake; though I thought at the time, and still do, that the greater error lay in perpetuating the huge formal no man's land which existed between the two sides of industry.

White Papers are useful to Government Departments as a means of demonstrating that they are still alive and have even been doing some thinking. They are also a means of impressing people; a glossy cover and a pretentious title – *Forging Ahead* was a recent example – can persuade those who don't delve too deeply into the contents that here is some important new initiative. The practice calls to mind a passage in George Orwell's *Animal Farm*.

> There was, as Squealer was never tired of explaining, endless work in the supervision and organization of the farm. Much of this work was of a kind that the other animals were too ignorant to understand. For example, Squealer told them that the pigs had to expend enormous labours every day upon mysterious things called 'files', 'reports', 'minutes', and 'memoranda'.

I recall with some pride a White Paper on port finances which I was obliged to produce. We started off with a draft of over a hundred pages, which, with much urging, I managed to get down first to sixty and then to twenty, before finally taking it home with me and reducing it to a mere three or four pages. 'Minister, this is going to look awfully thin,' was the response of one official. Since its message was that the ports hadn't got any money and the Government wasn't going to give any to an industry which wouldn't or couldn't put its own house in order, that seemed appropriate.

Towards the end of my time I was suddenly confronted with a draft White Paper on transport policy. Why, I asked, was it necessary? Did we have in mind some new ideas or strategy which required explanation? I was told, we did not, but that my colleagues were expecting one. That struck me as a bit odd, since none of them had ever expressed the slightest interest to me. I said, however, that of course I would look at the draft over the weekend and we could then discuss it. The paper said nothing that was new and much of which no reminder was necessary; moreover, being the work of many hands it lacked cohesion. I said when we met that I had read it, found it interesting, but thought that it would require a lot more work before it was given any wider circulation. Again I was told that my colleagues were waiting for it; it should be circulated and would no doubt be improved in the process. Unable to believe in such magic, I said that I was sorry, I could not and would not send it as it was to my colleagues, who were not short of reading material and would wonder what it was all about. In the event, it never saw the light of day. Nor, I think, did Idwal Pugh, the Permanent Secretary, who had felt obliged to bring the thing forward, lose any sleep at its demise. It was a good example of how intelligent and able people feel constrained by habit and routine to undertake useless labour.

The CEMT or, to give it its full name, the Confederation of European Ministers of Transport, was a most unusual international body; it generated goodwill and mutual understanding and never even looked for anything to have a row about. It met twice a year, a one-day meeting in Paris in the winter and a two- or three-day conference in the summer in the country of whoever was that year's President. I was myself Vice President in 1971, when the annual conference took place in Spain. By chance, the Spanish Government had not long before declined to receive Alec Home, the Foreign Secretary, simply because he had previously been in Gibraltar; it is possible that after that unpleasantness they looked around for someone not too important to whom they could be friendly. For whatever reason, I received an invitation to be the guest of the Spanish Government for several days before the CEMT Conference began. John Russell, then our Ambassador in Madrid, came to see me in my office to urge acceptance; the fact that he welcomed the idea stifled at birth the objections which the Foreign Office would otherwise have been likely to dig up. In the event, John, who had assured us that he would look after us, carelessly developed mumps, with the result that he was effectively out of action until officially cleared on the evening before we left. Aliki Russell and Nicky Gordon-Lennox, then Counsellor at the Embassy, took good care of us.

Mary and I had a wonderful time and enjoyed every moment. We attended the opening of a new reservoir not far from Madrid. The ceremony was performed by my opposite number, Gonzalez Fernando de la Mora, with some help from me in that together we turned the wheel which let in the water. The Spaniards don't, or at least in those days didn't, pay much attention to nagging criticism. A magnificent lunch was arranged on the spot by one of the best restaurants in Madrid; we visited the Prado with the

Director of the gallery; we saw palaces and pictures and were splendidly entertained, well above our level of importance. At the end, I was asked if I would like to meet General Franco; I said of course I would, I was a guest in his country. He lived, so far as I could see, rather simply in the Prado Palace just outside Madrid. He was smaller than I expected and spoke very quietly. With the Spanish Minister of Transport to interpret, I said how sorry I was to find so powerful a man almost brought down by the plague which affected lesser men like myself – there were papers piled two feet high on his desk. 'There is order in that chaos,' he said, and then asked, 'Do you know why I have so much paper? I have it to kill my Ministers with.' I said I understood the need to do so, but thought it should be done more humanely.

X

Politics and Parties

And now to Politics, a good amusement, though a bad employment.
Charles James Fox, letter from Naples, 1797

Political parties are unpleasant things, perhaps the only thoroughly unpleasant things of which you need to have more than one. Their annual conferences in the early autumn by the seaside are contrived, theatrical occasions which tend to show them, so far as the large outside audience is concerned, at their most fatuous, the worth of a speech being measured by the length of the standing ovation that follows. The message 'Look at what we have done! Hear what we are going to do!' is trumpeted out and received with such enthusiasm that rhetoric sounds like achievement and applause is mistaken for the prevailing wind, rather than just an escape of it. It is, of course, the business of the party machine to organize, to produce and to orchestrate; it is up to those who would lead to avoid becoming so enmeshed in such processes that the beliefs which are the basis of the party's existence are neither displaced by the desire to win, nor overlaid by mere posturing. Mark Twain had views on political parties, which I share:

Men think they think upon great political questions, and they do; but they think with their party, not independently; they read its literature, but not that of the other side; they arrive at convictions, but they are drawn from a partial view of the matter in hand and are of no particular value. They swarm with their party, they feel with their party, they are happy in their party's approval; and where the party leads they will

157

follow, whether for right and honor, or though blood and dirt and a mush of mutilated morals.

Alas, I cannot claim ever to have had the heady experience of a standing ovation at a party conference; rather the reverse. I recall with horror a particularly dreadful afternoon in Blackpool in 1973. The session, which began with education, found an audience eager, wide awake and ready for Mrs Thatcher, the first star of the afternoon. She got her spoon into the cup and stirred and stirred, winning rapturous applause which culminated in the expected standing ovation. Northern Ireland came next, with Willie Whitelaw as Secretary of State and Brian Faulkner as Prime Minister pulling out every stop as they revealed and anguished over the problems of the troubled Province. A second standing ovation followed, after which the huge audience, elated but exhausted, thrilled but wrung dry, rose to its feet and in desperate need of a reviving cup of tea and some fresh air left the hall, just as, when the plug is removed, water leaves a bath. I found myself with Mary and a Chairman, who seemed to have shrunk, alone on the platform, with a debate on transport on my hands. The hall in front of us, which had minutes before contained thousands of lively, cheering people, was by then drained and all but empty, the few who remained showing almost no signs of life. Two or three did struggle to their feet to mouth prepared speeches to the emptiness, after which I hurried through my own contribution, feeling rather as if I were being forcibly fed the contents of last night's ashtrays.

The closing months of 1973 were a bad time for the Government; its majority, already down from thirty-one in 1970 to about half that number, was beginning to look even more uncertain as the long-standing ties between the eight Ulster Unionist MPs and the Conservative Party in Westminster weakened. So, with the miners set on a collision course at the moment when the Government needed all the muscle and determination it could muster, it found itself uncertain of its support in the House of Commons. At such times, Governments begin to look foolish and things generally come unstuck. Ministers are driven, as they prepare for the next crucial test in the division lobbies, to all manner of shifts in policy, which tend only to make things worse. The disappointed ask for more; the opportunists feel the wind in their sails; the professionally nasty become nastier and every crunch is harder to handle. As each new initiative fails and each fresh lance taken down from the walls shatters in their hands at first contact with the enemy, nerve ends on the backbenches begin to twitch. Those who are seen to break ranks receive the prize of publicity; those who stay to support are ignored; it is a time in which the hyenas see and seize their opportunity. Meanwhile the change of wind and tide enables the opposition to look more like a possible alternative Government, its nakedness, for the moment at least, decently covered.

Since I had no particular involvement either in Northern Ireland or with the miners, I was not much more than a spectator of the events that followed. My view at the time was a simple one: the Government had been put there to govern; it should continue to do so up to that point at which it became impossible to pursue the policies it considered right. It seemed to me towards the end of 1973 that that point had been reached, and that an election should be held as soon as possible and certainly before Christmas. At one time I communicated my anxieties to Willie Whitelaw. Although he received them with courtesy and understanding and said that there was nothing very much dividing us, I left him without having any very clear idea as to where he or anyone else stood. Those who counselled soldiering on prevailed, suggesting that it would be wrong to hold a General Election on an old register. We drifted through the humiliation of the three-day working week and power restrictions, to the point at which the miners came out and it was far from clear what would bring them back.

The election, when it finally took place in February 1974, was a depressing affair which left our country wallowing uneasily in the doldrums. Even though, from the point of view of the Conservative Government, the verdict was nothing like as adverse as I had feared, it was a sad end to a Government which, in difficult circumstances, had achieved a great deal. 'The election result was,' as I said in a speech at the time, 'a defeat for elected government and a clear win for no one except the NUM, who got what they wanted.' There would be others in key sectors who would digest the lesson that muscle is more effective than merit. Mr David Wood commented in *The Times* that my argument went, and was intended to go, much deeper than the surface issue of incomes policy. 'He has returned,' he said, 'to the election issue of "Who Governs?" and many troubled Conservatives will be making the journey with him.' In the same article, he went on to quote the defeated Prime Minister as saying 'this nettle will have to be grasped again'. Economic expansion would not be achievable, he had added, without reasonably disciplined relationships within industry and between industry and Government.

Departure from ministerial office is a deflating affair, the gloom of which more than matches the excitement of arrival. The heady, though illusory, feeling that you are engaged in important work and that you are even of some importance yourself disappears overnight. There is no private office, no diary secretary, no red box with its load of paper to be absorbed, and, what is particularly hard to bear, no official car. Dick Marsh told me that, after being fired by Harold Wilson, he only woke up to what had happened when he saw the car drive away. The gloom of electoral defeat and the dismissal from office which went with it were to a point relieved by the knowledge that I had myself been re-elected; on the other hand, I had painfully little to do. Although Mrs Thatcher, who was to head the Environment team on the Opposition Front Bench, seemed to expect me to join in, I didn't find the prospect of continued involvement in the affairs of the Department of the Environment all that alluring, nor did I relish the confinement which being an Opposition spokesman would have involved.

I have often wondered whether Oppositions derive any great benefit from giving themselves Shadow status; the moon to the Government's sun. True, it gives those on the Front Bench some feeling that they are usefully engaged and some hope for the future, but at a price. For those who do so day by day it is for the most part unexciting: not unlike standing in a quiet, uneventful corner of a cricket field, becoming accustomed to nothing happening, until of course it does, and you drop the catch or see the ball which you should have stopped go by on its way to the boundary. Only the confusion or likely collapse of the Government gives its opponents something of a cutting edge. Until that time there will be little to cheer them on; resources will be limited, opportunities to shine hard to come by and achievements minimal. They can only hope that the usual message of by-elections and opinion polls will not be trodden underfoot, as the electorate returns to previously held opinions.

I was at the time fifty-five years old – it seemed a great age; it also seemed unlikely that I would ever hold office again. I had begun to think of the possibility of doing other things. Bill Harcourt, whom I had got to know and like in the course of dealing with the Channel Tunnel, asked me one day what I was going to do; 'Not much,' was the only answer I could find. Later he introduced me to David Culver of Alcan Aluminium, a Canadian multi-national company, with the idea that I might become a director of its subsidiary company in the UK. Philip Chappell, a director of Morgan Grenfell, told me that they had been asked by Texas Instruments to find a Chairman for their UK company. Lewis Whyte, Chairman of the London and Manchester Assurance Company, suggested that I might join the Board. I was lucky: all three prospects in due course materialized and lasted until I reached retirement age. Between them they gave me some acquaintance with North America, a sight of many other countries, some clue as to what commerce and industry were about and an idea of the almost unlimited potential of electronics.

I am, of course, aware, and we have all been recently reminded, that there are those who believe that the role of a Member of Parliament should preclude the acceptance of any part-time employment, though for some reason not immediately clear to me law, medicine and journalism are exceptions. This desire to confine MPs to the Westminster monastery makes nonsense of the other complaint that they are out of touch; moreover, it suggests that knowledge of the rather esoteric game that is played there is the only thing that matters. The House of Commons depends for its strength upon the fact that MPs are not all of the same mould; that they vary in age, character and skills; that they don't all spend every moment of their working lives there. If the rules required them to do so, the parliamentary institution would become over important; so immersed in the intricacies of its own business, fascinated with its own navel, monumentally dull and irrelevant as well. It may sound like a good idea to put MPs in a kind of regulatory cage, but where precisely to put the bars would be a continuing source of difficulty; adherence to the rules would come to mean more than integrity. I never had the slightest objection to people knowing of my outside activities; I had some reservations about entering them in a register. A further point which ought not to be lost sight of is that the House of Commons has its place in our affairs not because of the quality of its members, but because the people put them there.

Towards the end of 1974 – indeed, just after the second General Election of that year – I became Chairman of Texas Instruments Limited, the UK subsidiary of Texas Instruments Inc. (TI), the US electronics company. The company was the offshoot of an oil-search company, Geophysical Services International (GSI), started in the thirties by Cecil Green, Erik Jonsson and Eugene McDermott. Cecil, born in Oldham, moved as a baby to Vancouver, studied there and ended up in Texas. He told me of a dinner in 1930 which he and Ida, his wife, had had with Erik Jonsson and his wife. He had laid out all the money he could get his hands on to get into the business and had hardly enough left to pay his share of the dinner. When the meal was over Erik, who had been several times broke, put the question: 'Well, Ida, what'll you do, suppose we make a big pile of money?' Ida, without a cent in her bag at the time, had replied, 'I'd kind of like to be a philanthropist.' Forty or fifty years later she and Cecil, having made a fortune, laid out many millions of dollars for the benefit of charitable institutions in the USA and elsewhere in the world. Green College, Oxford, a postgraduate medical college which embraces the refurbished Radcliffe Observatory, is just one example. They didn't really look for thanks and seemed almost surprised when they came.

Erik Jonsson, who had been the guiding spirit of the company in its early years, became Mayor of Dallas following the murder of President Kennedy. He was proud of Dallas; when in his eighties he talked of the problems of the city as if they were to an extent his own. He too was immensely generous and had given huge sums of money to help make the city something special. Walking with him in downtown Dallas one constantly met people who greeted him, 'Good morning, Mr Mayor.' He took us to see the

new and splendid Civic Library; as we were leaving, a pretty girl
came up to him.

'I would like to shake your hand, Mr Jonsson.'

'Who are you?'

'It doesn't really matter. I just work here and I know what you
have done for all of us. I just would like to say thank you.'

Gene McDermott, another of the founders, had died before I
became involved with the company, but Mary and I stayed often
with Margaret, his widow, in the house they had built in Dallas.
She loved pictures and had, with Gene, put together a wonderful
collection. She was also one of the most generous and kindly
hostesses I have ever had the luck to come across; it was a joy
to have breakfast looking at two of Monet's waterlilies.

When the Japanese bombed Pearl Harbor in 1941, the company
had been told by the US Government that there was plenty of oil
available, there was no need to look for more, and its staff were
needed elsewhere. Second thoughts came with the realization that
the instruments which the company had developed for locating oil
deposits could be used to detect the presence of submarines, so the
company had been enlisted in the war effort. As soon as the war
was over Erik Jonsson suggested to Pat Haggerty, who was then
working for the Navy Department, that he should become Chief
Executive of Texas Instruments, the company which had been set
up originally to manufacture the instruments required for GSI. It
was, he said, one of the best days' work he ever did.

Pat was a man whose vision and energy were never blunted by
success or money or even by the years. He drove himself and the
company through a period of phenomenal growth to spectacular
success. The first transistor made from silicon put the company in the
forefront of the electronics technology which was to revolutionize
world communications. Pat was a leader and would have been
one in any sphere; he chose industry because he believed that
was where the important things were happening. He told of a
meeting he had once had with Christopher Soames, who had
chosen politics, 'because in this country that is where the action
is'. Under Pat TI developed a clear culture: regardless of status
and rank, all were TIers; they were known by their first names
and they used the same canteens, the same washrooms; they wore

identity badges the colour of which showed not rank, but years of service; they all had a stake in the company's success, with opportunities to become stockholders; there were special awards for special services.

The declared strategy was to turn a very good small company into first a very good medium-sized one and then into a very good big one. The people who ran it travelled the world, visiting the plants, getting to know the managers and being known by them. Pat, in particular, had a way when he spoke of treating people as partners with whom he very much wished to share his thoughts. He thus engendered a sense of common purpose and of belonging which I have not met elsewhere. While British audiences have, I think, a lower boredom threshold than Americans and usually find listening harder, those to whom he spoke in Bedford listened with the same attention as others did in Dallas. He saw it as the responsibility of management to create 'those conditions which upgrade the human spirit through opportunities to participate in a worthwhile endeavour'. 'There was,' he said, 'probably no greater waste in industry today than that of willing employees prevented by insensitive leadership from applying their energies and ambitions in the interest of the companies for which they work.'

His vision was something which he sought to share. It embraced all those who worked for the company, 'the kind of people with whom it is fun and an honour to be associated'. It took account of the customers and their needs: 'Texas Instruments exists to create, make and market useful products and services, to satisfy the needs of its customers throughout the world.' It included also the buildings in which these products were conceived and made: 'Good buildings which reflect differences in taste and judgment, based on caring and on knowledge, add to the beauty of a city'. On this side of the Atlantic, we tend to be so concerned to avoid anything which savours of paternalism that we do too little explaining and attach no great importance to example. Only Hector Laing, long-time Chairman of United Biscuits, showed the same deep concern as Pat Haggerty that those who worked for the company were entitled to an explanation from him of the problems of the company, how they as employees would be affected, and how he intended to handle those problems.

POLITICS AND PARTIES

It was during the time of my involvement with TI – which lasted, I am astonished now to recall, for more than fifteen years – that it began to dawn on me just how far the politicians had fallen and were continuing to fall behind the technologists. The arrangements of the politician, his habit of mind and his horizons, limited in both time and space, were becoming increasingly inadequate either to accommodate the products or keep up with the thoughts of the technologist in most of the major areas of human activity and concern: defence, law and order, communications, health and the environment. While the sprawl of government has increased, and its power over the individual remains, its capacity to handle effectively the major problems of the time has perceptibly diminished. Moreover, its almost total concentration on the problems of the present, its concern to answer at all times the unanswerable and often daft questions of the media, has dimmed its awareness, even its interest, in things which are not far beyond the rim of the horizon.

The second General Election of 1974 produced a win for Harold Wilson by a narrow margin, a majority of four over all other parties. I had just come back from Dallas at the end of October, having been formally approved and appointed as Chairman of TIL, when I had a call from Ted Heath. He wished, he said, to talk to me about the Shadow Cabinet.

I said I didn't think that I had any useful advice to offer him on that subject.

'I don't want your advice about it. I want you to join it.'

'Oh no, even less do I think I have anything useful to offer.'

'That's a pity,' he said. 'We have a new job which we think you could do well – Shadow Leader of the House of Commons.' He added words to the effect that I was the only one they had who was any good at being offensive. I saw him later that evening and accepted, on the one condition that I had a place on the Front Bench near to him and opposite whoever it was I was meant to shadow.

It was not, I think, a particularly popular move in some circles: Willie Whitelaw seemed not to welcome it all that warmly and Humphrey Atkins, then Opposition Chief Whip, was far from enthusiastic. Rather above my station, I found myself walking by

165

the side of Jim Callaghan into the House of Lords to hear the Queen's Speech at the Opening of the new Parliament. Later he sent me a picture of the two of us together on that occasion. His comment, 'Coming events cast their shadows before them: now we are neighbours', told of his recent purchase of the house next door to us in London. I could only reply that, with Denis Healey barely twenty yards away and Merlyn Rees not much further, if this inflow of eminent Labour politicians were to continue, my reputation, such as it was, with my own Party would be in jeopardy. I used to see Denis from time to time, usually on the way to collect the newspaper; I enjoyed doing so, for he always had something amusing to say. He had a particularly sharp eye for the first symptoms of age and decay, often in people younger than himself. I never really noticed him in the House of Commons until Suez, when he began to show his mettle, and particularly his hitting power. Had he ever become Leader of the Labour Party, he would certainly have presented Mrs Thatcher with something much less easy to wallop with a handbag than either Michael Foot or Neil Kinnock could manage. His book, *The Time of My Life*, was, to say the least, one of the star political autobiographies of my time; not the least of its merits was that it showed him as having had far more fun than most.

In my new role I had occasion to reflect upon the way in which Parliament works and the extent to which, over time, its powers have leached to the executive. In theory, Parliament is supreme, sovereign; it makes the law, it imposes taxes, it authorizes spending and it confers upon Ministers the power to govern in the Queen's name. In practice, its role is more that of lackey than master. Far from deciding upon new measures, it performs the functions of a laundry, washing, ironing and packaging the often ill-conceived and flawed proposals which Ministers put before it in ever-increasing quantity. A glance at almost any modern legislation will indicate the low priority accorded to clarity and comprehensibility. Our taxation measures are particularly horrible and long-winded: the 1995 Finance Act consisted of 387 pages. So far as I am aware, there is no reliable estimate of the number of accountants required to explain what it all means to their lay clients or how much those clients will have to pay before they can understand what precisely the law requires of them. It is a source of constant surprise that Governments should have the gall to boast of the mess which annually they tip out on to the Statute Book.

Two defeats in one year were a severe shock for Conservative MPs, a sufficient number of whom concluded, much as they had ten years earlier, that whatever it was that had gone wrong could not be their fault and must therefore be that of their Leader; another must be found, who would more faithfully reflect their merits. George Thomas commented, in his book *Mr Speaker*, on the uncertainty of the ties which bind the Conservative Party to its leader for the time being:

> The public school boys can be much rougher than the grammar school boys when it comes to guarding what they believe to be their own interests. If anybody is in their way, they are not going to stay up all night feeling embarrassed that they will have to get rid of him. They did it to Anthony Eden, Alec Douglas-Home and Ted Heath; and [he added prophetically] they will not hesitate to do it again, when they feel that it is in their interests to do so.

On the same page he quoted Harold Wilson: 'Our boys talk a lot but they never do anything. The Tories say very little and the man is out before he knows he is under attack.'

Alec Douglas-Home, similarly blamed in 1965, had stepped down with a generosity and dignity which others have found hard to match. Under the new procedure which Alec himself had then set up, Ted Heath had emerged as the victor. When, ten years later, the process was repeated, he received eleven fewer votes in the first round than Mrs Thatcher, who was still short of the overall majority required. I was myself in Ted's room when Tim Kitson, his Parliamentary Private Secretary, came in, handed him a piece of paper at which he looked for a moment and then indicated that things had gone amiss. There were only four or five people in the room: all were silent. I favoured his withdrawal at that stage rather than staying in the contest for the next round; those who had not voted for him in the first round would certainly not do so in the next, and some of those who had would be quick to climb on to her bandwagon; he should decide at once to quit a contest which he could not win. I also ventured the thought that, while people in our country often differed about winners, they loved and admired good losers. Although he did decide quite quickly to withdraw from the contest, Ted was never able to swallow the hurt.

There was still a second round to be settled. Thatcher, Whitelaw, Howe and Prior were in the lists. A few siren voices suggested to me that, with so many runners, one more would not make much difference and unwisely I allowed my name to go forward. Apart from a few TV appearances, some interviews and a speech or two in unusual places, I took no serious part; nor was anyone active on my behalf. In so far as I said anything of substance, it was to the effect that if we as a nation continued to pay ourselves more for doing less and doing it less well, without worrying about our customers, at the end of the day we would land ourselves with a good deal of pain and anguish. No one took much notice; such a message was either too unsophisticated or too uncomfortable, I was not sure which. I got eleven votes, which had no effect at all on the outcome, for Mrs Thatcher had a runaway win. Thinking that she might well prefer my room to my company, I offered to leave the Shadow Cabinet; too easily reassured and somewhat flattered by her request that I should stay, I agreed to do so. As time went on, however, I began to think that it might not be all that long before I was dumped and suggested again that it might be better if I left. It is always rather beguiling to be told you are useful and necessary, and I was all too easily persuaded to stay.

The entertainment value of Shadow Cabinet meetings was, to put it mildly, limited; nor was it a body in which friendships could be said to flourish. Peter Carrington, who had never been in the House of Commons and who found the routine wrangles boring, relieved the tedium of one meeting by composing this masterpiece:

I love the Shadow Cabinet, its meetings are great fun.
. . ., I love them every one.
I much admire the discipline of thought and speech and mind,
The way they never wander – or so at least I find.
What other body is there composed of men so great,
Noble, wise and splendid, every one first-rate.

Of course there is another view about that awful bunch.
They talk so much and drivel so, they're keeping me from
lunch.

Much of the time was spent discussing the subject for debate on
the next Supply Day. By a quaint and ancient custom, in every
session a number of special days are set aside for the Government
to ask Parliament, or rather the House of Commons, to vote a
huge sum of money for one purpose or another. The Opposition
could, if it wished, challenge and even vote against the proposal;
in practice, since spending is always popular and saving is regarded
as mean, it never does so. Instead, it usually moves a motion calling
for more money, not less, to be spent. The pattern is that of an
eighteenth-century minuet, in which everyone ends up pretty well
where they started, and no one, certainly not the Government, gets
hurt in the process: oddly, parties in opposition believe that it is a
useful weapon in their armoury.

In 1976 America celebrated the bicentennial of its independence;
there were ceremonies in Westminster Hall and in Washington to
mark the occasion. As Shadow Leader of the House of Commons
I was to some extent involved, though matters never rose much
above the level of an exchange of pleasantries and some competition
in ceremonial. It was a demonstration, if one were needed, of how
much more important the Americans are to us than we are to them;
we seem cast in the role of the tiresome maiden aunt, always pressing
for attention. The contrast between the proceedings here and those
on the other side of the Atlantic was evidence of this. For us it
was an important and historic event, which required thought and
effort; the ceremony in Westminster Hall was superb, reflecting
our concern with Magna Carta and those things which had held
us together since. In Washington the Declaration of Independence
made its appearance rather as an afterthought, printed on a nylon
scarf which was presented to the ladies; interestingly, it was made
in Japan. One had the impression of friendliness certainly, but of
a minor incident rather than of a great occasion.

The Parliament of 1974–9 was a rough one. Labour had at the start
only a paper-thin majority of four over all other parties. That was
quickly eroded, leaving the Government in a precarious position

and dependent upon a pact with the Liberals. Nevertheless, it survived for nearly a full term until it was defeated by one vote on a no confidence motion which had the support of the Liberals, eight Ulster Unionists and the Scottish Nationalists. Jim Callaghan's comment on the Scots, that they were 'turkeys voting for Christmas', seemed in the circumstances to be not all that wide of the mark. The remarkable thing was the way in which the Government, with total support from its backbenches, managed to struggle on through all manner of difficulties and to survive for so long.

The Chair of the House of Commons can be, and often is, an exceedingly uncomfortable place in which to sit. Horace King, the first Labour Speaker, who held the office from 1965 to 1971, found some of the pressures a bit too much for him. His successors, Selwyn Lloyd (1971–6) and George Thomas (1976–83), were, I thought, outstanding. Selwyn, complained of by that master cartoonist, Vicky, as 'almost uncaricaturable', had survived not only that deficiency, but also the trauma of Suez and his abrupt dismissal from the Treasury as one of the main casualties of the night of the long knives.

One day, sitting on the Opposition Front Bench, half listening to whatever was going on, I received this note from the Chair:

My dear John,

When will your colleagues realize that some approaches are counter-productive!!! The fact that a man is helping in the Committee stage is not a very good reason for calling him on 2R [Second Reading]. Anyhow, I do not like being *told* what I have to do.

Yours,

Selwyn

No action from you – but *you look* as bored as *I am*.

Enclosed with it was this message to Mr Speaker from Michael Heseltine's private office: 'Mr Heseltine is anxious that Mr Stanley should be called as early as possible. He is helping him on the committee stage of the Bill.' George, the son of a Welsh miner, had previously been Secretary of State for Wales. His sense of history, his ability to laugh, his willingness to take on the toughs and a fine voice all contributed to his considerable success as Speaker. Like his predecessor, he had his share of rough moments in a restless and volatile House. A thin Labour majority at the start had soon vanished, leaving the Government dependent upon others for survival.

It was in Selwyn's time that the protagonist of Irish unity Miss Bernadette Devlin made her appearance. She seemed only to come alive when there was someone or something around for her to hate: hatred was as necessary to her as air is to a balloon, and her maiden speech oozed with it. In 1972, when pregnant and in search of trouble, she first called the Home Secretary, Reggie Maudling, 'a murdering hypocrite', then moved from her place at high speed across the Chamber, pulled his hair, slapped his face, scratched it and then departed, leaving a disturbed House behind her.

Severely criticized for his failure to discipline her, Selwyn explained ruefully that the removal by force of a pregnant woman from the Chamber could have been a problem: he wondered who would take the blame if anything had then gone amiss. Faced later on with other ladies who had misbehaved, though they had stopped short of personal assault, George Thomas showed himself to be somewhat tougher. He had them locked up on the premises until such time as the House rose; by chance that night it was five o'clock in the morning.

As part of the changes which Mrs Thatcher made in her Shadow Cabinet in 1976, she wished me to move from Shadow Leader of the House to become Shadow Minister of Agriculture. I did not fancy the prospect: British agriculture, it seemed, was totally enmeshed in the EEC Common Agricultural Policy, which I felt was not going to be at all easy to master and impossible to change. Moreover, from a personal angle I suspected that I was being pushed just that bit nearer the door and into a position from which I could more easily be tipped out later. I suggested once more that she would get on quite well without me – that I would, at that stage, be quite willing to go without regret or recrimination. She replied that she was anxious to keep me and asked me to see Willie Whitelaw and hear his views. Some emollient words from him, and he is an artist at them, were sufficient to persuade me to accept; it was a mistake.

171

I spent much of the next two years or so learning about farming, fishing and food or, more accurately, the politics in which they were and are entangled. In this I had the help of Michael Jopling, who knew far more about farming than I did. He gave me generous support as my number two. Mrs Thatcher seemed, for a variety of reasons, not all that well disposed towards the farmers; nor did she think well of such advice as I had to offer. She was inclined to seize upon ideas which, while they could be easily put over on a platform, had no earthly chance of being accepted. She thought at one time that it might be a good idea to have a fifty-mile-wide cordon round these islands within which we would have sole fishing rights. Michael Jopling stressed the absurdity of it and told me that I must resist it: any party which adopted such a stance could hardly expect to be taken seriously. During a rather unhappy meeting, I just about managed to persuade her of this; I also convinced her that I was hopelessly wet and incapable of standing up for British interests. She never sought my opinion again. From then on, I suspected that I would be for the chop as soon as it became convenient; but I continued, rather foolishly, to hope that when she said she wanted me to stay, she meant something more than just for the moment.

On a number of occasions I predicted to Michael Jopling that, when the chips were down, we would neither of us be involved in Agriculture; my forecast was that he would end up as Chief Whip and that I would be out on my ear; and so it proved. He telephoned to me on the Saturday morning after the 1979 election. He said that he was speaking from Number Twelve Downing Street as Chief Whip and that I was indeed out. My place at Agriculture had gone to Peter Walker, who later wrote to assure me that he had had no part in my elimination.

The Prime Minister, on Michael's insistence, rang me minutes after the end of his call. She told me briefly that I had no place in her plans.

I said 'Oh' in as uncordial a tone as I could.

She then suggested that I should go to 'the other place'.

I replied that I could hardly do that since I had spent the last few weeks telling my constituents that I wanted nothing so much as to continue to be their MP. They would not understand if now, in the face of personal disappointment, I did an about turn and told them to find someone else.

She accepted this and added, 'Well, after the next election.'

Wishing to make my feelings clear without being too offensive, I replied, 'Prime Minister, in the circumstances, I am going to need that in writing.'

'You shall have it. And you must come and see me next week and I will explain.'

Soon afterwards, I received the following handwritten letter from her.

In Confidence 19th June 1979

My dear John,

First, I want to thank you for everything you have done during your years on the front bench and the way you have furthered the principles and ideals we both believe in. When we spoke, I mentioned to you that we shall need you in the Lords after this Parliament. The Chief Whip and I have talked about this – but for obvious reasons I should be grateful if, apart from Mary, this could be known only to the three of us.

I hope you will join us for dinner here one evening and at Chequers. I value your political advice and experience and always shall.

Yours ever,
Margaret

Some weeks elapsed before that promised meeting took place, and then only because Michael insisted that it should. 'Prime Minister,' I said, 'I have three things that I want to say, and if I don't say them now I will never get them out. First I want you to know how hurt and angry I was and am at the way you have behaved to me. Secondly, despite what I have just said, I shall not be looking for an opportunity to get my own back; I hope for all our sakes that you will be successful. Thirdly, I think you would do well to be more careful when it comes to choosing your friends; some of them may prove less reliable than you suppose when the weather changes.' I have seen little or nothing of her since and retain mixed impressions.

Her achievement in becoming the first woman Prime Minister and remaining for eleven years as the tenant of Number Ten Downing Street was astonishing. It was her particular strength that there seemed to be no room in her make-up for doubt. Had she so much as flinched or stumbled during the Falklands campaign, particularly in the early weeks, she would have put wind in the sails of the uneasy and turned their anxiety into open opposition. It was due largely to her robustness that the attitude of the United States was in such sharp contrast to what it had been over Suez. She had the courage to rely on her instinct rather than her intellect; something which, with a bit of luck thrown in, made her, for a long time, invulnerable. Her weakness lay in her lack of understanding of opinions which she did not share, and her impatience with those who held them. She gave the impression of having little concern for the underlying unity of the nation. I recall on one occasion giving voice in the Shadow Cabinet to what I regarded as something of a cliché about its importance, and my intense surprise at the brusqueness with which she rejected it. Had she supported both Geoffrey Howe and Nigel Lawson as they deserved, and listened less to outside counsellors who neither shared nor understood their burdens, she might well have remained in office for further years – invulnerable.

Being the only member of the Shadow Cabinet to be rejected was a considerable mortification. It meant that at the age of sixty my political career was over; it took time and the advice of friends to perceive that there were compensations. I remember being particularly shaken when Steve Hastings, an old friend, told me bluntly that I was making a fool of myself. Since I had expected to be in the Cabinet, I had rather abruptly to change gear. I told the Whips that I intended to change my name to Cinderella and to pay due regard to the Fairy Godmother's instruction not to stay out late. Cap in hand, I told TI, Alcan and the London and Manchester that my farewells had been premature and that I could and would stay on if wanted; I warned Renee Short, my friend and most obliging pair from Wolverhampton, that I would have increasing need of her help. My constituency chairman, when I told him that I would not be standing again, expressed neither surprise nor regret; clearly he thought my decision timely, that a new face would be no bad thing and that the seat would be quite safe. In 1983 he was proved wrong and the seat, which the Conservatives had held for seventy years and I myself for thirty-two, was lost to a Liberal; moreover it was a result against a trend which swept the Conservatives in with a greatly increased majority.

As soon as the Parliament of 1979 had been opened, we went with Maurice and Katie Macmillan for a holiday in Tunisia. Maurice had become a particular friend during the time of the Heath Government. That was rather against the trend, for being in office together tends to erode friendships rather than strengthen them. He had always understood my various problems and whenever possible helped. During the time when he was Secretary of State for Employment and I was Minister of Transport, a strike in the railways or in the docks used frequently to frustrate any plans we had made for a recess. Our continued presence in the country was on such occasions said to be essential, regardless of the fact that there was nothing useful that we could do; it was just necessary to be around, to look concerned and to make some anodyne comment if required. We both understood that anything which resembled intervention by us would be fatal, that peacemaking efforts by ACAS or some other masseur would only be effective if backed by the weariness of the strikers, the waning interest of the media and the evaporation of the public's patience. It took one or more of those factors to bring to an end those old-fashioned trials of strength which I think Sidney Webb described as the 'arbitrament of war'.

Even as a Treasury Minister, Maurice showed understanding and imagination; he once wrote me a letter from that citadel of power and short-sightedness. He looked forward, he said, to seeing me ride three separate horses – standing on two, straddling a third and driving a fourth in front of me. 'If there is anything I can do to help from this peculiar position which I now occupy, please let me know – and I will do what I can.' Although I cannot now remember who the four horses represented, I do remember how grateful I was for his understanding. From the earlier part of the letter, it would seem that the British Waterways Board was one; Jack Jones, the General Secretary of the Transport and General Workers' Union, and Toby Aldington, at the time Chairman of the Port of London Authority, were probably two of the others; of the identity of the fourth I have no clue. It was not always easy to follow Maurice's train of thought, the complexity of which caused him at times to lower his voice to something near a whisper. What was never in doubt was the firmness of his friendship.

We used to stay quite often at Birch Grove, the Sussex home which Maurice and Katie shared with his father. One night, Harold suggested that I should have a final drink with him before going to bed. 'I am so glad,' he said, 'that you are so friendly with Maurice – such a dear kind fellow. Of course, I've known him all his life. I've never known him do or say a mean or unkind thing.' As an afterthought he added, 'Very different from me – I've been a bit of an old trickster.' What an actor he would have made. In 1975, when we were both still in the House of Commons, Maurice wrote to thank me for having spoken at a meeting in his constituency. I quote it here because it expressed my own views about the importance of trying to tell people the truth, and by that I mean much more than merely avoiding what you know to be false. I quote it also because that is how I like to remember both the man and his generosity. 'They', he wrote, referring to his constituents, '*are* entitled to demand that we as politicians do our bit; by spelling out the dangers; by making it plain that these are not "normal" times; by telling them that it *is* their business, and not just ours. This you did very successfully. I wish more people would follow your example.' That, however, is far from being either our practice or our aim. Having voted, it is the wish of most people to detach themselves from what they see as just another spectator sport, inferior to football. It is not easy, however, in a climate of mistrust, which the media do nothing to dispel, to explain either problems or policies. It is the habit of interviewers on radio and television to appear in the role of counsel for the prosecution; they are skilled in the art of making their victims look at least foolish.

I had been a member of the Board of Alcan UK since 1974. In the years that followed, fierce competition between that company and the British Aluminium Company (BACO) had driven down prices to a point at which it looked likely that neither could survive the process of attrition; certainly neither had anything to spare for investment. The high hopes which BACO and those who worked there had for the great new smelter at Invergordon came to nothing. Low prices and a shabby let-down over the price at which the South of Scotland Electricity Board would supply power forced its closure. In 1982, terms for the merger of the two companies were agreed; Alcan Aluminium Ltd (Alcan UK's parent company) would provide the necessary finance, but only on condition that the arrangement was one which was acceptable to the British Government and that there would be no long delay. I was deputed to put the question to the Prime Minister. She said that, while it seemed sensible, the decision was one for Arthur Cockfield, Secretary of State for Trade and Industry, whom I should see as soon as possible; Ian Gow, her Parliamentary Private Secretary, would come with me. The outcome was that the merger was allowed to go ahead and without delay; the result was to preserve a significant aluminium producing capacity in this country and with it many thousands of jobs. George Russell, as Chief Executive of the new company, earned great credit for the success of the merger and for the fact that it was done as fairly as possible to both sides and with the minimum of pain. He has since shown his considerable qualities in various roles, including the chairmanship of the Independent Television Commission – surely one in which it is easier to make enemies than friends.

While there are, as I have said, those who think that MPs ought not to be involved in such matters, here was an instance in which, since I was aware of what was going on, I was able to do something which was of benefit to the country as a whole and particularly the North-East. So long as there is total disclosure, there seems to me to be no reason why backbench MPs should not be involved in commercial or industrial activities any more than they should be restrained from practising the law or medicine or writing for the press or broadcasting. It is, of course, in part a question of appearances; it is possible to make such extra-mural activities look suspect – 'sleaze' is the word currently in vogue. It is also possible, indeed likely, that there will be abuses from time to time. A system of rules not easily put into words and enforced by outsiders would soon put paid to any notion of the sovereignty of Paliament. Let us hope that the new Committee of Privileges has teeth and the will to use them on those who show themselves to be short on integrity or who are so crassly stupid as to accept money for doing what is their duty as Members of Parliament.

On 2 April 1982, Argentine armed forces invaded the Falkland Islands, 400 miles away from its mainland. Somehow we had drifted into supposing that the Argentine leaders, an unprepossessing gang, would not be so foolish as to resort to force. They had done so, believing that we would never go to war to defend them. A most hazardous operation across eight thousand miles of ocean to recover the Islands suddenly became not a remote possibility, but an immediate prospect. The general reaction of most people to the fact that we were at war was one of huge surprise mixed with very real anxiety. Three days after the seizure of the Islands the carrier group departed on its long sea journey, followed soon after by the remainder of the task force which had been assembled and made ready with amazing speed. Attitudes too changed with equal rapidity: relaxation and unconcern gave way to a determination to recover the Islands almost regardless of cost; prudent housekeeping, which had been the rule only a week or so before, was put into cold storage. The Prime Minister and those who ran the operation must be given tremendous credit for the unwavering determination which they showed. Most of us found ourselves as rather unwilling and exceedingly anxious spectators of a venture, the failure of which would inevitably bring consequences both unforeseeable and agonizing. To enhance the suspense and the shock the Ministry of Defence seemed to have explored the world beyond the tomb for a voice tailor-made to carry bad news and to make sure that no one missed a word of it.

It must have all been very different for those who looked at the near prospect of battle against the background of the cold grey seas of the South Atlantic. One of my constituents, Captain Burne RN, who commanded the *Canberra* and received a CBE, wrote to me after it was all over. Being a very modest man, he had these comments to make:

I am proud of my South Atlantic medal; but the CBE makes me think. First of my Naval Party who did it all. Second of my mistakes – there were many – and how lucky I was they

178

did not come home to roost. Third, of all those not honoured who did so much more than I. Above all one remembers those superb young sailors who fought and died and have no grave but the sea.

Charles Stewart, a naval chaplain, wrote an account which moved me at the time and still does:

As we left the warm and pleasant climate of the region [Ascension Island] and headed for the stormy and unpredictable waters of the South Atlantic, the chilling realization gradually evolved that a bloody confrontation was on the way . . . To say that it was a terrifying experience fails to capture the intensity of the emotion. The chilling sound of the Action Stations alarm will forever send shivers down my spine . . . the utter calm and peace that I received that, whatever happened, I was secure in the presence of God . . . I well remember the bitterness I felt. We had just committed a young man from one of those ships when the Action Stations alarm sounded. The planes, whose results we had so clearly witnessed, were back again. As our Harriers took off to engage them, my thoughts were only for the victory of their action . . . You learn down here to weep silently in your cabin at man's folly . . . Much of the veneer, which so often attends professional life, has been removed, exposing how vulnerable we are. We are indeed frail children of dust, needing to love and be loved . . . I have no idea what the future may hold for us here in the South Atlantic. I do know that it has been my privilege to minister in God's name to a remarkable group of people, some of whom are only $16\frac{1}{2}$ years of age, whose professionalism, courage, devotion and compassion – not to mention their own distinctive sense of humour, which, alas, I doubt I could use at the Women's Guild – has for me returned, for the highest reasons, the Great back into Britain.

His words tell a tale of courage and endeavour which soon and sadly became overlaid by the garbage which is the tabloids' view of ordinary everyday life.

WITHOUT BENEFIT OF LAUNDRY

Some weeks after it was over, I went to Yeovilton to see some of the Harriers which had played so important a part in the operation fly in from the carriers which had brought them home. The young men who flew them had not changed outwardly, but they had had a part in something which they would never forget; the rest of us probably would, but should not.

XI

India Half a Century On

God is love. Is this the final message of India?
E. M. Forster

I have tried to think what it is about India which has led me, for no particular purpose, to return there again and again and why, having spent less than a year there during my life, I am now impelled to include in this book a further chapter about that extraordinary country. It is not as if I have some special knowledge which I am tempted to display, nor do I have a host of close friends there; nor is it simply the memory of glorious places and beautiful things made by men's hands. If they were the sole causes of my fascination, there would be no need to explain. Rather, I think it is because India, more than any other country I have been in, reveals, without any attempt at concealment, all the muddle, confusion and contrasts of humanity. The splendour and the ugliness, the riches and the grinding poverty, the fertile and the barren, the clean and the foul, the purity and the corruption, the wisdom and the folly the order and the confusion: all those apparent opposites are in India close, inseparable companions, with love somehow coming out on top of the heap. A month or so in south India became, to my surprise, something of a spiritual experience, in which an image of Shiva or some words of Krishna caused me to think of Christ; to reflect upon man's need for God and to puzzle about the much more difficult question, God's need for man.

When he was Governor of Maharashtra, Ali Yava Jung, my old friend of Hyderabad days, had pressed me to go back; but with inconceivable foolishness, I had not done so. Zehra, his widow, as full of grace and beauty as ever, came to stay with us in Somerset

181

in 1981, reminded me of my folly and suggested that I should now redeem that error and return. We arrived in Delhi in January 1982 in time to see the Republic Day Parade; it was a magnificent and unique affair. While orderliness and precision are not perhaps the most pre-eminent of Indian virtues and the armed forces normally play only a rather subdued role in the nation's everyday life, on that day there is a display which begins as a parade and ends as a pageant. India's armed forces show themselves to be as smart and as disciplined as any in the world; they bring with them not just their guns and their tanks and the normal accoutrements of war, but also elephants and bands and floats depicting the huge variety of India and its peoples, stretching from the tropical south up to and across the great mountains of the north to Kashmir and into the heartland of Asia. This extraordinary revelation of India moved with immaculate timing from New Delhi through India Gate towards Old Delhi, through crowds to be counted in millions. We were fortunate to be in the President's stand, from which we enjoyed a wonderful view of the whole scene; not least was a first sight of Indira Gandhi, standing up as she was driven through the vast crowds, her arm raised in response to their welcome.

Van Kataraman, the Minister of Defence, who subsequently became President of India, asked me on the following day if I had seen the parade and what I thought of it.

I replied that it was spellbinding, unique.

'Ah, that is what they all say.'

I asked him – what else could I have said – how he would have responded if I had said it was commonplace, that its like could readily be found elsewhere.

'I am sorry,' he replied at once. 'You were our teachers in all this. We don't really mind what others say, but we want you to think well of what we do.'

As impressive, in some ways even more moving, was the ceremony of Beating the Retreat two days later, carried out with the same breathtaking smartness and precision. The massed bands of India's armed forces marched and played old tunes, hymns and marches, many from Britain, which they had made their own; amongst them was 'Abide with Me', said to have been Gandhi's favourite hymn. The Presidential Palace, built by Lutyens half a century before as the home of Viceroys, and the principal Government buildings, designed by Baker at the same time, provided a tremendous background. High above the crowds on the ramparts of the Palace, outlined against the sunset, mounted and motionless, stood a line of six members of the Camel Corps, three on each side facing inwards; they seemed like sentinels guarding the margin between day and night.

Zehra had secured for me a meeting with Mrs Gandhi; I saw her in the house where she was later murdered by a Sikh from her own bodyguard. The daughter of Pandit Nehru, she gave the impression of being engaged on a mission which would last a lifetime rather than just holding an office for the time being. Into that mission went everything she had: the problems facing her country absorbed her totally; questions of her personal safety seemed not to interest her. Small in stature, but majestic and simple, even austere, in style, she gave the impression of being more comfortable with the crowds to whom she belonged and who were hers than with more formal occasions. At the end of her first term in office she had been routed and left without a party; yet after only a short interval she had returned in triumph with a new one which had even adopted her name. I had the impression that the mean and vindictive way in which her successors had harassed and humiliated her had done much to keep her in politics. 'They took away my passport. They wouldn't allow me to attend an environmental conference in Helsinki. They stopped me from going to Vienna. They even sent snoopers into my bedroom.' Her anger was real and it had driven her on.

Her son, Rajiv, whom I met at much the same time, said to me, 'My mother is never so formidable as when she is under attack. At such times she knows exactly what to do.' I despaired on arrival of ever seeing him, for half India seemed to be encamped on the lawn. I gave my name at the door and was shown into a small, simply furnished room. Two minutes later Rajiv entered, saying quietly that he was sorry to have kept me waiting. He had only recently emerged from the withdrawn and rather solitary life of an airline pilot to take his place as one of the most prominent of India's politicians. He talked unhurriedly and easily of the huge change there had been in his life following the death of his brother,

Sanjay. Far too intelligent to be unaware of what might lie ahead, he seemed to be untroubled and serene and to have about him a quality which I could only describe as purity. I thought him one of the most immediately attractive people whom I had ever met; I never saw him again.

Old Delhi station, where we waited three hours for our train north to Jammu, is a place which teems with life and incident. There were welcomes and goodbyes; there was a notice which seemed at first sight to suggest that those with upper-class connections would be executed there; there were people sleeping in unlikely places; there was a procession, a politician on his way home with a band and a few applauding, with a photographer to record the scene and provide evidence for those at home that the man at the centre was an important figure in the capital. When we arrived we were welcomed by the Governor of Jammu and Kashmir, B. K. Nehru, a relation of Pandit Nehru. We had three wonderful days with him and his wholly delightful Hungarian wife, Fori; she had given her heart to him and to India as well. He had been High Commissioner in London and Ambassador in Washington, and was at that time still carrying out duties at the United Nations in New York. While I had met him years before when he was in London, there was no possible reason, save for the urgings of Zehra, why they should have had the two of us to stay and have looked after us so kindly.

Here in England you can have British MPs for two a penny or even less; but in a remote Indian village the visit of one of whom they have never heard, but who they readily assume to be important, is an event. We received an almost royal welcome at a small village a few miles out of Jammu: why, we were asked, did not more British MPs come to visit Indian villages? A very old man was introduced to us as a hero who had fought for the King Emperor in the First World War; as evidence of this, he wore the Defence Medal of the Second. We were given a sight of the whole pattern of the life of the village and were offered refreshment; we managed to drink only tea and to eat the minimum, but still my over-sensitive Western stomach protested subsequently. At a Hindu temple which we visited one had first to pass along a line of beggars who attended every day at regular hours, rather like a club

184

for men who hadn't much else to do. They gave no impression of being particularly poor and their begging was discreet, restrained and gentle. Urged by the Nehrus, the best and most generous of hosts, to return in the summer when the snows would be gone and stay with them in Srinagar, we gave the only possible answer: of course we would.

Inexplicably I had somehow failed to see the Taj Mahal on early visits to India; so, on leaving Jammu, we embarked upon a tour of Rajastan, Agra, Fetipur Sekri, Jaipur and Udaipur. First encounters with beautiful things are important; a bad guide can ruin it all with a commentary delivered in a monotonous drone which, like a dirty window, interposes its stain between you and the splendour of what you are trying to look at. We were fortunate in the guide we had in Agra, who insisted on taking us first to the tomb of Itimad-ud-Daula, a gem which would surely be world-famous if it were not so near to and surpassed by the Taj itself. You see it and wonder if anything could be more beautiful; then you pass on to have the question answered by the Taj, serene, timeless, perfect. Built by Akbar's son, Shah Jahan, in the seventeenth century as the tomb for his wife, Mumtaz Mahal, it is so lovely that it is hard to believe it to be the work of human hands. Breathtaking in design and perspective, built of marble inlaid with semi-precious stones, it has a lustre of its own, scarcely needing to borrow from the light of sun or moon, always changing and seemingly celestial. Now, a decade or so later, this most beautiful creation is threatened by pollution. An oil refinery positioned twenty miles away upwind – an act of unrivalled vandalism – disgorges its acid wastes, which are powerfully reinforced by the thousands of mini-taxis with their primitive phut-phut engines burning dirty fuel.

British respect for India's monuments was not spontaneous. The Itimad-ud-Daula tomb had served at first as the mess for some British officers who had whitewashed the walls, and with them the paintings, and partitioned the building to meet their needs, until, the merits of the place recognized, they were very properly turned out. The debt owed to Lord Curzon for what he did to restore and preserve Indian heritage when he was Viceroy can hardly be overstated. Fetipur Sekri, beautiful and solitary, demonstrates marvellously both the skills and the foolishness of man. Akbar's

185

intention to make it his capital, the centre of his Mogul Empire, ensured its beauty and magnificence: the fact, which came to light only after it had been built, that there was no water rendered it unusable – not much more than a folly. The lotus throne had originated in Akbar's thought that man, like the lotus, having his roots in filth, could still grow through and rise above the dirty water to achieve purity. We spent a few days in Bombay, mostly with Zehra. She had started a school for children who lived in one of those areas of unbelievable squalor, a short distance from the road leading out of the city to the airport. It was hard to envisage anything human or clean emerging from such a place; yet these children were both and more besides, showing what they, having started with little hope, could do if someone with imagination and drive lifted them out of the mire and gave them the chance to be human.

In 1983 we went back again, in response to the Nehrus' invitation. It was a chance which we would have been mad to miss. On the way we paid a visit to my son Tom, who was working for BP in Bahrain. I had not been there since 1956 and found it much changed. A good deal of land had been recovered from the sea in order to bear the burden of concrete and asphalt which are the usual features of modern civilization. While in Bahrain, I spent an hour with the Foreign Minister. Tolerant and broad-minded himself, and anxious that Bahrain should be so too, he was aware that not all of his neighbours were of the same mind. He was very conscious of the pressures they were generating throughout the Middle East. His hostility to Israel was formal, sufficient to satisfy those who considered that no true Arab should be without it. Ayatollah Khomeini he described as a man who sits in a cell seeing no newspapers, watching no television, receiving no outsiders, just reading his 'yellow books' (I wasn't clear exactly what they were). The Ayatollah had been an exile in Paris; he was now in his own country but still an exile from the world; possessed of power and influence, full of prejudice, hating people whom he hadn't met and things of which he knew nothing. The Russians, the Foreign Minister thought, had made a monumental error in invading Afghanistan; it had cost them the goodwill of the Third World.

In Delhi we steamed gently in the August heat for two days, but achieved some sightseeing before going on to Kashmir where, for a month or more, we were either staying with the Nehrus or at least under their wing. As hosts they would be hard to equal: their friendship is pure joy, full of laughter, wisdom and that quality called grace, which we in the West have come to regard as unnecessary but which in India is still cherished. They lived in a house in the hills high above the Dal Lake, looking towards the sunset. As Governor of Kashmir, he ruled over a territory as beautiful as any on earth, and at that time peaceful. There had been trouble with China in 1962; Pakistan was showing itself to be increasingly an unfriendly, troublesome neighbour. Not long after our visit, Mrs Gandhi, concerned at the way things were going, replaced B. K. Nehru with a man who, though readier to fall in with her views, was not of his quality, and it did nothing to avert the coming storm.

Fori Nehru is her husband's match. Warm-hearted, welcoming and perceptive, she devoted much of her considerable energy to 'my women', seeking to woo them away from unquestioning acceptance of the notion that men were the masters and women merely there to cook and bear numerous children. She introduced us to 'Suffering Moses', whose shop was a treasure house of beautiful things and who spent the first ten minutes lambasting the British for ever leaving India. He thought worse of the Americans who, he said, always wanted to buy everything he had in his shop: thinking about them caused him to smile upon us.

B. K. had a remarkable tale of an incident at the start of a visit of Pandit Nehru as Prime Minister of India to the USA, when President Kennedy had welcomed him as his personal guest at Hyannisport. There were only two others present, J. K. Galbraith, US Ambassador to India, and B. K. Nehru, Indian Ambassador to the United States. After lunch on the Kennedy yacht, the President had turned to the Prime Minister and told him how welcome he, as the premier statesman of Asia, would always be; but now, particularly with all the problems of South-East Asia, they knew little; they needed and would be grateful for his advice. Nehru remained silent; the President waited, clearly puzzled, as were the other two present, by the lack of response, and then

187

repeated what he had said. Again Nehru was silent, and a moment at which much of modern history might have been changed passed unnoticed. It was only later that Nehru was found to be suffering from a liver complaint which at times so affected his brain that he neither received nor understood what was said. A few days after in Washington, when the Indian Foreign Minister, Moraji Desai, said that he was going to see the Secretary of State, Dean Rusk, Nehru cut in, 'You must tell him, and tell him from me, that on no account must they get entangled in South-East Asia. It would be a disaster for all of us, and most of all for themselves, from which they would never be able to extricate themselves with credit.' That warning, if indeed it was passed on, was delivered by the wrong person to the wrong person and changed nothing.

On our first night in Srinagar there was a dinner to say goodbye to the local corps commander who was leaving to take up an appointment in Delhi. General Chibba, the Army Commander, asked if we were going to Ladakh, said we should, and told us if we did to let him know; he could and would help. A visit to the Mogul Gardens, Shalimar and Nishat offered glimpses of paradise against a backdrop of mountains, sheer and splendid, from which flows the water which refreshes the gardens and holds them together. Notices stating 'This is your garden, please don't pick the flowers' had the effect of encouraging the numerous gardeners to do just that and to proffer them to any visitor on sight. Arrangements for mowing the extensive lawns were aimed more at the preservation of jobs than at getting the best results quickly. Three men were the crew of a small, light mower. One guided and pushed it while the other two, bent double, held it down with one hand so that it actually cut, the thick grass instead of just bouncing over the top of it; with the other hand they held between them a sack which caught the mown grass. Their wage for such work is small. We in the West, of course, do things differently; we mechanize and modernize; the machine does it all, with the result that there is nothing for many people to do.

An evening trip by shikana, a long, narrow boat with room for two passengers either to sit or lie down, on the Nishat Lake: smooth water with vivid reflections of cloud and mountain; a wealth of bird life; floating gardens (made of weed gathered and compounded together). Small children wept at the sight of a camera, fearing that it contained a demon. Even in this idyllic world of peace, stillness and beauty, there is no escape from the crime and noise of our times: thieves can easily tow away a floating garden with its crops without fear of subsequent detection; water skiing provides with sudden intrusive bursts of noise a sharp reminder of how fragile a thing silence has become everywhere. When, after some hours, we landed and thanked the official of the Governor's staff who had arranged it all, he replied with warmth and that wonderful courtesy which India preserves, 'Not at all. It is absolutely our duty, and our pleasure.'

Another trip by boat, this time through Srinagar. The water, in which women washed clothes and small boys bathed, was like thick grey-brown soup, which made it impossible to see too much of what it carried. The banks, piled high with buildings, mostly of timber, provided a huge congestion of dwellings, shops and factories, with gaps only where one had recently fallen down. We visited an ancient mosque, many times destroyed and rebuilt finally by the Moghul Emperor Aurungzeb in the sixteenth century. An unusual example of tolerance in these times of fundamentalism, it carried in addition to the crescent of Islam the symbols of Hinduism and Buddhism. Its roof is supported by the massive trunks of some 370 shobar trees.

The Chief Minister, Dr Farook Abdulla, the son of Sheikh Sahib, the Lion of Kashmir, was a hollow echo of his father. An unorganized, knee-jerk man of confused instincts, he was incapable of distinguishing the things that mattered from those that did not. He had none of the good manners of India. Arriving late for an important occasion, he would offer only the tame explanation, 'I was held up.' He travelled around on a motorcycle, 'getting the feel of things' and 'keeping close to the people'. He made a practice of calling on people late at night and asking them how they – and he – were doing. He was said to talk incessantly at meetings without having first read the relevant papers. His colleagues were an unimpressive and inadequate bunch. He moved straight and honest civil servants to positions from which they could not obstruct and replaced them with those who were more accommodating. When some taxi drivers fleeced passengers

189

from the airport, the Chief Minister, as was his way, threw the baby out with the bathwater and decreed that no taxis could pick up passengers from the airport. The alternative public transport could not cope; total confusion ensued and the tourists suffered miseries. By way of contrast, when a seven-year-old Harijan girl was raped, her twenty-year-old attacker boasted that he had taught the untouchables a lesson – a lesson which, he said, had been called for because most of them had voted for Mrs Gandhi. The Chief Minister and his colleagues took no steps to bring the rapist to justice. Nor could he be relied on to stick to any undertaking; having agreed that the Chief Justice of the state should, like the Governor, come from outside, he later professed dismay that his administration should be so dictated to and refused to accept the appointment proposed. Suspension of the constitution and direct rule by the Governor began to look more and more likely.

Politicians in India are viewed even less favourably than those in the West – incompetent, arrogant, short of understanding and on the make being the usual verdicts. There, as here, the word 'politician' has almost become a term of abuse, with the result, of course, that in India, as elsewhere, better people keep away and more and more of the cheap, the conceited and the glib come crowding on to the stage. Mrs Gandhi herself seemed sharply aware of the inadequacy of most of her colleagues and associates, both at the centre and in the provinces. She reacted by keeping as much as she could in her own hands, and by bringing power to the centre to such an extent that urgently needed decisions were long delayed and fundamental issues such as constitutional reform and the appalling pollution were put aside altogether.

In a land where disorder and muddle seem at times overwhelming, the smartness and discipline of the armed forces offer a striking reminder of the contrasts which India offers. Newspapers, full of stories of brutality and extortion by the police, carry no such tales about the Army. The officers whom we saw were as disciplined as the men they commanded. Dedicated to the service of their country, they were as determined to secure that military decisions should be for them as they were to keep out of political involvement. The Governor's ADC, who had charge of us from time to time, explained that to become an officer you must first undergo four years' training, the first two devoted to character-building. Whereas in earlier times officers came from the educated and moneyed classes, this had changed, and although army pay was not generous, it was sufficient. The police, on the other hand, were so grossly underpaid that extortion and bribes were common practice. He had no criticism of the generals, whom he admired for their dedication and professional skills; he had little regard for politicians. Arms were bought even-handedly from East and West. Those from Britain, he said, were supplied with complete up-to-date material and with the full technology; those from Russia were old and used, but cheap – tanks designed for use in Siberia were apt to become overheated in the plains of India.

In due course, we took General Chibba's advice and went to Ladakh; it was in many ways the high point of our visit, perhaps one of the most memorable experiences of our lives. Our flight took us across the Himalayas along the Indus valley and into Leh, the capital, 11,000 feet above sea level. The area around Leh is a rocky, bare plateau, with few trees, sparse vegetation and not much oxygen; one needs time to get used to the height and the thin air. On the first morning I awoke with a headache which might well have been the product of a wild night, though I had on advice drunk nothing. From the moment of our arrival until our departure, the Army took us in hand. The Divisional Commander, General Rodriguez, and those under his command welcomed us, planned our visit and made arrangements which we could not possibly have expected and certainly could not have made for ourselves.

The General suggested that we might go to the Pangong Lake on the Tibetan border on the far side of the Karakorams, forbidden territory to all except the military. He would lend us his jeep, complete with driver, and provide an escorting officer. Before we were allowed to go we were given a very thorough medical check-up at the military hospital, which they claimed was the best of its kind in Asia. In a country which has its full share of poor people it is striking, particularly in a remote area such as Ladakh, how the Army, far from provoking resentment and hostility, is respected and welcomed. The Division which was then based on Leh had, since 1962, been kept on full alert and at full strength. In 1962 Chinese forces had entered Ladakh, the frontier of which was undefended. On the orders of the Minister of Defence, Krishna Menon, troops from the south had been sent up in the light uniforms they wore and without any training in mountain warfare, with inevitable results; the Army had then resolved that purely military moves would only be made on orders given by its own commanders. There were outposts more than 200 miles from Leh, one in the mountains at a height of 19,000 feet.

Although races were mixed, with battalions of Dogras, Sikhs, Nagas and Mahrattas, there were no communal problems, since there was no one whose interest lay in stirring them up. Communications are difficult, particularly in winter when the mountain passes are blocked. Aircraft cannot be sure of getting in: even in July, the month before we were there, only one civil flight got into Leh. The temperature ranges from 60 or 70 degrees Centigrade in the summer to minus 40 degrees in the winter. The Army has two roles, first to defend the frontiers of India and second to care for the civilian population. The Development Commissioner, an able and charming Ladakhi, told us that he had once been asked what problems he had with the Army; 'Problems with the Army?' he had replied, 'The Army solves our problems.' A school run by the Army, to which children from a vast and barren catchment area came to live, was convincing evidence of that.

We visited Hemis, travelling on oiled roads along the sandy floor of the valley in sight of the fast-flowing Indus. Apart from occasional oases, there was no vegetation; no trees softened the fierce façade of the hills. At the monastery we were received by the head Lama: aged forty-six, he had been selected for the post when he was four as a result of long prayerful procedures which had shown him to be the reincarnation of his predecessors. He felt the heat in summer, but – and he attributed this to a physical abnormality – the cold in winter not at all. Tourists, he said, were disturbing to the peace and contemplation of monastic life and they were coming here, as everywhere, in ever-greater numbers. The building, four hundred years old and in poor repair, offers little protection against extremes of heat or cold. It is also a treasure house, with a massive statue of the Buddha made of gold and silver; there are manuscripts in Tibetan with lettering of solid gold; there are frescoes of beautiful colouring, all valued not for material worth, but as spiritual heirlooms. When I asked if they were worried about thieves, the head Lama replied that they were not; the manuscripts were in Tibetan and therefore not of interest to Westerners who didn't understand the language; maybe, I said, but they were well aware of the value of gold. He was a man wise and unstained, who seemed not to care for the things which we think matter most.

In mid-August we visited Tangtse, headquarters of the 114th Infantry Brigade. In the course of a four-hour journey by a road at times more of a hope or a line on the map than a means of passage, we crossed the mountains in a blizzard by the Chang La pass at over 17,000 feet above sea level. There is a temple there, near the top of the world, where all can worship God without being told or telling others who God is. 'There is one God,' we were told, 'but wise men know him by many names.' Just after we started the descent from the top of the pass, our driver, who had been wonderfully skilful in negotiating the hazards of the road, failed to observe a substantial boulder: our vehicle shot up in the air and descended with a shattering bump. Although we didn't realize it at the time Mary had cracked two vertebrae, a source of pain for a long time to come. On the next day we made another four-hour drive, again along crude tracks, to the Pangong Lake, which we reached at the point where it turns north into Tibet. The water is beautiful, its bright colour changing with the wind and light from turquoise to dark blue; coming straight off the high mountains, the water is so cold that you couldn't live in it for more than a minute. We saw yaks and goats which seemed able to manage the climate; we were welcomed, at the few settlements we passed, by friendly people – the women generously decorated with turquoise, but with few other possessions. A box of matches, since it saved the labour of making fire by other more primitive means, was a most welcome gift.

In the Brigade mess in the evening the conversation showed how successful the Russians had been in suggesting that it is the Americans who are the exploiters and the destroyers and themselves the saviours; Afghanistan had begun to give rise to second thoughts. Reagan was spoken of as one akin to the Devil, his only human trait being a likeness to Machiavelli. The Falklands and the success of British troops had impressed and pleased our hosts and caused them to favour British weapons, despite their cost, of which they were very conscious. Again we encountered that same hostility towards and massive mistrust of politicians; but, as elsewhere, low opinions did nothing to damp down expectations; miracles could still reasonably be expected.

The journey back was in better weather, with wonderful scenery, this time clearly visible – but with agony for Mary. In Leh the General moved us from the hotel into the HQ mess, where we were well looked after. We saw Stok, the only royal palace still used. The Queen or Ranee was away: she has much treasure but little money, her income arising from rent received from peasants who farm her lands – they pay only what they can afford. We wondered at the way in which such gentle people contend with the ferocity of the climate; we wondered too how Buddhism, with its message of loving kindness, could survive the fierce intolerance of Islamic fundamentalism and the harshness of Chinese Communism. We had a splendid soldier servant, who did his utmost despite some language difficulties. When I asked him one morning if he had seen my razor, which I couldn't find, he was much upset by the idea that I suspected he had stolen it. It took time and the help of an officer to reassure and comfort him and to explain that nothing was further from my mind. He could not be persuaded one evening that Mary, in bed and in pain, wanted only a boiled egg for supper. In the hope that he was married or contemplating marriage, I bought him a bracelet to give to his beloved: he thanked me profusely and said she lived in Jammu. It transpired that he had neither a wife, nor the prospect of one; he hadn't liked to say so because it would, he felt, have disappointed me. He spent, I was told, an afternoon of anguish wondering how he was going to explain it all.

We left India in 1983 and, forgetting what a magnet that huge reservoir of humanity is, had thought it unlikely that we would return. Ten years later, in 1993, we did so, largely because B. K. Nehru had told us firmly that his travelling days were over and that we must go to him. We thought we should take the opportunity to see something of the south. With some advice from B. K. and from Robert and Sally Wade-Gery – Robert had been High Commissioner in Delhi ten years before – and with the expert assistance of Mr Shuban from Pleasure Seekers travel agents in the Haymarket, a plan was produced. It set out a tour of just over a month, during which we were to stay in nineteen different hotels, visit more than a hundred sites and travel by train or taxi over considerable distances. Air travel would be impossible for most of the time, since Indian National Airlines pilots would almost certainly be on strike. The plan was a mixture of his suggestions and our stated requirements, which we changed many times. Moreover, only days before we were due to leave an outbreak of communal troubles and the advice of the Indian High Commissioner in London that we would be unwise to go caused us to cancel the whole thing. Happily, after a few hours' dithering we reinstated everything. Mr Shuban took it all with that unruffled calm with which India accepts the upsets of life. In the morning he cancelled and in the afternoon resurrected, whole and unscathed, the plans he had made for us.

Bombay, normally free of communal troubles, had had a burst of rioting stirred up by politicians who, not unusually, saw advantage for themselves in acting as mouthpieces, even amplifiers, of every opinion which had in it the seeds of conflict. To the fury of the Muslims, a mosque at Ayodha had been pulled down to make way for a Hindu temple marking the birthplace of Rama, one of the incarnations of the god Vishnu. Legend has it that he had been in some difficulty when engaged in a war against the demons and had sent Hanuman, the Monkey God, to obtain supplies of a certain herb which would revive his soldiers. Hanuman flew off at the speed of light but, unsure on arrival as to which herb was required, brought back the mountain on which it grew.

Rather than face the awful journey into the city of Bombay, we spent a night at the airport hotel before going on by air to Bangalore, the principal city of Karnataka – a journey which we achieved despite the Indian Airlines pilots' strike. The name Bangalore had evolved over time from Bendakalooru – town of boiled beans – given by a king to commemorate the diet on which he had been fed by an old woman who had found him when he was lost in the jungle. From a brief visit in 1946 I had memories of a well-ordered city with rather stately buildings and excellent roads. Since then the ocean of modern India had flowed over it, leaving the racecourse, some parks and gardens and buildings of obvious British origin as islands in the tumult and confusion of what had become an important and thriving industrial centre. The road system and the infrastructure generally are barely able to handle the phenomenal growth which has taken place; massive congestion and heavy pollution are the price of years of neglecting basic needs. Our hotel, with a garden of its own, quiet, peaceful, and of a very high standard, seemed far removed from the throng immediately outside its gates.

While in the cities congestion is such as to eliminate the possibility of speed, elsewhere it is a frequent hazard. Men who not all that long ago drove carts as fast as they could persuade bullocks to go now do the same with modern heavy trucks, competing with each other to occupy the often narrow strip on which it is possible to travel at speed. Indifferent maintenance of both roads and vehicles; determination on the part of the drivers to get there fast and ahead of the pursuing demons; a fair quota of the traditional bullock carts driven by people who don't seem to notice the change and to whom the rules of the road are totally alien; these together make road travel in India speculative and hazardous. Many drivers wisely avail themselves of the protection of one or other of the gods, a model of whom is prominently displayed on the dashboard. Ganesh, the remover of obstacles, having the head of an elephant, is perhaps the most favoured. It is said that Shiva, returning from a long absence, found his wife Parvati tucked up in bed with a young man and, failing to realize it was his own son, in a rage cut off the young man's head. Repentant and full of apologies when he understood what he had done, he promised to provide his son with the head of the first living creature to appear; it chanced to be an elephant.

Pushpa, our guide, was a Hindu studying for her doctorate in Sanskrit. Charming and intelligent, she guided us expertly through the labyrinth of the Hindu hierarchy. She explained that, since few found it possible to meditate upon the wholly abstract, there had been a need first for symbols, which, to make things easier, had tended to take on human form and character. Thereafter it was only a matter of time before legend provided them with the paraphernalia of human existence. At the top there are three, Brahma, Vishnu and Shiva. Brahma created the universe and so perhaps because his task is over and not therefore a source of future favours, attracts little popular support compared with the other two. Vishnu the preserver has hosts of followers and many temples are sacred to him. There will, it is said, be in all ten incarnations of Vishnu; of the nine who have already made their appearance, Rama, Krishna and Buddha are the most recent. Kalka, a messiah and a warrior mounted on a white horse, is the one still awaited; his role will be to bring the world and the mess which man has made of it to an end.

It is, of course, easy to mock Hinduism, based as it is on myth and legend, with a legion of gods and goddesses round whom is woven a fabric of fantastic tales. It is less easy and certainly wrong to ignore the devotion of its followers, whose varied needs it meets, or to dismiss the wisdom of its teaching. It is hardly possible, save with closed eyes, to be unaware of the great flowering of artistic skill which decorates its places of worship, and it is a supreme irony that with Hinduism, as with other faiths, all that is most pure and gentle is trampled underfoot by zealots who claim to know the mind of God. Without basic awareness of what Hinduism consisted of, our visits to numerous temples and the sight we had of the marvellous stone carvings would have had much less meaning.

The three wonderful Hoysala temples, Somnathpur, Belur and Halebid, we saw almost on our own, since the airline strike had pretty well wiped out the package tours. Only at one temple did we have to wait for a massive German lady wearing strong and unsuitable colours to remove herself almost from the arms of Vishnu before it was possible to take a photograph. Like other temples in south India, their entrance is known as the Gopuram, the place of the cow, the idea being that man entering the presence of God should seek to emulate the cow, which can apparently only handle one idea at a time, and centre his thoughts on God. Halebid has been compared and contrasted with the Parthenon. One expert on Indian architecture, James Fergusson, wrote: 'All that is wild in human faith and warm in human feeling is found portrayed within these walls.' Such wonders as these, with their outpouring of human skills and imagination, all of them dedicated to an unending search for God, offer even to the restless tourist an extraordinary and unforgettable spiritual experience.

Before we started out Robert and Sally Wade-Gery had rightly insisted that we must on no account leave out Hampi (Vijayanagar), of which we had never heard but which they described as the Angkor Wat of India. It entailed a long and hazardous drive, the last fifty miles being by a road of which the crown was a strictly one-way affair, for which vehicles travelling in opposite directions were forced to compete; this usually meant that at the very last minute the smaller lurched to one side and off the road, hoping to make a soft landing. The hazards of the journey and the austerity of the hotel at Hospet were, however, a small price to pay for what we saw. For three or four centuries, until it was sacked by Aurungzeb in 1565, Hampi had been a rich and civilized community of a million or so people. Despite systematic looting and massive destruction by the Muslim conquerors, many beautiful buildings still survive.

It is a wonderful legacy from what must have been a prosperous community, talented and peace-loving to a degree rare in human history. The temples, the palaces, the guard house, the elephant stables and the market survive as symbols of an artistic and civilized people. In the courtyard of the Vitthala Temple, which is the centrepiece of this amazing place, there is a chariot, carved out of a single piece of granite and raised from the ground, with wheels which can be turned. The stonework of the temple itself is exquisite. A vegetarian establishment next door to our hotel provided basic requirements; its proprietor, friendly and welcoming, besought us to visit him in his house for a meal, which was quite a ceremony and beautifully cooked. Only when we insisted did he agree to join us; the ladies just brought in the food and watched us eat it. The seven-year-old son of the house, under no such restraint, ate with his hands, but, lacking the necessary skill, fed more or less equally all parts of his face.

Having survived the perils of the return journey, we spent a night in luxury in Bangalore before taking the train to Madras. As we drew into the station, I caught sight of a large and splendid lady bearing down the platform towards us like a ship under full sail. She had, she said, been receiving daily messages from her office in Delhi instructing her to take utmost care of us; we were regarded clearly as being both difficult, which we may have been, and important, which we were not. Some simply beautiful bronzes of the tenth and eleventh centuries in the Museum; the Kapaleeshwara Temple, dedicated to Shiva; and St Mary's church, built by the East India Company in 1653, made an odd mixture – the church seemed not to belong, to have been left behind. From Covelong and Fisherman's Cove, some ten or twenty miles out of Madras, we made visits to Mahabalipuram and Kanchipuram.

The former was certainly, with Hampi, one of the high points of our tour. There are a series of temple-like structures hewn out of granite monoliths on the site where they had always been. So skilful is the sculpting that only when you get close do you see that the structure is a monolith without interiors: a massive wall of granite with a relief of elephants and, above them, a whole host of figures carved in the solid rock. One can only wonder at the patience and skill of those who, with the primitive tools available, brought these amazing things almost to life out of that hard material. Kanchipuram (Kanchi), a city of temples and silk and pilgrims, is one of the most sacred cities of India. Our guide – and she was almost a teacher – was concerned to explain how for her the Hindu religion was an attempt to bring God and man closer together and in the direction of mutual understanding, towards a world in which each would care for the other. The joy that she derived from the Hindu faith was a world away from the ferocity and violence of fundamentalism.

It is a sad fact of modern life that many, if not most, airports are such ghastly and unwelcoming places. They seem too often to be packed with people whose skills lie in composing fatuous rules for passengers to comply with or perhaps were acquired in cattle markets. Delhi Airport is no exception, though there we did manage to dodge one queue by presenting our passports at a desk marked 'Diplomats Only'. In a contest, however, to make the visitor feel that he is of no importance, that he is unwelcome and that he has made a mistake in coming at all, Miami Airport would come out an easy winner, with perhaps Athens second.

XII

People of Influence: Jones, Buggins, the Duke of York – and the Media

Evil communications corrupt good manners.
Corinthians I 15:33

By the early eighties I had been more than thirty years in the House of Commons, had no prospect of being in office again and was well on the way to an old age pension. It was not difficult to call it a day, particularly as I was at least likely to be made a peer. I hoped that some of what I had been able to do in my constituency would prove useful, and I knew – and this was important to me as well as to them – that from time to time I had been able to give some help and comfort to those who had been in need or distress. Beyond that, I felt as if I had been following the course of a river, sometimes carried along by its flow, at other times walking rather slowly along its almost dried up bed or along its banks, or stuck in some backwater into which I had somehow wandered. It was a process which affected in many and different ways those who took part in it; some it drowned in the force of its passage; others it left washed up on its banks; some it carried to modest achievement; others, just a few, to the edges of greatness.

There must have been around two thousand individuals who were Members of Parliament in my time; few can have remained unaffected by the experience. Belonging to an institution which has been so long at the centre of the nation's life, which has absorbed the convulsions of change without being buried in its debris is a long way from the merely humdrum. On arrival, the newcomer, one of a collection of disparate individuals, will be

200

linked up, as it were, to a central nervous system and subjected to restraints and pressures which only an ancient institution with deep roots in history can exert. First and foremost, there is the intricate web of its own procedures, rituals and rules; then there are the attitudes and habits of those who have been part-digested by the system; there are also the influences and the expectations of Whips, constituents and the media; last, but perhaps not least, there come the hopes and ambitions of the individual.

It hardly needs to be said that the institution of Parliament requires to be propped up and sustained by a scaffolding of popular regard and respect: without that, it would soon take on the sad look of a dead tree or an empty house. Those who make a practice of showering the individual politician with the acid rain of contempt and derision should at least take care that they don't in the process do too much damage to an institution which it would be difficult to replace.

One of the trials of the modern world is the unceasing battery of instant communication, which keeps us abreast of all that is unpleasant, wrong or alarming. We are forever being reminded of the blemishes and wrongdoings of individuals, the misdemeanours of government, the imperfections of institutions and the general unfairnesses of society. Politicians and governments, shocked by the barrage, tend more and more to run for the cover of short-term, popular approval and get themselves involved, as a result, in measures which irritate and annoy but do little to solve the problem. I have in mind measures such as the Dangerous Dogs Act, the Firearms Bill and, in early 1997, the proposed BSE-related selective cull of cattle – the latter without any firm undertaking as to when or even if the ban on the export of British beef would be lifted. There used, not many years ago, to be a gloomy archway leading from Whitehall to Richmond Terrace Mews; on either side and rather in shadow was a notice: 'Commit No Nuisance'. Perhaps that laconic instruction, which sought to restrain those who had in mind the relief of a temporary and personal need, should now be reissued to those in Whitehall and Westminster who intend things far more disturbing.

Such measures are undertaken either in response to great pressure or simply because it has become necessary to be seen to be doing something. Even worse is the habit of tampering for no very sound reason with things which are part of the equipment of government without first explaining, discussing and even doing a bit of listening. Some Ministers seem unaware that that is what ears are for, and believe that they are for ornamental purposes only; as a result they get into bad habits. The Government, in selling for a relatively unimportant sum the Recruitment and Assessment Services of the Civil Service of the Civil Service, and in its plans for the Whitehall Estate, has shown blinding arrogance – an updated definition, for those who seek one, of the Greek word *hubris*.

No commentary upon government and upon the way we conduct our affairs would be complete without some reference to three legendary characters who wield a great and continuing influence: they are Jones, Buggins and the Duke of York. The first is the man of the moment, the one in fashion, with whom you must keep up; the second is the one who, for no better reason than that it seems fair, must be given a turn; the third, and perhaps the most influential, is the one who marches us first up the hill, then down again – an expert in U-turns. Anyone seeking to understand how other supposedly sensible people came to do things plainly futile, might be well advised at least to consider the possibility that it was the influence of one of these three which brought it about.

In 1983 I was made a peer. Alec Home and Solly Zuckerman made an unusual and distinguished pair of sponsors when I took my seat; I wasn't at all sure how well they knew or liked each other. I have spoken of Alec elsewhere; all I would add now was that he had about him a quality – perhaps grace is the right word – which made him all but invulnerable and certainly secure against the maggots who find dismantling reputations profitable. I had been reluctant to ask him, but was encouraged to do so by his wife, Elizabeth, who said of course he would. She was one who lived on a different level from most of us, seeing and caring for the things that are important, but which too often we contrive to miss.

Solly was unique; he arrived in this country from Cape Town University in the early twenties, bringing with him no assets other than his considerable talents. His first move in a long and remarkable career was to the London Zoo, which as Secretary and President he was to run for some fifty years. As Chief Scientific and Defence Adviser to successive Governments over many years, he enjoyed in war and peace the confidence and trust of a succession of Prime Ministers from Churchill to Thatcher. Few have remained so long in such a position or survived so many changes of government. By the end of his long life, his experience and knowledge covered a great range of people and events. He was on terms which allowed him access to many eminent persons in all parts of the world, whose doors were barred to most. Discreet in what mattered, he made no attempt either to adjust or conceal his opinions of people – and yet he survived. He ended as a peer with the Order of Merit, an honour which still deserves its name.

It would be wrong, and Solly himself would have been amazed, to paint him as altogether immaculate; he was not. He could be, and often was, intensely irritating and seemed to enjoy being so. One sign both of his unusual endurance and of the position he had carved out for himself was his continued tenure of two rooms plus a secretary in the Cabinet Office for some years after he had reached the age of eighty and had ceased to occupy any official position. Space in such places is jealously guarded, and such is the strength of the Establishment's excretory muscle that an occupant is ejected immediately he ceases to be whatever he was. Exceptionally, Solly remained sitting there in the very centre of the web; no one seemed to know why, or if they did, they were not in any hurry to explain. Since it was he who, at about that time, had persuaded me to become involved in the affairs of the Zoo, I felt that the least he could do was to make himself responsible for me on my introduction into the House of Lords.

The ceremony is a piece of historic ritual, which, rather surprisingly, has escaped that paint-stripping process to which we are inclined to subject traditional courtesies. The newcomer and his sponsors wear robes, usually borrowed, and carry hats of a kind you would never wear or expect to see anyone else wearing outside a theatre. Without them, the new entrant and his sponsors would be unable to salute the Lord Chancellor, who, so that he can respond, wears a three-cornered hat on top of his full-bottomed wig. Preceded by Garter King of Arms, who, parcelled up in the Royal Arms, looks rather like a King from a pack of cards, and followed by Black Rod, they march in, in line. When the new peer, on one knee, has presented his writ of summons to the Lord Chancellor and taken the oath, the three of them, guided by Garter, take their seats on one of the backbenches, put on their hats, rise, take them off again and bow; having done so three times, they process out of the Chamber. It is a ceremony which could easily be made to sound ridiculous and which those of a modernizing turn of mind might be tempted to do away with; there are other and more serious obstacles to progress which could be tackled first.

I made my maiden speech opposing a motion that the proceedings of the House should be televised. It was moved by Christopher Soames, who told me that I should have supported my friends. I believed that the introduction of such an intrusive and powerful medium, the principal aim of which is to entertain, stir up or shock, would unduly change the ways and manners of the place; in that I was wrong. My other thought, and here I was nearer the mark, was that all that the TV moguls really wanted was the key to the House of Commons; they realized that if the Lords were well received, the Commons would not wish to be left out in the cold. The motion was carried, the cameras were duly installed and the House of Lords received for a time much unaccustomed attention; seeing which, the Commons were quick to follow suit. The television people, persistent, concerned solely with audience ratings or profits, got, as usual, what they wanted. What, if anything, the House of Commons gained is a matter of opinion: the ridiculous, the rowdy, the rude and the discreditable are highlighted, the more serious stuff neglected.

No one seeking from a scratch start to plan and establish a second Chamber would be likely to come up with the idea of the House of Lords as it is. Unelected, with a substantial hereditary element, having very limited powers, and none at all over money, it lacks the muscle to take on a determined and extremist House of Commons. Yet, with the duty to review legislation both generally and in detail, it is able to remedy at least some of the defects in the torrent of legislation which flows through Parliament and which, like other torrents, carries a quantity of garbage with it. Abolition of what can easily be portrayed as an antiquated and anachronistic institution may seem at first sight to be easy and popular. On the other hand, admiration for and trust in the House of Commons is not so widespread and unqualified that people would be entirely happy to see it set free – free, if it saw fit, to prolong its own life and that of its masters. Moreover, a second Chamber which was simply a mirror image of the Commons might strike some as a nightmare prospect. Since neither saints nor angels are much in evidence, it would be going too far to describe the House of Lords as Heaven. Only when it is compared with the House of Commons does it begin to take on something of a celestial aura.

While the Commons may regard the Lords as a bit of a nuisance from time to time, they might well find an alternative with new and added powers much less easy to live with. While they might cheer the disappearance of the hereditary element, they would certainly not welcome any proposal that they should yield some of their powers and privileges to a reformed second Chamber – even less one that involved a reduction in their own numbers. Do we really need as many as 650? The United States, rather bigger than we are, makes do with a lot less. Would a reformed second Chamber be elected or nominated, and, in either case, by whom and for what term? How many members would there be? Would there be a place for crossbenchers, or would they all be party nominees? It might prove quite difficult to find an acceptable replacement which did not involve a huge extension of the Prime Minister's powers of patronage. The additional cost might also be something of a stumbling-block.

The process of debate and reform could well be so protracted that a new Government with many other problems on its hands would be tempted to settle for some fudged measure, which would solve nothing and please no one. Meanwhile, something of value could be lost. The House of Lords does offer at a modest cost a convenient way of leavening the lump of professional politicians, of involving in the process of Government men and women from the Church, the law, the Civil Service, medicine, the universities, industry (both sides), the armed forces and more recently, not before it was due, the police and the social services. The truly remarkable Lucy Faithfull, who died in March 1996 aged eighty-five, was, so far as I am aware, the only peer who had spent her life as a social worker. It was her particular belief that, in order to achieve 'a relationship of lasting value, a social worker must surely have touched the garment of God', something which she surely achieved.

I was privileged to give the address at her Memorial Service; some words from it push to be included here:

Lucy was first and last a social worker, a role which she so lit up as to make it at least the equal of any other. Her concern for the vulnerable, the lonely and the dying was an imperative and a source of almost unceasing energy; children unloved, neglected, abused and damaged were her especial care. She enjoyed the House of Lords, which did not, in her view, stand in quite such urgent need of reform as some now suggest. She respected it, and she was angry when a rather tiresome person with one of those in-built sneers which are the fashion of our time set out to trivialize it in a film made for television. She welcomed and used to the full the opportunities which the House of Lords gave her to speak for those whose voices are barely audible above the din of modern times.

It was characteristic of her to want to share such an institution with people, particularly the young, who might not otherwise see it. On one occasion a number of those whom she had come to know through their problems – she called them 'my children' – arrived on a visit. A watchful attendant pointed out to her that they were all chewing gum, a habit not generally indulged in within those precincts. She issued instructions that the chewing should cease and was at once obeyed. Reflecting upon this later and wondering what had happened to the gum, she went back along the route which the group had taken and retrieved a quantity of it from various places in which it had been hurriedly stowed away. Most of us would have let things be; not so Lucy. In that, as in so much else, she was different.

Few, if any, such people would even think of fighting an election; yet to remove them and put in their place a crowd of party liners and hacks, easy meat for the Whips, would not be much of a forward step. One wholly undesirable, but likely, consequence of reform could well be the disappearance of the crossbencher, who would

206

follow the independent MP into limbo. In parallel with that would be a further enhancement of the power and influence of 'the Party'. Knowledge of the ways of political parties would be all-important to the new entrant; a period of time as a research assistant to a Minister or MP would be an altogether better qualification than a career, no matter how successful, in industry, business or one of the professions.

The storm of change which has been shaking the world for the past two centuries has made it a smaller and more dangerous place, in which the problems, already daunting, are likely to increase. The need will be for people with something more than the parlour tricks of party politics to handle them. The fact that Governments and Ministers are regularly dwarfed and made to look silly by events, and the dimension of change has not, oddly enough, caused them to look for better ways of doing things. In their war with the media, they have seen the need to be more for clever presentation and attractive packaging than for coherent thought.

Politicians are not and probably never have been well thought of at any time anywhere. It is their misfortune that the low regard in which they are held is not matched by correspondingly low expectations; very much the reverse: miracles are regularly looked for. Aristophanes saw 'a horrible voice, bad breath and a vulgar manner' as the characteristics of a politician. Swift, in *Gulliver's Travels*, saw 'ignorance, idleness and vice as the best ingredients for qualifying a legislator'. 'An honest man in politics shines more than he would elsewhere,' was the view of Mark Twain. Hilaire Belloc's verse echoes the thoughts of many:

> With pomp and ridiculous display
> The Politician's corpse they laid away.
> While all of his acquaintance sneered and slanged,
> I wept for I had longed to see him hanged.

There have been numberless occasions when irate or disappointed people have emptied out over me their stores of invective; two were unforgettable. Some years back, I was travelling in a London taxi when the driver asked me if a group of hippies, who had taken possession of a house in Piccadilly, were still there.

Without pausing for an answer, he launched into a vigorous and colourful denunciation of people who neither washed nor worked. I listened for a while until my attention wandered. When I came back to him he was still in full flood, but aiming at a different target – politicians, whom he put on much the same level as the hippies. I felt I had better come clean and confessed, with some trepidation, that I was one. Silent for a minute or so, either from shock or because of the traffic, he half turned his head towards me and, with a contempt that was monumental, delivered this memorable judgement: 'Guv, you ain't got a fucking clue.' I told him rather feebly that he was probably speaking for the whole of the British people about those who were so unwise as to become involved in handling their affairs.

A letter from a chartered accountant in Northwood conveyed a similar message, though in different language. He attributed the grossly inflationary situation in which we found ourselves to many years of incompetent intervention by government. 'It is *your* fault,' he wrote, 'Ministers and MPs alike who, with typical arrogance, claim to have the knowledge and ability to run the country. Some of you could not run successfully a Sunday School Summer Outing.' He went on to deplore 'the holier-than-thou tone of voice which you people use'. 'You are not better than us, in most cases, you are worse – conceited, vain, voluble, tricky, unreliable', etc. etc. Comments such as those can hardly be shrugged off as expressions of an irritation which will pass; they seem to me to reflect a distaste – to use no stronger term – altogether more deep-rooted. Convictions such as the cab driver's that politicians don't begin to understand how life appears to ordinary people, and the anger of the chartered accountant at finding himself represented by and his affairs in the hands of people at once inadequate and presumptuous, are both widespread and deep-rooted. The politician, in peace at any rate, cannot bring himself to say that events are more powerful than he is, and that the world's problems are not mathematical conundra to be solved with time and thought but the winds of a storm which has not ceased to rage.

Expectations would perhaps be more modest if people were to have in mind the fact that we not only have representative government but studiously avoid anything that smacks of an elite.

It ought not to be a cause for surprise if, among those whom we choose to represent us, there emerge from time to time some undoubted villains and charlatans: John Wilkes, Horatio Bottomley and, more recently, Robert Maxwell, as well as a number of other more minor defaulters, come to mind. Such names should at least remind us that the House of Commons is an assembly which is, above all, mixed; mixed, that is, in terms of age, sex, experience, ability and integrity. It manifestly is not an assembly of the elite – the very word sends shivers down sensitive egalitarian spines – of wise men and women, all in their prime, especially selected for their expertise in anything. While with time knowledge does rub off on some, MPs would, if that knowledge or even the ability to acquire it were a pre-requisite, have to be chosen by very different means.

The House of Commons is, and is designed to be, a mirror echoing and reflecting what is going on now; its concern is to redress, even exploit, grievances, misfortunes or disasters, rather than prevent them. It registers rather than initiates changes, and it does that quite quickly: 'A week,' said Harold Wilson in a much-quoted sentence, 'is a long time in politics.' Less well known on this side of the Atlantic is the reply of Lyndon Johnson, another consummate politician, to a journalist who accused him of inconsistency; he had dismissed Nixon as chicken shit one week and welcomed him as a hero the next. 'Son, in politics you've got to learn that overnight chicken shit can change into chicken salad.' In echoing, as it does, public moods, concerns and discontents, the House of Commons acts as a kind of ventilator, letting in the fresh air and releasing to the atmosphere the toxic gases which have been generated by the community as a whole – in much the same way as the exhaust pipe on a motor vehicle.

Expectations might be further modified if we were to reflect upon the process by which acceptable candidates for Parliament are selected. The first step for the aspirant is to assert, without being called upon to provide supporting evidence, that he or she is a fit and proper person to have a part in the government of the country; the second, since there are now, sadly, no independents, is to secure the endorsement of one or other of the major political parties. Since they are normally ready to welcome anyone who is neither seriously unpopular nor a proven criminal, this presents no major difficulty. The third and final step, which may take time, is to find a constituency in which his or her chosen party needs a candidate, and to persuade those who do the selection that he is the one they need. The committee will be largely self-chosen, with no particular qualification other than being able and willing to find the time. The questioning will be prolonged rather than penetrating; the essentials for the occasion will be a loose acceptance of the policies of the party, the ability to string together a few sentences into the form of a speech, a measure of self-confidence and a presentable spouse. They will be looking for someone who broadly shares their views and will fit in locally, rather than one cast in a more heroic mould; someone who will take care of local matters and won't be diverted into larger issues.

It all rather fits in with the views expressed by Garry Wills in a discerning article in the American *Harper's* magazine. It was entitled 'Hurrah for Politicians'. 'Politicians', he wrote, 'have many virtues which ignorant people take for vices.' He went on to list them: compromise of principle, egotism and mediocrity. 'People do not like', he wrote, 'to be ruled by their superiors. They will settle for their equals, but prefer their inferiors. They like to feel that they are too smart to be deceived by a politician; so just to be safe they choose politicians too dumb to do so.' Egotism he thought particularly important; 'it is flexible, it relaxes to the tickle of acclaim'. He ended the article thus: 'virtue and brilliance are uncommon, volatile, distrusted. We need men we can trust.'

If what Mr Wills wrote is even halfway to being true and fair – and I believe it comes a great deal nearer than that – we ought not to be too surprised when it turns out that some of those elected possess neither exceptional talents nor impregnable virtue. Plainly, it is not sufficient to keep banging on about either the inadequacies of politicians or the future of our institutions. There is nothing new in such complaints; history affords few examples of times in which people considered themselves to be well governed and not many in which, with hindsight, they were. Politicians are not well thought of and probably never have been at any time, anywhere. Perhaps Charles James Fox saw things in a truer perspective; in a letter written from Naples in 1796, he abruptly changed the subject from his own sexual activities to politics, which he described as 'a good amusement, tho' a bad employment'. Whether they are still as amusing as he found them depends upon your point of view; certainly, as many have found since, they remain, if not a bad employment, at least somewhat precarious.

Realising Our Potential – something which, incidentally, we have long failed to do – was the title of a White Paper in May 1993 which contained a strategy for science, engineering and technology. It was presented to Parliament by William Waldegrave, surely one of the most modest as well as the most intelligent of our Ministers. The paper defined an area in which we had markedly failed; it signalled a welcome conversion on the part of the Government from the old detached hands-off approach to something more positive. It was not long, however, before Waldegrave was moved and the Office of Science and Technology, which had been set up to oversee the new policy, was removed from the Cabinet Office and gobbled up by the Department of Trade and Industry, a huge octopus which has never shown any great liking for strategies. The move remains a cause for concern, even dismay.

Failure to accord their proper place to science and engineering has long been a source of weakness; there is, I have been told, one engineer in the Treasury – a single David in a regiment of Goliaths. There have, of course, been other sources of weakness less easily defined: the ingrained addiction to self-disparagement and to confrontation; an ambivalent, even hostile, attitude to success – 'fat cats' and similar gibes. Perhaps Reggie Maudling, in a single sentence in an article in *The Times* not long before he died, came as near the mark as anyone: 'We have lost our pride, but kept our conceit.' Those words were certainly a necessary reminder to me that, although they are both as close to each other as are the two sides of the same coin, they are at least as different. Whereas the former carries with it standards to be observed and ideals sustained, the latter teaches only rights and entitlements; it suggests that you can call the tune without worrying who will pay the piper.

It was pride which somehow carried us through the war; we believed, and not without reason, that had this country not miraculously survived the first tremendous onrush of Hitler's armies; had it not refused to accept that its own defeat would inevitably follow that of France; had it not withstood with courage and determination the years of bombing, the whole of Europe, including Russia, and the Middle East would have fallen and been reduced to vassalage; there wouldn't have been anything that could be called peace. All of that ghastly paraphernalia which Hitler required to sustain himself and his regime – the Nazi Party, the Gestapo, the concentration camps and the ultimate obscenity of the Final Solution – would have survived. Without this country and without its determination to resist and to endure, there would have been no platform from which to launch a new crusade.

Thereafter, it was not pride but conceit which led us to believe that we had earned a rest and even some reward; that we were and would always be better than others, without effort, and that we could now go back to where we had been in 1939. The harsh reality was that the huge turmoil of the war had left nothing unchanged; whereas America, the powerhouse of the war effort, had emerged from it as the richest and most powerful nation in the world, we were both weaker and poorer. Not only were we not in line for the aid poured out to others, but even Lease-Lend ceased within weeks of the war ending. Our overseas investments had been largely liquidated to repay the Americans what we had borrowed from them, at a time when we, together with our Dominions and Colonies, had been on our own. Moreover, our industry had been driven without renewal during the war years; our currency was shaky, and as a sign of the times the meat ration was at a level of not much more than a cutlet a week. The fat was gone and we had to learn a living.

The world was grey with a disappointment which pervaded everything. The peace for which we had struggled was shaky; the Russians, recently our allies, showed themselves unable even to spell good faith, let alone observe its requirements: an Iron Curtain divided, if not the world, at least Europe. Nuclear weapons, with all their hideous potential for destruction, made their appearance on both sides of the divide. The Empire was in the process of dismemberment; the Commonwealth, a larger association with looser ties, could not be counted on always to see things our way. In short, we began slowly and painfully to wake up to the fact that the world, though hugely changed, was still dangerous and that we were smaller, weaker and less important than we had been. At home the state proved less competent and much less wise than people had hoped, and certainly less able to meet the demands laid upon it. The more it provided, the more people wanted and the less keen were they to pay. Its cumbersome machine, incapable of the innovation and enterprise that were needed, discouraged them also in others; crippling taxation and a cloying cobweb of regulations ensured that enterprise didn't get out of hand.

To harp back for a moment to conceit; it is hard to avoid the conclusion that in nothing has our conceit been so monumental as in our approach to the new Europe. It almost blinded us to the reasons which led the nations of Europe to come together and to seek a means of avoiding another catastrophe. True, the vision has been muddied by every kind of stupidity; the absurd bossiness of an unelected Commission and a Franco–German axis which regards any questioning of its diktats as bloody-minded have not been helpful.

Against that, our own responses have been paralytic. At first, we applauded; then for a time we said no, it may be a good thing for you, but it is not for us; we have our Empire; we are the centre of a worldwide Commonwealth; we have our special relationship with America; we have no need of further entanglements. There followed a time in which we dithered, hoping, or seeming to hope, that the whole thing would go away. When it didn't, we said, please, we would after all like to come in, but were rejected as unfit; we tried again and were allowed in on terms. By that stage, however, the influence we might have had on the framework and the procedures had vanished; the others had come up with arrangements which suited them and which they had no mind to change just to suit an uncertain new recruit. Moreover, having joined, far from seeking friends, we have clouted everyone with our handbag and have indulged in an unending stream of petulant criticism, thus diminishing even further our influence and giving the impression to others who were there before us that we wanted nothing so much as to frustrate the whole venture.

A quite small group of Conservative MPs, whose importance has stemmed less from their qualities than from their number, have been able to hold the Government to ransom and make it look stupid; they have seemed not to understand the extent of our present involvement in Europe; that since we swim in the same quite small pool as our neighbours, we had better make sure that we have some say as to the temperature of the water. The irony is that they have done much to weaken, maybe destroy, a Government which favoured a gradual approach and sought cooperation as opposed to federation. They will have helped to bring in one which will happily go along with just those things to which they are vehemently opposed.

There has been another factor eating away at our confidence and self-respect. We have been increasingly provided by our media with an impression of ourselves, our conduct towards each other and of our institutions, which is profoundly discouraging. The message which is put out is that we are poorly served. The Crown, Parliament, the Church, the law, the Civil Service, the police; all of them are given a regular dip in sulphuric acid and, not surprisingly, little emerges looking its best.

I listen most mornings with millions of others to the *Today* radio programme, always with admiration for the skill with which it is put together and presented, but with increasing gloom as the staple diet of incompetence, injustice, failure, scandal, disease and disaster is dished out. As Ministers and others are barbecued in turn and revealed as stupid, vain, useless or worse, I wonder if those who present it with such skill pause to ask themselves what kind of impact this has on the morale of the nation as a whole. Injustice and incompetence may be shocking, but they are not new; they have been with us from the beginning and they tend to be always just that bit stronger than our desire to eliminate them; 'If', wrote Hazlitt, 'mankind had wished for what is right, they might have had it long ago.' Dwelling too much and too constantly on what is wrong, amplifying every protest and airing every grievance, real or imagined, is profoundly discouraging for all. It not only spreads a belief that the task of putting things right is beyond us, but makes service of the community appear unrewarding and hazardous.

I wonder too about Rupert Murdoch and how he intends to use that huge influence which he has acquired in our affairs. I find it difficult to understand what he wants; he is not, after all, a British citizen and he does not seem either to like us, or admire us, or even wish us well. William Shawcross, in his excellent account *Murdoch*, makes this judgement, 'and of course he took the paper into that netherland where he always goes, down market'. He quotes Murdoch himself as saying, in his early twenties, 'I hate this bloody place [London], all snow, slush, shit and starch'; it seems that he still does. Mrs Murdoch, surely a reliable witness, has this to say: 'If Rupert was a pilot, I wouldn't want to board the plane, he cuts too many corners.' To me he seems like the captain of a ship who spends his time not on the bridge, but in the engine room piling on the speed, unconcerned where the ship he is driving is going or who it hits or hurts on the way.

Having acquired great influence in this country, does he aim to make it a better place to live in? Maybe he just doesn't care. Or does he believe that power such as he possesses carries with it no responsibility? But if, contrary to appearances, he does care and does accept at least a measure of responsibility, does he believe that in order to do so it is necessary first to clear the decks of all or most of what is there now? Is the problem which would then arise – the problem of what to replace it with – a matter of concern to him?

The 'Establishment', a word which we use with a vague hostility, denoting something from which we are excluded, is useful to Mr Murdoch as a dartboard is useful in a public house – and for the same purpose. What is the purpose of flaying those who at least try to make things better? What will be gained by pulling down Mr Major, who, drenched in ridicule more than any Prime Minister in my lifetime, still survives in a way that he quite certainly would not if he were just the pitiful pygmy which Mr Murdoch's papers make him out to be? Mr Murdoch makes war on respectability, and it is always easy to deride those who seek it. But how should we judge those who seek to dismantle it? Are we to conclude that they favour what is manifestly not respectable? Many people would like to know his answers to such questions; few have such easy access to so wide an audience as he has, if he were minded to give them.

No one would be so foolish or blind as to suggest that any system of government that we might devise would ever come near to perfection; much less that any group of individuals to whom power was entrusted would ever show themselves free of fault. At the same time, those who hold the power to influence opinion need to be careful that they do not act in such a way as to make impossible the already difficult business of democratic government. If they do, and if, in addition, they make life intolerable in that already hazardous arena, they could find themselves confronted with a regime of a different order – one which regarded dissent and criticism as sinister, and opposition as treason.

XIII

Treasurer of the Zoo

Animals are such agreeable friends – they ask no questions, they pass no criticisms.

George Eliot

There wasn't, in 1984, any compelling reason for me to become involved in the Zoological Society of London. Although I had been a Fellow for some years, I hadn't taken any great interest in its affairs and had no knowledge of its problems. Yet there I was, all of a sudden its Treasurer, and as such called upon to face problems which had been piling up for years and to which there was no obvious solution. People looked at me pityingly and suggested that I had taken total leave of my senses. All that I can now say by way of explanation to myself is that, having left the House of Commons, I had some spare time, I was willing to do something for nothing, and I drew some comfort from the thought that no great shame would accrue to me if I failed to perform what was regarded as a miracle. Solly Zuckerman's powers of persuasion and, I suppose, my own vanity, upon which he played with skill, were the deciding factors. Whatever it was, I found myself landed with the role of persuading the Government to rescue from bankruptcy a Society which, for all its run-down state, possessed not only a considerable collection of creatures but a body of knowledge and expertise which in the modern world is needed and ought not to be lost.

The problems were considerable. Resources were meagre and management threadbare: John Boyer, recently retired from the Hongkong and Shanghai Bank, was brought in as Chief Executive to bring some order into the situation: it was a tough assignment. The days when Solly could go off fishing and come back with a

217

million pounds or so in his bag were gone; visitor numbers were declining; the cloud of dilapidation and decrepitude which hung over the premises in Regent's Park would do nothing to bring them back. Poverty was, as always, a torment. There were times when I thought it might be a good idea to keep the tigers on short rations for a period, then bring one or two of them down to the House of Commons and let them loose there on some occasion when the House was full; it would have drawn attention to our needs. One alternative with which I toyed was a programme in which selected animals would be shot in front of television cameras to draw attention to the fact that we could neither feed nor house them adequately: it failed, however, to attract support. Lack of funds had caused maintenance to be neglected; the Mappin Terraces were closed as being unfit for man to visit or beast to occupy; the Aquarium and other structures were in a dicky state; there were eight or nine listed buildings; there were the restrictions attaching to a Royal Park – you can hardly blow your nose there without asking someone's permission. For good measure, there was a group of residents from the Regent's Park area who were something short of neighbourly: an angry lawyer; a retired civil servant who never tired of proclaiming that, whatever we said, we were not to be trusted; and an ex-MP who dealt in ultimatums, contributed all they could by way of discouragement. They even suggested that, if the Society did not comply with their wishes, they would cease to restrain the Animal Rights people from taking a part.

A feeling that it was wrong to confine animals, that they should be allowed to remain where nature had put them, in the wild, was also a cause for concern. Those who hold such views tend to ignore the fact that the wild offers no sanctuary for endangered species and that space for habitat is rapidly being encroached upon by man, the one living creature who endangers all others, who needs the land to live off and is a poacher on the grand scale. It was impossible to persuade such people that zoos, run as they should be, are not only repositories of knowledge but also provide opportunities for research in animal health and welfare which would certainly not be available in the wild. So concerned were some of their number to sustain their arguments intact that they wouldn't take the risk of coming to see for themselves and face the possibility that they

218

might be wrong. To fulfil its purposes, an institution such as the Zoological Society of London needs the understanding and support of both the public and the Government, and, of course, it needs money. It finds itself saddled with additional roles in informing, educating and entertaining, for which special skills are required.

The Society had, as a matter of history, not just missed the bus of Government support; but, when offered it in the last century, had actually turned it down. It had then preferred to remain a private club belonging to its Fellows, enjoying the privilege of occupying forty acres of land in Regent's Park and allowing in visitors on terms. As a result of this, the public perception of the London Zoo became and remains that of a menagerie, or a collection of live fauna, to be visited in warm and fine weather by those with young children to amuse. By contrast, Kew Gardens and the Natural History Museum, with their concerns for live flora and dead fauna, enjoy the status of scientific institutions. Whereas they had the respectful support of the Ministry of Agriculture and the Department of Education respectively, the London Zoo had somehow drifted within the orbit of the Department of the Environment, which was always looking for water with which to wash its hands of this unlooked for responsibility. Visits to San Diego, the Bronx and Toronto Zoos showed me what could be achieved with the different attitudes of North America.

The modern world resounds to the noisy boasts of the immodest and the strident; those who cherish and seek after knowledge leave those less encumbered to do most of the talking. The scientific community, with a huge diversity of interests, is more concerned with understanding the natural world than it is with proclaiming either its past achievements or its hopes for the future. For those entirely respectable reasons, my constant and repeated pleas to the eminent scientists who were members of the Zoo's governing body not to hide their own light or that of the Society under too large a bushel met with little response. The Secretary, the late Sir Barry Cross, told me sharply on more than one occasion that, if scientists did as I was suggesting, they would lose the respect of their colleagues. My role as Treasurer was to persuade a succession of Ministers that the merits of the Society were such that it should be supported. It involved seeking help and support from a number of eminent people, who all had other things to do, to help in one way or another. In particular, in 1987 I managed to persuade Michael Heseltine, who was out of the Government at the time, to join the Council of the Society, believing he would provide invaluable support and advice; indeed he did, until he returned to the Government in 1990. My main concern was, however, with Ministers and particularly at that time, 1985–7, William Waldegrave, to whom I must have been a source of considerable irritation; he, unfailingly patient, polite and intelligent, declared that he did want, if at all possible, to find 'a structured solution'. He suggested that as a first step we should appoint consultants.

In due course a helpful and positive report emerged which led the Government to make a grant to the Society of £10 million. I paid a kind of ceremonial call one morning upon John Major, then Chief Secretary to the Treasury. He remarked that it must have seemed strange that the Government had taken so long to make up its mind about so important a national institution, and asked whether I would like the money in instalments or in a lump sum. Having the very high current rate of interest in mind, I opted for the latter, thanked him and said that, since he was the most hard-pressed member of the Government, I could best show my appreciation by taking up no more of his time. He said, 'No, sit down and talk for a bit.' After some while I said that I didn't wish to exhaust any lingering goodwill by staying a moment longer. He then walked down the stairs with me and said goodbye in the street. Such good manners are far from being the rule with Ministers, some of whom see themselves as masters or managers, others as public servants; only the latter find time to be polite.

I felt that I had secured a great triumph and was delighted to receive a more than generous letter from Solly, which I cannot resist the temptation to quote in full.

Dear John,
   It would, I suppose, have been unseemly of me to have embraced you in those noble precincts yesterday (although I imagine that nobles who are given to a preference for other nobles may have slipped into dark corners since the Magna Carta), but I was so pleased with your news that I all but did

so. I *am* glad that despite the occasional impulse you may have had to drop the whole thing, you went on to the successful end. When I sucked you into the Society's affairs, I literally did so because I could not think of anyone other than you to do the necessary bullying. When I left, all we had was a remission of sentence for a couple of years. Now you've got the wolf away from the gates long enough for the cubs inside to grow to maturity.

Bless you and thank you. I now feel that the some thirty years I put into the job won't be wasted.

Yours,

Solly

Later on, however, relations with the Government became rather less friendly. Michael Heseltine, who had returned to the Government as Secretary of State for the Environment, sought to distance himself from a concern with which he had recently been involved and put the Government's relations with the Society in the hands of David Trippier, one of his junior Ministers, who proved somewhat wooden and unsympathetic. When one day he seemed particularly so, I said that I assumed that he and the Secretary of State were of the same mind. He assured me that it wouldn't be possible to get a razor blade between the two of them. I was left muttering that I wouldn't at all mind trying, on a bad day and with a shaky hand.

The relief that at last we had some funds was quickly balanced by the realization that we did not have enough. A thorough survey of the premises at Regent's Park, the first for many years, revealed that, quite apart from the derelict and unusable Mappin Terraces, the state of other buildings left a great deal to be desired; arrears of maintenance were of the order of £16 million. Since the Society had no prospect whatever of finding such funds, I inclined more and more to the view that, since our resources would not stretch both to putting Regent's Park in order and to developing Whipsnade, we had much better opt for the latter and close Regent's Park altogether.

Quite apart from the cost of putting things right there, there were other serious disadvantages: limited space in which to provide better accommodation for the animals and improved facilities for those who came to see them, the problems of being in a Royal Park and the burden of the various listed buildings. Differences of opinion between the other Officers of the Society and myself, which had long been simmering, became with time rather sharper. Although, in May 1991, the Council decided to announce that the Regent's Park Zoo would close in eighteen months' time, there were those amongst the management who took a different and what seemed to me a short-term view. I could, I suppose, have stayed on and brought about a showdown, but, since I had only a few months to run before my seven years as Treasurer would come to an end, and since the mutual trust and confidence necessary for progress had evaporated, I concluded that resignation was the better course. Robert Armstrong, Stanley Clinton-Davis, John Walton, Alcon Copisarow and Alistair McAlpine took the same course.

That was the rather sad side of it all; the arrears of maintenance, far larger than we had feared, meant that to some extent Solly had been right in saying that nothing had changed. Moreover, we had not helped ourselves by spending money on plans which we had not the resources to carry out. It is always easy to get advice if you are willing to pay for it; Mark Twain's comment, 'The first consultant was Satan', is one to remember. There had, however, been some gains; it had been possible for the first time for many years to take stock of the situation, to do the place up, to make it more attractive to visitors and to improve the accommodation of the considerable collection of creatures. In particular, the centre had been greatly improved with money provided by David and Frederick Barclay. New buildings had been put up and a good deal of old and useless clutter had been cleared away; one particularly important development was the new life which had been breathed into Whipsnade, which offered space that was not available in London and had for too long been its poor relation.

The rather sour and unhappy climate which developed towards the end of my time served to cloud over what had been achieved; it meant also that those responsible were barely thanked. Andy Grant, who was the hub of the management team, made a huge contribution with fresh vision; Andrew Forbes revitalized Whipsnade; Gregor Henderson as President gave me staunch support in the first half of my time. More, I know, should have been said and done to acknowledge the contribution of the staff in tidying the place up and for the care which they lavished upon the creatures in their charge; thanks were owed in particular to those engaged in the research side, of whose existence few visitors are even aware.

There were others too who were brought into my life by the Zoo and its affairs and who have, to my good fortune and joy, stayed there. Sir Gordon White (later Lord White of Hull), having been prevailed upon to come up with some money for Somerville College, Oxford, by the Principal, Daphne Park, was quick to recognize her merits and established her in Regent's Park to run the Society's appeal. She lists as her recreations good talk, politics and difficult places: a star in the first, wiser by far than most professionals in the second and hugely experienced in the third. It is a combination which, to put it mildly, makes her unusual. She was a FANY in the war, engaged in training people who were to parachute into German-occuped Europe. In peacetime she served in the Foreign Service and in MI6; Leopoldville, Lusaka, Hanoi and Mongolia all figured in the itinerary of her career. When in the Congo, she was stopped by some disorderly soldiers and told that she could not go on, they were shooting Europeans; she replied that she was sorry, she had to go and was going to go to Stanleyville; she would be back tomorrow, they could shoot her then. What then made them allow her to go on can only be understood by those who know her. As Principal of Somerville College she must have been a delight to the undergraduates, though I suspect something of a surprise to the dons. She speaks powerfully with great knowledge of Defence, though so fast as to make it difficult for her audience to digest the worth of what she has to say. In a speech made in July 1995 she expressed 'very grave anxiety about the state of morale in the services and about the creeping privatization that could turn a magnificent fighting machine into a failing business'. I often have the feeling that Ministers react to such speeches as pedestrians do to a shower of rain, putting up their umbrellas to ensure that it doesn't soak in. I haven't ever met anyone quite like her before and don't expect to do so again.

Rather to my surprise, I was able to persuade Alistair McAlpine to involve himself in the affairs of the Society and had good reason to be grateful to him for his support. It isn't, I think, unfair to say there were always those who frowned upon the proposals of others without coming forward with something better of their own. Alistair did give me all the support he could before finally warning me that someone was going to put a knife in my back before long. Apart from supplying much-needed encouragement, it was he who brought David and Frederick Barclay into my life. We met for lunch at his Cork Street gallery. 'Go on,' said Alistair, 'tell them about the Zoo.' When I had done so they offered wise advice, to which I could only reply that our resources were so meagre that we could not afford to follow it. After a pause, one of them asked, 'Would half a million pounds help?' No one had ever spoken to me in such terms before; 'Thank you, yes it would' seemed a bit inadequate. It was, of course, tremendously welcome and doubly so, since at that time the Government was matching pounds with whatever we could get from the private sector. I had grown accustomed to the glazed look which comes into people's eyes as soon as they realize that they are being asked for money, followed by a quick look at the clock and a dash for the door. Some, and these have usually come from the ranks of the rich, are so upset even to be asked that they cannot bring themselves to refuse politely. The response of the Barclay brothers at a time when we seemed to be getting nowhere and I was near to despair was one of the best surprises that has ever come my way; it wasn't just the money, but the encouragement and understanding which went with it.

David and Frederick Barclay are twins; they are very much alike in appearance; they think on similar lines; they enjoy each other's company; the illness of one is not far from being the illness of both; their self-respect and the standards according to which they live and run their business are the stronger for being shared. In any discussion between them – and I don't believe that there are many thoughts which they do not share – they have the huge advantage of mutual regard and affection and the complete certainty of being understood; no trace of jealousy or suspicion disturbs the regard they have for each other. Their firm rule never to take any important step unless both agree is one which, because of their unusually close mutual understanding, is free of the frictions which ordinary partnerships bring. I have never met two people who have such a clear and effortless understanding of one another. They started in life with no advantages save their own talents, which include an unusual ability to focus upon what is important and a rare perception of what is likely to happen next. The immense debt they owe to their mother is one which they readily acknowledge, even though they didn't fall in with her advice to find a nice safe job in a bank.

The Barclay brothers operate in different parts of the world and have been involved in real estate, hotels, construction, investments, brewing, container shipping (including the largest independent liquid natural gas shipping company in the world), mining, oil prospecting and newspaper publishing – quite a list. They have been through difficult times; they worked in the early years for long hours and without holidays; their close resemblance to each other led those who worked for them to think that the one who had just come in was the one who had gone out minutes before and that neither of them ever slept. They have been prodigiously successful, but their outlook on life has not changed; they work hard and enjoy it; they know the value of money and are generous with it. Many of those who work for them have done so for years, and are remembered if ill fortune strikes. The brothers shun publicity, not because they have anything to hide or are secretive, but because they wish to be free from intrusion and the questions which come in an unceasing tide from those who insist that everyone has some God-given right to know everything about everyone.

We have, perhaps, allowed envy to permeate our thoughts to such an extent that we have become comfortable with failure, which weakens us all, and suspicious of success, which we are encouraged to believe has something sinister attaching to it. It is hardly sensible to spread abroad the impression that all rich and successful people cheat and are greedy. Americans tend to respect success, and perhaps for that reason have more of it than we do.

It is not at all difficult to get to like people who give you the kind of encouragement and help which David and Frederick Barclay gave me, and I have since rejoiced in a friendship which had so unusual and welcome a start. In 1989, a few years after I had first met them, Freddy said to me, and I well remember his words, 'David and I have been very lucky in the things we have undertaken. We think it right to put something back and we intend to start a charitable trust to support medical research and do something for the young, the old and the disabled; we would like you to be Chairman.' I replied that, while I was greatly flattered by the suggestion, I had never done anything of the kind in my life and would have no idea how even to begin. That, they seemed to think, was no objection; so I accepted.

The Foundation which they then set up has opened for me doors that I would not otherwise have even knocked on. One half-respectable reason for passing by the problems of other people is that you lack the resources to do much about them. In providing me with the means, the Foundation obliged me as a first step to have a look at things which had not seemed previously to be concerns of mine. I am not suggesting that in doing so I discovered anything, simply that I began to see rather more clearly what a prison old age, disability and poverty can make of life, death being the only exit on offer. The young too can find themselves ill equipped to find their way, short of useful guidance – full as the world seems to be of counsellors – and without the possibility of a job or prospect of escape from one of those ghettoes of hopelessness where the only comfort to be had lies in congregating with others in similar plight and learning from them of the relief that drugs and crime appear to offer. The poorer the areas and the more meagre the amenities, the more they become the gathering point of the problems to which society either cannot find the answers or won't even look for them. Differences of language and race add another layer to the puzzle. It is possible in some areas in our inner cities to walk for ten minutes and encounter as near as fifty main languages, English not included.

There are those who are willing to battle with the modern world's prevailing winds, to swim against its tides and soften its harsh materialism with pity. Against a background of muddle and ignorance on the part of authority, they bring help to the disabled and protection to the weak; they provide shelter for the homeless, salvage the drop-out and the drug addict and bring some light and joy to the old and the lonely. Such people, poorly rewarded and often derided as 'do-gooders', put the rest of us in their debt, for they make bearable things in our society which might otherwise become an explosive mixture. I give the names of two such people who spend their lives helping others.

Andrew Mawson, a Minister of the United Reformed Church, who was sent by his church some ten years ago to revive a derelict centre at Bromley by Bow in the East End of London, brought intelligence and guts to the task and has been wonderfully successful. A nursery school, a cafeteria, classes in wood and ceramics and transport arrangements for old and sick people are there to prove it. Fifty people work there and a thousand visit it every week. Now he is well on the way to establishing a health centre.

Maria O'Dwyer runs a hostel for Turning Point in Hackney. It caters for the young who have drifted into drugs and alcohol, but who with encouragement make wonderful efforts to confront their problems and find another way. One young girl whom Maria had rescued from a male predator, and to whom I had been able to give some modest help, wrote to me,

'I am pleased to tell you that I have done really well. I have successfully finished the City Lit Access Course and I have enclosed a copy of my pass certificate for you to see for yourself. I just received my certificate and I must admit I was overjoyed. I have come a long way since I admitted myself to Lorne House and I am eternally grateful for the kindness and support people have shown me to make this possible, yourself included.'

If we want to find answers to the problems of the inner cities, and we must, it would be as well if we started to listen to the Andrew Mawsons and the Maria O'Dwyers. Those who look at these things through Whitehall windows will not achieve much unless from time to time they get a bit nearer to the action in the streets and hear what those most closely involved have to say.

We live in a society which has been dubbed affluent and caring, but is neither as affluent as we would like it to be nor as caring as it ought to be. The huge paraphernalia of the state, insensitive and remote, tends to replace compassion with procedures and to blunt the edge of pity with rules. Officialdom, if it has imagination, is not encouraged to use it; it can see and understand the shape of the wood, but it has no idea how dark it is under the trees.

XIV

Pictures, Pots, Gardens and God

> We must be still and still moving
> Into another intensity.
> T. S. Eliot

Looking back now at what I have written, I feel rather as a fisherman must, seeing the contents of the net which he has just pulled in: a mixture of relief, satisfaction and disappointment. I have also some concern that I may have got the balance wrong and allowed the times of sadness and desolation to overshadow the rest.

My capture by the Germans in 1940 was a personal disaster, infinitely worse in that it was a microcosm in a massive and seemingly irreversible defeat for our country. It brought me, as the numbness wore off, to the edge of despair; hope at that time had only the flimsy quality of a dream. The death of my brother in the raid on St Nazaire in 1942 seemed to shut out whatever light remained, with the Germans, and all that they stood for, triumphant. The sudden and totally unexpected death of a five-year-old son in 1960 seemed again to empty the world of joy, but this time it was only the small world of a single family. In 1993 Mary's almost disastrous illness, with both pulmonary arteries blocked, was another time when the whole landscape of life was hidden in shadow. Her life was saved by two remarkable men, Professor Kakkar, who recognized the danger, and Sir Magdi Yacoub, who performed a near-miraculous operation.

Such events have a cutting edge so sharp that they are etched deep into the memory, their imprint clear in outline and detail. The debris of the years may give them a covering, but can never wipe them out. Other better, happier times have more of a dreamlike

229

quality about them, their shape half hidden in yesterday's summer haze. Permeating my own story is a concern, which at times has become an alarm, at the decline of our country; a decline to be measured not in terms of wealth and influence – they go together – but in terms of those intangible things which we once shared and which, to an extent, held us together. Some, of course, will shrug that off and say that it is the kind of thing which you must expect from the old and the peevish as they see the world slipping away from them. I wish it were so, for then it would be just my worry.

What troubles me and, I suspect, many much younger than I am, is that in our supermarket society – not all of it affluent nor all of it caring – the individual, who is the source of all creativity, is lost sight of, if not trampled upon in the herd. The herd, to which we all belong, is seen by its managers and those who supply its needs as a source of power and profit. As such, it is something to be watched rather than listened to; manipulated rather than respected; tricked rather than trusted; sedated rather than stimulated. Since its one observable shared value is money, success lies in providing it, and since the appetite for it is insatiable, there is no alternative but to promise more – more than even with the most skilled management is likely to be available. There is, of course, nothing inherently wrong with money; it is a necessary alternative to barter. But when its glitter outshines all other values, forces are released which are not easily put back in the bottle. Some it prompts to steal, others to cheat and defraud and others again to furnish such examples of greed that liberty, degraded into licence, becomes hard to defend. Mark Twain had an eye for such things; in his 'Battle Hymn of the Republic (Brought Down to Date)' he had some sharp darts to throw:

> In a sordid slime harmonious Greed was born in yonder ditch
> With a longing in his bosom and for others' goods an itch
> As Christ died to make men holy, let men die to make us rich.

It may not be all that easy in practice to distinguish between greed, which we tend to see in others, and that legitimate self-interest which we allow in ourselves; but we ought at least to try.

George Orwell may have had such thoughts in mind in the last scene of *Animal Farm*. The pigs and the humans have been celebrating their reconciliation and affirming that there was not and need not be any conflict between them. A game of cards is in progress. Suddenly, a fearful row breaks out: Napoleon, the leader of the pigs, and Mr Pilkington, the principal human, have both played the Ace of Spades together. The lower animals outside in the dusk, aroused by the commotion, rush to the lighted window and, looking in from face to face, from pig to man and man to pig, find it is no longer possible to tell which is which. Maybe the time has come when we should remind ourselves of the differences and even to cherish them. Pigs, so far as we are aware, are not much bothered with notions of service, discipline, responsibility, respect or reverence. Civilized society, however, dispenses with them at its peril: there are times when we seem to have come close to doing so.

I must now turn back to the chapter heading, 'Pictures, Pots, Gardens and God'. It would never have occurred to me when I began to write to make more than a passing reference to the first three, for I have no expert knowledge. Yet now it seems that to leave them out would be wrong; for they have over years become a source of interest and joy, part of the backing into which is stitched the tapestry of my life. Still less, for fear of seeming sanctimonious and hypocritical, did I have in mind even the most hesitant approach to the impenetrable mystery of God; yet now, not to do so, no matter how lamely, would seem a greater error, even a betrayal.

While I was still at school it began to dawn on me that, although the past will always be another time, another country, pictures bring another dimension to the written word of history and shed light on those who were part of its procession. They tell you of the kind of people they were; they give you a glimpse of their towns and cities and houses and furniture; they show you the clothes they wore, the way they travelled and the weapons with which they fought. With such thoughts in mind, I wandered in a rather unconstructed way round the principal London galleries and acquired a sort of album of the mind which stayed with me through the war years and until such time as I was minded to refresh it. It was not, however, until the war had been over for some years, 1950 perhaps, that I even thought of buying a picture.

Those which I have collected over the years are mostly of still and quiet places, distant from the turmoil of the modern world. In one gallery I received this simple advice: 'Never buy anything you don't like and look for things once admired, but which for one reason or another are out of favour.' Albert Goodwin, who had died not long before the Second World War, was given as an example. His sister, to whom he had left many of his pictures, rather ungratefully dumped a quantity of them on the market, driving the price through the floor where it had stayed. I bought my first one that morning for ten guineas. Knighton Hammond lived at one time in my constituency; he had been thrilled to hear Augustus John's reported comment that he was the greatest watercolourist of his time. Hammond continued to paint until he was ninety in order to pass Michelangelo, who had given up at eighty-nine. He still had, however, when I first met him in the sixties, an almost inexhaustible store of watercolours of landscapes in which men guided ploughs pulled by horses and stooks of corn told of the harvest; of old men with scythes and wagons with wooden wheels which looked as if they were part of the land. They are reminders of a countryside which now exists only in the mind, one in which farms had not become food factories and pigs and chickens spent time in the fields and the open air.

We bought from Alistair McAlpine on very generous terms a large and glorious watercolour by an Australian aborigine artist: it shows what light and water can do for each other. Mary and I each paid half, a present to the other after twenty-five years of happy marriage. A sleeping rhinoceros, some surprised-looking sheep and a feather are marvellous reminders of Wendy Taylor's skills as a painter; she is better known as a sculptress. A small oil painting of Salisbury Cathedral was given to me by a New Zealand artist. He had come to Britain to improve his art, but, having been found to be merely painting instead of studying in an art school, was adjudged by the authorities to have deceived them and told he must go. I was able, after knocking rather loudly on a few doors, to get this oppressive decision reversed; he sent me the picture as a way of saying thank you. Such things are available; they do not cost a fortune; they can be lived with and enjoyed.

Great masters, on the other hand, are, for the most part, only to be seen jostling with each other on the walls of galleries, their splendour in danger of being submerged in the crowd. Occasionally – and it is something of an event – you see a great picture where it ought to be, in a church or chapel or some other place by itself, its glory enhanced by the solitude. El Greco's *Burial of the Count of Orgaz*, in a small chapel in Toledo, is an example. You can stand, sit or kneel in front of it and take it in, and you feel as if you were alone with the painter.

The chapel at Vence in the South of France built by Matisse for the Dominicans as surely reflects the man who created it as if it had been his home. I saw it first in 1950, and was wondering what it was when an old Sister of the Order invited me in and showed me round. She told me of Matisse's illness and how they had cared for him and he had promised to give them the chapel. She pointed to the Stations of the Cross and explained how he had seen the crucifixion not as incidents separate from each other, but as one terrible and deeply shocking whole. He had heaped them together on one wall in a pyramid of black lines on stark white tiles, so as to tell of the terrible thing that had been done. She rejoiced in it all, St Dominic, the Madonna and Child with the single word 'AVE', a door, the panels of which represent the falling tears of Christ, the crucifix on the altar, the colours of the windows. Matisse himself wrote of what he had done: '*Cette chapelle est pour moi l'aboutissement de toute une vie de travail et la floraison d'un effort énorme, sincère et difficile.*' I have been back many times since and always with the same feeling as then, stained on going in and cleaner, grateful, uplifted on leaving.

Those qualities of stillness and grace, which are part of that chapel, are to be found in pots. It was a Grecian urn which inspired Keats to write lines that reach out to its beauty and encase it in words:

Thou still unravished bride of quietness
Thou foster child of silence and slow time,

– language so lovely as to take the breath away.

My interest in pots originated with the Leach family: Bernard, the doyen of modern English potters, his son David and his grandson Johnny, who lived in my constituency. David gave me a book by his father, *Drawings, Verse and Belief*, about himself and about potters. 'Man needs humility,' Bernard wrote, 'he has to get rid of himself, his egotistic self'. Potters, it seems, manage to do so; politicians are not alone in finding it hard. David in his mid-eighties continues to make beautiful things, though from time to time he disturbs himself without cause, worrying that time has eroded his skill. I used to cherish the hope that Johnny might one day vote for me; he tells me now that he never did. I did manage, however, to persuade him to make twelve chamber pots to mark the candidature in 1974 of a Mr Tippett, who, though a member of my own executive committee, stood against me as a Conservative Anti-Common Market candidate and so deprived me of five hundred votes. The outside of the pots bore the date of the election: the inside was inscribed, 'Tip it out'. I kept two and gave the other ten to those who I felt had worked particularly hard on my behalf.

Lucie Rie from Vienna and Hans Coper from Saxony were both refugees from the Nazis. Their qualities – her delicacy and serenity and his strength and originality – are enshrined in their work. From time to time Lucie made larger, heavier pots, and she agreed to make one for me. When, two years later, I enquired as to how it was progressing, she replied, 'Your trouble is that you are so patient. I will make you one now, if you still want me to do so.' A month or so later she rang to say that the pot was ready; I need not have it if I did not like it, but if I did, the price would be what it would have been if she had made it when she should have done; it was almost a gift. She once mended for me a pot with which Mrs Thatcher, our daily help in London for many years, had had a bit of bad luck. Lucie did so beautifully and refused to charge for it, saying, 'I don't mend pots.' After arriving in England in 1938, she moved soon afterwards into a small house in Albion Mews and remained there until her death in 1995. She and Hans Coper worked together; each must have influenced the other, but never to the point of copying. It was said of him that he knew the nakedness of emperors.

PICTURES, POTS, GARDENS AND GOD

Pictures and pots lead on easily enough to gardens, places where stillness and silence and love come to restore themselves. In a marvellous book, *The Purest of Pleasures*, Jill Parker has compared a garden with a work of art; 'what work of art grows and dies, changes its appearance, asserts its own will, fades away and then returns – in fact lives? Only a garden.' The one which Mary and I have been making at Hinton St George for nearly twenty years is small – not much more than an acre. We had at first no plan; we bought trees and shrubs and put them where they looked right and there was room. We became aware that our problem lay in its shape; a rectangle of length six times its width, it needed to be broken up into rooms, with hedges doing duty for walls. Colonies of winter-flowering heathers, a rampart of eleagnus, clumps of red and yellow cornus stems here and there which make the most of the sun in winter, and rather more trees than perhaps you would expect in a small garden combine to stop the eye from drifting on and seeing little. A host of hellebores, snowdrops, crocuses and primroses are an unearned gift of nature or our predecessors; their function is to tell of the coming spring. Five yews in a new moon curve have grown to form arches, and an old oak stump which revolves on a spigot shows nature's skill as a sculptor. Some small granite figures carved in Brittany by a Frenchman, the sixth in direct line to work in that hard material, now have their home with us.

At the far end, across a vale of rich farming land, you look north towards Langport and Sedgemoor, flanked to the west by the Quantocks, to the east by Glastonbury and the Mendips. Near at hand is Ham Hill, the source of the honey-coloured stone which glows in the sunshine and provides so many of the churches, houses and villages of south Somerset with the warmth that adds to their beauty. A garden may be demanding, but the rewards it offers are almost unequalled. No matter how familiar, it can always shock by either some disaster or some quite unexpected beauty. 'God Almighty first planted a garden'; maybe, but Bacon's beautiful words take us back to the beginning and to the legend of Genesis, which has it that the garden, which God made, was the place where all our troubles began; where discontent and the gnawing need for more led Adam to put Paradise at risk and lose it.

That story and Horace's question, 'How is it that no one can be content?', go on echoing down the centuries to remind us that, however great the pace and size of change, whatever else many appear or vanish, discontent will be always with us; what we have will never be enough. Perhaps seeking is the essence of life itself. Moses, asking to see the face of God, was told, 'There can no man see my face and live' and was allowed only to see 'the hinder parts'; the face and the full glory would be more than a man could bear. Man has been sitting so long in judgement upon God and hovering in the neighbourhood of a 'doesn't exist' verdict as to overlook the possibility that things may be the other way round; that it is he who is on trial. I do not believe either that the mystery of God can be unravelled in words or that because something is beyond the reach of human language it cannot, for that reason, exist. It seems to me better, but not necessarily easier, to accept what Henry Vaughan in a marvellous phrase called 'the dazzling darkness of God' than trust to attempted explanations which, in ironing the creases out of mystery, leave behind them something which is flat, ordinary and dull. A mere dauber might have the same effect if he sought to improve upon a Rembrandt masterpiece. I have come by slow steps to regard God as a problem with whom or with which we all must seek to come to terms; that the gifted intellectual will have no advantage over the humble worshipper.

The notion that life is a journey to be made, a river to be crossed, is familiar; what lies at the end of the journey, or on the other side of the river, is for most of us an area where faith and hope are jostled by doubt and fear. It is a place from which the traveller cannot return to tell of what he saw; nor can the visionary and the mystic convince those more earthbound of what it was that they may have glimpsed. We have perforce to be content to see through a glass darkly until the moment when, with all our hopes and fears, we either cease to be or learn what is until then a matter for faith.

Since there is no bridge or boat by which to make the crossing and it isn't possible to swim, we have need of stepping-stones to save us from being either swept away in the swirling waters of despair or left to wallow in the stagnation of materialism. I have three; their meaning has survived the tread of the centuries and can still pierce the fog of doubt and uncertainty of our own time. First, 'Be still then and know that I am God' is the Psalmist's warning that without stillness there will be no knowing. Second, 'The Father spoke but one word, this is his Son; he speaks it forever and in eternal silence and it is in silence that the soul should listen.' That message of St John of the Cross is similar; without silence there will be no hearing. The last of my stepping stones is the single word 'Master', spoken at the sepulchre by Mary Magdalen on that first Easter morning. Despair and misery are swept away in a tidal wave of joy, wonder and homage as, hearing her own name, she realizes that the man who spoke it was not the gardener, but the one whom she believed dead; the one for whose body she had been searching.

To these I would add, by way of ballast, those words of Hazlitt which I have quoted elsewhere, 'If mankind had wanted what is right, it could have had it long ago.' We still enjoy the right to choose for ourselves; we show no signs of wanting to give it up or even seeking guidance as to how we should exercise it. What is right may or may not be plain to see; it is seldom, perhaps never, easy or popular. Christ's choice, made alone and in the silence of the wilderness, was to reject the easy ways of enticement and persuasion, abundance, power and magic, and to take instead the awful way of the Cross. Had he done otherwise, his story would by now have been part of the compost of history. Faced with a less stern choice, we in our time opt for abundance, only to find that it is not enough.

Index

INDEX

INDEX

INDEX